JENNI CALDER was born in Chicago, educated in the United States and England, and has lived in or near Edinburgh since 1971. After several years of part-time teaching and freelance writing, including three years in Kenya, she worked at the National Museums of Scotland from 1978 to 2001, successively as education officer, Head of Publications, script editor for the Museum of Scotland, and latterly as Head of Museum of Scotland International. In the latter capacity her main interest was in emigration and the Scottish diaspora. She has written and lectured widely on Scottish, English and American literary and historical subjects, and writes fiction and poetry as Jenni Daiches. She has two daughters, a son and a dog.

By the same author:

Chronicles of Conscience: A Study of Arthur Koestler and George Orwell, Secker and Warburg, 1968
Scott (with Angus Calder), Evans, 1969
There Must be a Lone Ranger: The Myth and Reality of the American West, Hamish Hamilton, 1974
Women and Marriage in Victorian Fiction, Thames and Hudson, 1976
Brave New World and Nineteen Eighty-Four, Edward Arnold, 1976
Heroes, from Byron to Guevara, Hamish Hamilton, 1977
The Victorian Home, Batsford, 1977
The Victorian and Edwardian Home in Old Photographs, Batsford, 1979
RLS: A Life Study, Hamish Hamilton, 1980
The Enterprising Scot (ed, with contributions), National Museums of Scotland, 1986
Animal Farm and Nineteen Eighty-Four, Open University Press, 1987
The Wealth of a Nation (ed, with contributions), NMS Publishing, 1989
Scotland in Trust, Richard Drew, 1990
St Ives by RL Stevenson (new ending), Richard Drew, 1990
No Ordinary Journey: John Rae, Arctic Explorer (with Ian Bunyan, Dale Idiens and Bryce Wilson), NMS Publishing, 1993
Mediterranean (poems, as Jenni Daiches), Scottish Cultural Press, 1995
The Nine Lives of Naomi Mitchison, Virago, 1997
Museum of Scotland (guidebook), NMS Publishing, 1998
Present Poets 1 (ed, poetry anthology), NMS Publishing, 1998
Translated Kingdoms (ed, poetry anthology), NMS Publishing, 1999
Robert Louis Stevenson, (poetry, ed), Everyman, 1999
Present Poets 2 (ed, poetry anthology), NMS Publishing, 2000
Scots in Canada, Luath Press, 2003
Not Nebuchadnezzar: In Search of Identities, Luath Press, 2005

Scots in the USA

JENNI CALDER

Luath Press Limited
EDINBURGH
www.luath.co.uk

First published 2006

The author's right to be identified as author of this book under the
Copyright, Designs and Patents Act 1988 has been asserted.

The paper used in this book is recyclable.
It is made from low-chlorine pulps produced in a low-energy,
low-emission manner from renewable forests.

Printed and bound by Scotprint, Haddington

Typeset in 10.5 point Sabon

Maps by Jim Lewis

© Jenni Calder 2006

Acknowledgements

This book would not have happened without the one that came before, *Scots in Canada*: thank you again to all those who encouraged me on the North American trail. For particular help, thanks to Hugh Cheape, David Forsyth and Geoff Swinney at the National Museums of Scotland. Thank you also to Angus Calder for the Lone Ranger, to staff at the National Library of Scotland, especially Kevin Halliwell and Diana Webster; to Jim Lewis for drawing the maps, and to all at Luath Press. Jennie Renton's guiding editorial hand has been invaluable.

For permission to quote from 'Charles Kerr's Praise-Poem to the Appalachians' my thanks to Tom Hubbard; to James Kelman and Hamish Hamilton for permission to quote from *You Have to Be Careful in the Land of the Free*; and to Duncan McLean and Vintage for permission to quote from *Lone Star Swing*.

And thanks again to AMB.

Contents

CHAPTER ONE   I Should Like to Be an American   1

CHAPTER TWO   Take Courage and Come to this Country   27

CHAPTER THREE   The Most Plentiful Country in the World   47

CHAPTER FOUR   American in my Principles   65

CHAPTER FIVE   Ideas of Living More Comfortably   87

CHAPTER SIX   Within Reach of All   113

CHAPTER SEVEN   The Lure of the West   139

CHAPTER EIGHT   Muscle and Brain   169

CHAPTER NINE   Fire on the Mountain   191

Map 1: Scotland   216

Map 2: North America – Thirteen Colonies   217

Maps 3–8: USA   218

Chronology   224

Places to Visit   228

Bibliography   230

Index   236

My Scotland, my America; oor Alba, oor Appalachia.
Tom Hubbard,
'Charles Kerr's Praise-Poem to the Appalachians'

CHAPTER ONE

I Should Like to Be an American

If I were not a Scotsman,
I should like to be an American.
THOMAS CAMPBELL, 1840

ALL ALONG THE west coast of Scotland, from the Solway Firth in the south to Loch Inver in the north, broad firths and deeply penetrating sea lochs reach inland. In the days when Scotland was a maritime nation these were highways to the Atlantic Ocean. On the other side of the Atlantic Ocean was a continent that over the centuries changed the lives of millions of Scots.

The broadest and most far-reaching of all these highways was the Firth of Clyde and its satellite lochs. It was the Clyde more than anything else that brought America to Scotland and enabled so many Scots to voyage west to America. Two advertisements in the *Glasgow Mercury* of 12 May 1784 bear witness to the relationship. The brigantine *Janet* is preparing to sail for Norfolk, Virginia, 'ready to take on board goods at Greenock by the 15th of June next, and will be clear to sail by the 10th of July at farthest'. Below this a second sailing is announced for Philadelphia:

The brigantine BETTY and MATTY, ARCHD.MOOR, Master, a stout new vessel, has good accommodation for passengers, and will sail positively on or before the 20th of May instant, wind and weather permitting.

The Clyde's direct connection with the USA has only recently come to an end, with the dismantling of the US submarine bases in the area.

There is not much remaining now to remind us of the huge numbers of ships that in the eighteenth and nineteenth centuries slipped downriver with cargoes of coal, linen, domestic goods, harness and haberdashery, tools and trade goods for the Americas, and returned with tobacco, sugar, rum, rice, indigo, timber, skins, raw cotton, to supply Scotland's commercial and industrial endeavour. Alexander Carlyle, who was a student in Glasgow in the 1740s, referred in his memoirs to the 'large warehouses full of manufactures of all sorts, to furnish a cargo to Virginia'. The harbours and docks have mostly vanished, as have the shipyards that responded to the voracious demand for the vessels required by the trade. But without America, the city of Glasgow would never have become a great manufacturing and merchant city. Without America, Port Glasgow downriver may never have existed at all, and Greenock a little further down would certainly never have become Scotland's largest port. As George Blake, who wrote extensively about the Clyde valley, put it: 'The story of the Clyde as a port is in essence the story of Glasgow's effort to bring the Atlantic to the doors of its warehouses.' For many decades it was an extraordinarily successful effort.

In 1700 the population of Greenock was 2,000. In other words, it was a village. By 1755 it had almost doubled. By 1801 it was over 17,000 and in another 30 years it was more than 27,000, making it one of the six largest towns in Scotland. This rapid expansion was the result of Atlantic trade, and the foundation of Atlantic trade was America. Not only did Greenock receive and send out Atlantic cargoes, it built ships and fitted them out, fostered a great range of shipping-related trades and skills, and furnished crews. John Galt, who partly grew up in Greenock and lived there in the latter period of his life, described it as 'savory with shipping, herrings and tar'. Until the mid-twentieth century ships and the sea still dominated the lives of large numbers of men and women in Greenock, Port Glasgow and the other Clyde ports. This was the American legacy.

The impact of North America on life and work in Scotland has been immense, from the early eighteenth century when the union of the Scottish and English parliaments legalised trade between Scotland and the American colonies, to the present day. Even before that, Scots were profiting from illegal transatlantic trade. The impact of Scots on Canada, where from the early years of settlement Scots were part of the fabric of an evolving nation, is without question. The part Scots played in the evolution of the USA is harder to identify. But play a part they did, settling the first colonies, fighting imperial rivals, shaping political ideas and educational institutions, pioneering the movement west, and providing initiative, labour and finance for commerce and industry. Although the title of this book is *Scots in the USA*, the story begins well before the Revolutionary War brought independence to Britain's thirteen American colonies. In fact, it is in these early decades that the Scots were most conspicuous.

In the seventeenth century Scotland's connections with the colonies were not auspicious. Although England and Scotland were part of a single kingdom, Britain's imperial activities were dominated by English mercantile interests. Scottish merchants were excluded by Navigation Acts from trading directly with the colonies, where products such as sugar and tobacco were becoming increasingly lucrative. This did not stop them. Even before 1664 when the Netherlands relinquished its hold on what became New York (named for Charles II's brother the Duke of York) Scottish traders were nibbling at New Amsterdam. By the 1640s Scots were shipping tobacco from Virginia and Maryland. The extent of their illegal trade is indicated by the fact that Port Glasgow was constructed in 1668, nearly forty years before the Act of Union, to accommodate ships involved in transatlantic commerce. Smugglers made use of less conspicuous landing places, for example along the Solway Firth.

While Scottish traders could establish only a furtive foothold, the colonial possessions were seen as a useful dumping ground for Scottish undesirables, which in the seventeenth century meant predominantly defeated Royalists and Covenanters. After Cromwell's victory at the battle of Dunbar in 1650, over a thousand prisoners were sentenced to be transported to Virginia, with a smaller number destined for New England. Those who arrived at Boston on the *Unity* were sold into indentured service. Their masters paid £30 for seven years service. Many were purchased to work in the Massachusetts ironworks which were hungry for labour. Cromwell's success the following year at Worcester again resulted in transportation sentences for Scottish prisoners. The *John and Sara*, sailing from Gravesend, brought around 250 of them to Boston, where they were sold.

These were the first significant numbers of Scots to settle in the American colonies, not from choice, not because they were inspired by visions of a productive and prosperous life overseas, but forced to leave Scotland. Some clearly did well. Charles Gordon from Aberdeen wrote in 1685 to a correspondent in Edinburgh that he had been 'sent away by Cromwell to New England; a slave from Dunbar, living now in Woodbridge like a Scots laird, wishes his countrymen and his native soil well, though he never intends to see it'.

Covenanters defeated in their last-ditch attempts to resist the impositions of Charles II on religious worship were similarly dispatched overseas, and others went into voluntary exile. Some of these made their way west by way of Ulster, which had seen the settlement of large numbers of Lowland and Border Scots from the 1620s. Attracted by the prospect of religious freedom, some Scottish Quakers also chose to make new lives on the other side of the Atlantic, encouraged by William Penn's success in settling Quakers in New Jersey and Pennsylvania. Scottish and English Quakers were in close contact. Alongside the identification of the colonies as a repository for troublemakers was a growing perception of them offering opportunities for underdogs and misfits. Some of those sold into indentured labour did better than they could ever have hoped to do at home, as Charles Gordon exemplifies.

The Act of Union of 1707 gave Scottish merchants legitimate access to transatlantic markets. They were quick to take advantage of this, particularly in the Caribbean and the Chesapeake Bay area of the American colonies. Daniel Defoe, in his book describing his *Tour Thro' the Whole Island of Great Britain* (1726), commented on the transatlantic traffic:

> the Union open'd the door to the Scots in our American colonies, and the Glasgow merchants presently fell in with the opportunity… I am assured that they send near fifty sail of ships every year to Virginia, New England, and other English colonies in America.

He and a later traveller in Scotland, Thomas Pennant, were both very impressed by the city. In his *A Tour of Scotland in 1769* (1773) Pennant noted that tobacco and sugar were the main imports and that Glasgow's textile trade was beginning to rival Manchester's. Glasgow, in his view, had 'in point of the conveniency of its port, in respect to America, a great advantage over [Manchester]'. Sir Walter Scott, looking back around half a century later, in his novel *Rob Roy* (1817) has Bailie Nichol Jarvie extol the Union as 'the treaty that opened us a road west-awa' yonder'.

Most of the Scots who crossed the Atlantic for commercial reasons did not intend to settle permanently. Their aspirations were generally to make enough money through planting and trade to enable them to return to Scotland and become owners of estates in a country where those not born to land ownership were very unlikely to achieve the status of lairds. This applied not only to those from landless families, but to younger sons of lairds who could not hope to inherit. The colonies proved to be promising territory for younger sons, although expectations often proved illusory. Plenty of Scots did extremely well, but those who actually went to the colonies were less likely to make their fortunes than those who directed operations from Glasgow.

The Clyde gave Scots a distinct advantage in British trade with the colonies, as Thomas Pennant pointed out. The transatlantic voyage was shorter from the northern half of the kingdom, and Clyde-based ships were able to make two trips in a season while further south normally only one was possible. As Defoe put it, Scottish ships were 'oftentimes at the capes of Virginia before the London ships are clear of the channel'. At first Scottish merchants were using ships from elsewhere, Holland for example, or acquiring ships built in America, where an abundance of wood favoured the industry. (Scots would later participate distinctively in American shipbuilding, particularly in the nineteenth century.) But Clyde shipbuilders, who had for generations produced smaller craft, began to respond to the need for ocean-going vessels. The coming of steam in the early 1800s initiated the Clyde's dominance in shipbuilding, which stamped its character for the best part of a century.

The demand for ships was not just in order to transport goods to lucrative markets. Increasingly, another valuable cargo was involved: people. The ship masters who in the seventeenth century took Scotland's rejects across the Atlantic did so because it was a profitable activity. They touted for business, offering to take convicts and others off the hands of the authorities. In 1668 and '69 James Currie, lord provost of Edinburgh, helped to finance the dispatch of undesirables to Virginia. Twelve years later Walter Gibson, a Glasgow merchant, advertised that he had a ship 'lying in Port Glasgow bound for America and is willing to receive thieves or robbers sentenced by the Lords of Justiciary or other judges to be banished thither'. Gibson also recruited voluntary emigrants. In 1684 he announced the departure of a ship for Carolina, New Providence and the Caribbean, proposing to charge passage at £5 for adults, half that for children. The same year he shipped around 180 Covenanter prisoners across the Atlantic on the *Pelican*. Ten years later James Montgomerie, another Glasgow merchant, petitioned Edinburgh Town Council with a proposal to transport prostitutes from the correction house to America, charging 30 shillings each to clothe and ship the women, who would then be sold into indentured service. There were opportunities at several levels for money to be made from human traffic.

Further shiploads of undesirables were disembarked in the Chesapeake area after the abortive 1715 Jacobite Rising. In the summer of 1716 four ships left Liverpool with nearly 300 Jacobite prisoners on board, destined for seven years indentured service. Many more would follow after the final defeat of the Jacobites in 1746 on Culloden Moor. But it was the 1730s that saw the real beginnings of systematic emigration. The frontier colony of Georgia needed men to hold it against the Spanish. They, with their families, were recruited from the Highlands in 1736. Another organised group of Highlanders left Argyll in 1739 to settle in North Carolina. At around the same time Captain Lachlan Campbell brought over 400 people from Islay in response to encouragement from the governor of New York, who wanted to settle the north of the colony with reliable Protestants. These migrations were harbingers of a Highland exodus to the New World which continued for over a century and a half. The reasons were various, depending on the ebb and flow of economic and social conditions, and on proselytising and pressures from landlords and agents on both sides of the Atlantic. Even before the Jacobite Rising of 1745 it was apparent that the traditional structures and relationships of Highland society were beginning to break down. New and commercially more productive ways of using the land were being introduced. Rents were going up. Clans people were realising that they could no longer depend on their chiefs when times got hard.

Similar pressures were driving another exodus of people of Scottish origin. By the 1720s Ulster Presbyterians were leaving in substantial numbers. Most of them were the descendents of Scots, mainly from the Borders and the southwest, who had migrated to Ulster in the early seventeenth century. Some of them were Scottish born, for contacts between Northern Ireland and the west coast of Scotland remained strong, with considerable traffic in both directions. The Ulster Scots had for some decades also had strong links with the American colonies, largely the consequence of the linen trade. Ulster imported flax from the colonies for its all-important linen trade, and exported linen cloth back. Like Glasgow, Belfast and Derry were accustomed to a constant transatlantic traffic; increasingly these ships were carrying people westward. Just as in Scotland, fluctuations in the economy directly affected the numbers of Ulster people who felt they had little choice but to leave. Another key factor was the marginalisation of Ulster Presbyterians. America offered freedom of worship and freedom from want. A succession of failed harvests fuelled departure. It is estimated that by 1775 more than 100,000 Ulster Scots had crossed the Atlantic.

The 1745 Rising accelerated a process that was already under way. Many Jacobites were forced into exile. Some went to America, either because they had no choice or because they already had contacts there. There were by this time established Gaelic-speaking communities where newcomers from the Highlands were likely to feel reasonably at home, even if the terrain was totally alien. The Highland connection with the colonies strengthened with the recruitment of Highland soldiers to fight in the French and Indian War which established British supremacy in eastern North America. In Edinburgh's Museum of Scotland there is a powder horn carried by one such soldier, carved with a map of the colonies he was there to defend. It is hung on a quillwork strap made by an Iroquois or Huron woman. It is an object that vividly links individuals (although it is not known who they are) with a significant episode in the story of Scots in America.

Between 1756 and 1763 thirteen Scottish regiments were raised; only one of them was Lowland. The preference for Highland troops was only partly in recognition of their abilities as soldiers. It was also a way of ensuring that young men, of whom there were thousands dispossessed and disaffected in the aftermath of the Jacobite defeat at Culloden, were removed from the places where they might cause trouble. These regiments saw service in Europe and India as well as in North America, but the Highlanders seemed to do particularly well in frontier terrain. Indeed, there were those who considered them kin to the native allies of the French they were fighting. The campaign did not start well, however, and the 42nd Highlanders, the Black Watch, under Glasgow-born Lord James Abercrombie, suffered heavy casualties in a fruitless attempt to take Fort Ticonderoga at the foot of Lake Champlain. Further south Highland troops were also involved in suppressing Cherokee attacks which erupted in response to incursions into their hunting grounds. With British victory many Highland soldiers remained in North America, settling on land grants in New York's Mohawk Valley as well as Upper and Lower Canada. But even if they did not remain in the Thirteen Colonies the word was out as to the nature of the country and the opportunities available. Reports from the troops coming home meant that more and more Scots were forming a picture of the New World.

The end of the war in 1763 brought a decade of relative stability. This coincided with increasing pressures on Scotland's population, particularly in the Highlands. It has been estimated that between 1760 and 1775 around 40,000 Scots departed for North America. There was, in the words of Norman McLeod who wrote a memoir of the period, 'a strange passion for emigrating to America'. Nearly three hundred people left McLeod's native Skye for North Carolina in 1772. In July 1774 over 800 left from the island of Lewis alone. Highland landlords needy for cash, often to sustain lifestyles divorced from their traditional responsibilities, were raising rents. Tacksmen, the more substantial tenants, were among the first to see that the old ways were disappearing irrevocably, and some persuaded families from their communities to accompany them to America. These were people who could afford to pay their way. Their example triggered the interest of others. As McLeod put it, 'their ideas of America were inflamed by the strongest representation and the example of the neighbouring clans'. But although many emigrants at this time were Highlanders, Lowlanders were also turning their thoughts westward. Poor harvests in the 1770s affected Lowland tenant farmers and farm workers and sent prices up. The textile trade, which had been employing increasing numbers in central Scotland and the Glasgow area, faltered and weavers found themselves out of work. It was natural that they should be tempted by the other side of the Atlantic.

For the years 1774 and 1775 records were compiled documenting the reasons for departure of emigrants from England and Scotland. Although some, like John McBeath who left Sutherland for North Carolina because crops failed and rents went up, clearly believed themselves to be on the edge of destitution, others saw America as an opportunity rather than a refuge. William Monro, a shoemaker from Tongue, departed with his wife and two servants. Aeneas Mackay, young and single, had learned 'to read, write and cipher, and goes to Carolina in hopes of being employed as a teacher or as a clerk', a prospect which was probably not open to him in Scotland. James McLeod yielded to temptation only because he felt he could not 'live decently by my industry at home'. He went to Virginia with the intention of making enough in the tobacco trade to enable him to return to Scotland and live according to his aspirations: 'you will excuse me,' he wrote in a letter of September 1776, 'if I think it would be more agreeable to me to live at a distance from my former acquaintances till such time as I can get something to enable me to live on a good footing with them'.

Scottish newspapers and journals took a keen interest in the other side of the Atlantic. Letters, pamphlets and advice to emigrants also spread information and a largely positive portrayal of colonial society. A pamphlet entitled *Information to Emigrants* had little doubt of the advantages: 'Liberty and plenty has induced many of our countrymen to seek after more benign skies, and a more bountiful soil; they have found them in America...' This kind of promotion added fuel to emigration plans born of deprivation and despair. But not everyone who set off for a new life found 'benign skies' and a 'bountiful soil'. 'We've turned into Indians right enough,' mourned one Gaelic settler in the New World; 'in the gloom of the forest none of us will be left alive, with wolves and beasts howling in every cranny.' A correspondent from Baltimore tried to deter people from 'abandoning their own homes to such a precarious subsistence so many thousands of miles across the Atlantic Ocean' and asserted that there was 'not one in a thousand of these deluded people, who, after twelve months experience do not wish themselves at home again'. There were descriptions of Highlanders arriving bewildered and destitute in New York. 'They were in the utmost distress,' reported the *Edinburgh Advertiser* in May 1775 of a group of new arrivals, 'sorely lamenting their departure.'

In 1772 the Scots American Company of Farmers was formed, based at Inchinnan in Renfrewshire. These were tenant farmers and artisans, 139 of them at the start, who got together with the aim of making a collective purchase of land in the American colonies. They raised £1,000 and sent two of their number, James Whitelaw and David Allen, to investigate the possibilities. The two men travelled hundreds of miles through New York, New

Hampshire, Pennsylvania, Maryland, Virginia and North Carolina before making their choice of land at Ryegate, New York, on the Connecticut River (now Vermont). Whitelaw reported to the company that 'no place we have seen is better furnished with grain, flesh, fish, sugar, roots, and other garden stuffs than this' and added 'here can be had all the necessaries of life and several of the luxuries and we think any that hath joined this plan and comes here and settles and is industrious may have a very genteel and comfortable way of living in a few years'.

The land was duly acquired. The first task was to prepare it for settlement. Tools were purchased in New York City and with the help of a third member of the company, James Henderson, the land was surveyed and cleared, and houses were built. The first settlers arrived in May 1774, to be followed by the remainder the following year. Other groups, for example the United Company of Farmers of Perth and Stirling and the Arnprior Society for Emigrants, also Stirlingshire, settled on land along the Connecticut River. Vermont's Caledonia County bears witness to the origins of the first settlers.

Not all emigrants showed the same care and circumspection as the Scots American Company, but the successful transplantation of such groups inevitably encouraged others. Every downturn in the economy was accompanied by a renewed interest in the other side of the Atlantic. In April 1783 the *Aberdeen Journal* commented that 'a spirit of emigration is spreading fast', adding 'considering the extreme scarcity, even bordering upon want, that prevails in many districts, it is no wonder that emigrations should take place'. At times the level of departure was of great concern to the authorities and efforts were made to discourage emigration. Landlords saw their workforce vanishing and as those who left Scotland were often among the better off – only they could afford passage money and resources to establish themselves in a new life – there was worried comment on the fact that cash as well as labour was leaving the country. Those who could not afford to pay their own way could volunteer themselves for indenture, which meant signing up to anything from four to seven years labour in exchange for free passage and the chance of owning land at the end of the period. Unscrupulous agents did not always wait for people to volunteer. Cases of kidnapping young men and boys were not unknown. Robert Louis Stevenson was drawing on the practice when he has David Balfour, hero of *Kidnapped* (1886), bundled on board the brig *Covenant* bound for the Carolinas. The wreck of the *Covenant* on the Hebridean coast saves David from becoming a transatlantic commodity, sold into indenture. In 1755, the year in which *Kidnapped* is set, the Maryland census recorded about 7,000 indentured servants, including convicts, with around 2,000 being released each year when their period of service came to an end.

Although some indentured labourers were recruited directly by landowners and businesses, others were taken across the Atlantic as a speculative venture. 'They arrive on board ships, entirely in the style of the sale of cattle at a fair in Scotland,' commented a letter from New York to the *Caledonian Mercury* of October 1774. The letter enclosed a notice taken from the *New-York Gazetteer* advertising the sale 'on board the ship Commerce' of 'Weavers, Tailors, Blacksmiths, Nailers, Shoemakers, Butchers, Sawyers, Wheelwrights, Hatters and Spinsters, from 14 to 35 years of age' who had just arrived from Scotland. A British army officer writing home to his father made a similar comment on this trade in human beings. 'They sell their servants here as they do their horses, and advertise them as they do their beef and oatmeal.' John Harrower from Shetland, who himself had a positive experience of indenture as a tutor, referred to 'soul drivers' who boarded newly-arrived ships to buy up groups of immigrants 'and then drive them through the country like a parcel of sheep until they can sell them to advantage'. Some indentured servants managed to escape, before or after they reached their destination. Numbers simply vanished into the back country. Others were shackled, like slaves, as they were marched from place to place in search of a buyer.

Official attitudes to emigration fluctuated, depending on circumstances both in America and in Scotland. During the Napoleonic Wars there was a rising demand for kelp, a seaweed abundant on Scotland's west coast, which provided alkali, an important ingredient in the burgeoning industries of linen, glass and soap production. Gathering kelp was labour intensive and west coast landowners were anxious to retain their tenants as a workforce. The government was duly lobbied and the result was the first of several Passenger Acts, passed in 1803. It introduced rigorous regulation of conditions on board ship which reduced passenger numbers. This made the Atlantic voyage less grim, but inevitably the cost of passage increased.

With the end of the war, cheaper overseas sources of alkali again became available and the demand for Hebridean kelp ceased. The men, women and children who had undertaken the backbreaking work of collecting and burning the kelp were no longer required. At the same time, discharged soldiers were returning home and looking for work, and industry's adjustment to peacetime lessened the demand for labour. All of a sudden, the notion of offloading what was looking like a surplus population seemed attractive. When a rash of emigration societies spread particularly around the Glasgow area, government support was forthcoming to help them on their way. A combination of self-help and official encouragement, plus increasing levels of information about what life might be like in North America, spurred the departure of thousands.

Factory weaving was driving handloom weavers out of work, and many felt they had no choice but to leave Scotland. Towns such as Paisley, Lanark and Renfrew lost large numbers. In February 1774 the *Caledonian Mercury* reported that 500 Paisley weavers were about to emigrate. Local factory owners, fearful that a potential workforce was disappearing, petitioned parliament to provide relief in order to stem the tide of emigration. The early decades of the nineteenth century saw an intensification of clearances in the Highlands, which had begun several decades earlier but were renewed as landlords sought to increase the productivity of their land. Many saw sheep as their salvation. They could feed on land that wasn't much use for anything else, and minimal manpower was needed for their care. Large tracts of land were being cleared of people to make way for easy-maintenance sheep. This displacement of population did not necessarily result in departure from Scotland. Many families were moved from inland straths to newly-built coastal villages, and thousands left the Highlands to seek work in central Scotland's mines, mills and factories. But large numbers nevertheless embarked on the voyage across the Atlantic, and many of those whose first steps took them to Glasgow's mills or Lanarkshire's mines later found themselves continuing their journey on a westward bound ship.

The descriptions of parishes in the *Old Statistical Account* (1791–99) are full of references to migration. The causes were clearly identified by the minister of Glenelg in Inverness-shire:

> Emigration is thought to be owing in a great measure to the introduction of sheep, as one man often rents a farm where formerly many families lived comfortably; & if the rage for this mode of farming goes on with the same rapidity it has done for some years back, it is to be apprehended emigration will still increase. But this is not solely the cause; the high rents demanded by landlords, the increase of population, & the flattering accounts received from their friends in America, do also contribute to the evil.

He added that a more equal distribution of land would enable families to stay put. The minister for Jura and Colonsay was less sympathetic. His view was that if the islanders worked harder they could improve their circumstances without having to leave: 'Instead of trying the effects of industry at home, they foster the notion of getting at once into a state of ease and opulence, with their relations beyond the Atlantic.'

The departure of emigrant ships became a common sight, not just from the Clyde but from ports all round Scotland's coast, from Leith to the Solway. In his novel *Lawrie Todd* (1830), John Galt writes of emigrants from Scotland to New York State as 'a caravan of human cattle'. Alexander Sutherland in 1825 witnessed emigrants at Cromarty in the northeast about to leave for America, their baggage 'piled in heaps on the quay'. They were the victims of clearance, men, women and children, 'one and all quitting their fatherland to seek an asylum in that of a stranger... the dejected looks of those who had reached maturity declared that to suffer in crowds scarcely lessens the poignancy of misfortune'. For ships departing from the east coast the voyage was much longer and often more dangerous than for those leaving from west coast ports, because it involved negotiating the notoriously unpredictable Pentland Firth. When the *Bachelor* left Leith in 1772 the intention was to pick up 280 emigrants at Thurso for passage to North Carolina. The emigrants were duly embarked, but it was already half way through September, late in the season for crossing the Atlantic.

Soon after leaving Thurso storms forced the *Bachelor* to put in at Stromness in Orkney. On a second attempt she was driven even further off course and forced to put in at Walls in Shetland. The ship needed repairs. Months passed and eventually the *Bachelor* returned to Leith, by which time the emigrants had exhausted their supply of money and had become dependent on the Shetlanders for help. Twenty-eight of the passengers remained in Shetland when the *Bachelor* left; the others were deposited in Leith, destitute. It is believed that some of the original 280 eventually made it to North Carolina, but most never did.

Many emigrants were picked up from remote west coast sea lochs and inlets by ships which then headed west. Others went first to Greenock, whose residents became accustomed to a large transitory population waiting for passage to America. Agents for ship owners and for those involved in land speculation in the New World increasingly played a part in recruiting emigrants. The usual practice was for individuals, or groups of individuals, to take up large land grants on favourable terms but with an obligation to settle them. To fulfill this obligation, and to recover their financial outlay, agents had to persuade hundreds of people to cross the ocean. Often agents and land speculators themselves never did.

Sir William Johnson, an Ulster Scot, was initially highly successful in peopling the 20,000 acres he acquired in the Mohawk Valley west of the Hudson River. He went there originally in 1738 to act as land agent for his uncle Sir Peter Warren, but was soon operating on his own behalf, acquiring land direct from Native Americans with whom he established good relations. He recruited Ulster Scots, New Englanders and Scots from the Highlands and the Borders as settlers. Whitelaw and Allen of the Scots American Company inspected his land but ultimately opted for settlement further north.

With the American Revolutionary War the pattern of settlement changed and existing settlers found their lives turned upside down. Although a few were able to maintain an uneasy neutrality, most had to make a choice between siding with the rebels who rejected government from Britain and remaining loyal to George III. There were Scots on both sides of the divide, but many, particularly those from the Highlands, joined the British forces or were compelled to leave their homes and either return to Britain or trek north into Canada. Emigration to the Thirteen Colonies drastically diminished. When it resumed after the peace of 1783, those intending to settle in the new-fledged United States of America had a changed prospect in front of them. Although part of the appeal of the colonies had always been the potential of a freer, less constrained society, where anyone might own land and do well whatever their background, now these colonies were an independent republic. Paisley-born Alexander Wilson, weaver, poet and ornithologist, left for the US in 1794 after his radicalism had landed him a spell in a Paisley jail. Four years later his belief in the US had not declined: 'men of all nations,' he wrote to his father, 'and all persuasions and professions find here an asylum from the narrow-hearted illiberal persecutions of their own Governments'. As *The Scotsman* was to comment in 1817: 'political feelings induce many to emigrate, who have no reason to complain of their worldly circumstances'. There were those who preferred British North America, Canada as it would become, which seemed to offer the same opportunities while retaining the authority of the British crown. But Scottish communities in the US which had survived the revolutionary war still attracted other Scots to join them, especially kith and kin. These connections were maintained, even when Scottish settlers moved west with the moving frontier. 'The Anglo-American republic is a pole-star to guide the people in their course towards freedom and prosperity,' announced *Chambers Journal*, which was consistently pro-American.

If the reasons for choosing to go to the USA were not quite the same as before, the reasons for choosing to leave Scotland remained, although they fluctuated in intensity. Most of those who left felt driven by deprivation and lack of opportunity. In John Galt's second emigration novel, *Bogle Corbet* (1831), the hero explains his motives: 'I saw before me the contraction of employment. I had five sons to be sent into business; no opening could be discerned for young men.' Some were forced to depart, although most of those who were evicted from their homes with passage paid to North America were destined for Canada rather than the USA. There was a growing, and convenient, belief that Scotland was simply overpopulated and that emigration was the only answer. The potato famine of the 1840s brought a renewal of efforts to organise large scale departures, as families struggled to feed themselves. Although there was aid from church and government, and a few landlords made efforts to sustain their tenantry, the overwhelming pressure was to reduce the population. Grim scenes of dispossession were enacted which often left whole families, including the very old and the very young, without any means of support. The minister of Sleat in Skye in 1851 summed up the consequences of evictions by Lord Macdonald, who had accumulated massive debts. Around 60 tenants in the area had been cleared, although they were all up-to-date with their rent:

> All their land is now in the hands of four or five men, and these small tenants have been driven up the hillside to trench more ground, to be at some future period pounced upon by a large farmer; or you will find some of them in lanes or closes, or dark areas in Edinburgh.

It is not surprising that many felt that leaving Scotland altogether was preferable, especially if there was a place to go where land was plentiful and productive. Not everyone who crossed the Atlantic would become a landowner, but they knew that in Scotland there would never be the opportunity of cultivating their own piece of territory.

Around the middle of the nineteenth century, clearance to make way for vast sporting estates brought another wave of devastation to Highland communities. By 1884 there were nearly two million acres of deer forest. Growing anger and resentment culminated in the formation of the Highland Land League in 1883 and direct action through rent strikes and land raids. While the Crofting Act of 1886 brought fairer rents and protection from eviction, it did not make more land available. For many, emigration continued to be a tempting prospect; for some it was a necessity.

Whatever the inducement and whatever the goal the experience of actually crossing the Atlantic was not to be undertaken lightly, especially before the days of steam. Conditions on board early emigrant ships were often appalling: overcrowded, poorly provisioned and insanitary. James Borthwick, who in 1733 sailed for the Rappahannock River in North Carolina, commented tersely on the ten-week voyage. There was, he said, 'much ill usage, many hardships and perils at sea'. Half of the two hundred on board died during the voyage. When in 1774 Janet Schaw sailed from Burntisland, Fife, on the *Jamaica Packet* she and her relative Fanny Rutherford shared a cabin six foot by five. They had bunks and their maid slept on the floor. Schaw soon became aware that their small cabin was luxury compared with the steerage quarters occupied by their fellow passengers, emigrants who had been illegally smuggled on board and had to be kept under hatches until they were well out to sea. Their weekly rations consisted of 'one pound neck beef, or spoilt pork, two pounds oatmeal, with a small quantity of bisket, not only mouldy, but absolutely crumbled down with damp, wet and rottenness'. To drink there was 'a very small proportion of brakish bad water'. When they ran into storms Janet's cabin was flooded, but it was a great deal worse for the emigrants. The sea poured into steerage:

> For many days together they could not ly down, but sat supporting their little ones in their arms, who must otherwise have been drowned. No victuals could be dressed, nor fire got on, so that all they had to subsist on, was some raw potatoes.

In the midst of all this a woman had a miscarriage.

The year before, the *Nancy* had sailed from Dornoch in Easter

Ross for New York with 250 passengers on board. On the voyage over 50 children under four died, and six women died in childbirth. They arrived at their destination in a wretched state. The *Edinburgh Advertiser* printed a report from New York which stated that they would have 'died in the street' if local people had not helped them. A later report commented:

> The unfortunate situation of such of these unhappy emigrants as have of late been brought to this colony is beyond description; almost the one half died on the passage, owing to hunger and the bad accommodation on board the vessels that carried them... although it may be an advantage to the rich who have estates in the colonies, to get people, yet the poor emigrants cannot be placed in worse circumstances than by being brought to any of our colonies, where they may expect the very worst treatment without the least hope of getting back to their native country.

Bunks 18 inches wide with 24 inches of headroom were common. On the *Fortune*, which left Skye in 1791, 480 steerage passengers shared the use of two cooking pots.

Steamships, which were beginning to supplant sail by the middle of the nineteenth century, made a striking difference to the time it took to cross the Atlantic. Ten weeks – or longer – could become ten days. In August 1856 Robert Leggat was writing from New York to his mother in Glasgow that he had crossed on the ss *Clyde* in eleven days and seventeen hours. The passengers were so satisfied with the voyage that they produced 'an address' complimenting the captain and crew.

But conditions for steerage passengers were still generally overcrowded and insanitary, and the experience of crossing the Atlantic far from pleasant. RB Cunninghame Graham, who would later have a notable career as writer and politician, made the journey on the ss *Atlas*. It was 1873 and the fare across the Atlantic was £10. He described his departure from Glasgow's Broomielaw:

> Rain, fog and coal-dust, and the lights of whiskey shops glaring like ogres' eyes upon the crowd, decks filthy, crew either half drunk or else disabled by disease; the skipper sulky, mates thinking about home and surly, the boatswain almost inaudible through a bad cold, and the poor draggled drabs upon the shore looking like animated ragshops in the December gloom. Scuffling and cursing, creaking of blocks, throbbing of the screw, and their vessel slides out into the foul-smelling, muddy drain they call the Clyde.

After seven days at sea the galley fire was out, which meant no hot food; on offer was cold salt horsemeat and biscuit. There were storms, water running into the cabin, rats and seasickness. The whisky continued to flow and the chief engineer, from Greenock, continued his yarns.

Six years later another Scottish writer, Robert Louis Stevenson, crossed the Atlantic on the ss *Devonia,* which he joined at Greenock. The *Devonia* was a state-of-the-art steamship built for the Scottish Anchor Line in 1877. Promotional literature described her as a 'floating palace': 'every appliance that science or ingenuity could suggest has been adopted with the view of ensuring safety to both ship and passenger'. This pitch, of course, was directed to the 200 or so who travelled first or second class. Steerage passengers were packed together, as many as 24 in a space measuring 5 by 3.8 metres. The *Devonia* could carry about 1,000. The American critic and commentator Lewis Mumford highlighted the phenomenon:

> What the steamship companies discovered in the 19th century in their exploitation of the steerage passengers, the ground landlords discovered long before: maximum profits

came, not from providing first class accommodation for those who could well afford them at a handsome fee, but from crowded slum accommodation, for those whose pennies were scarcer than the rich man's pounds.

Stevenson witnessed this at first hand. A steerage ticket cost £6. He paid an additional £2 for slightly better accommodation but shared much of the steerage experience, which he vividly described. 'The stench was atrocious, heavy and sour and rancid; each respiration tasted in the throat like some horrible kind of cheese; and the squalid aspect of the place was aggravated by so many people worming themselves into their clothes in the twilight of their bunks.' In spite of this – the terrible food, the impossibility of keeping clean and the sea-sickness – the Scots, Irish, Scandinavians, Germans and one Russian on board managed to keep cheerful with ceilidhs on deck bringing together the 'fiddle, the accordion and the songs of all the nations'.

These were people whom Stevenson, in his book about the voyage, *The Amateur Emigrant* (1895), described as 'broken', failures in one land now 'fleeing pitifully' and with almost childlike optimism to another. 'In America,' said one steerage passenger, 'you get pies and puddings.' When they disembarked at Manhattan's Castle Garden they entered a maelstrom of confusion and bewilderment. For most of them this was not the journey's end. They had to cross by ferry to Jersey City in order to board the trains that would take them onward. It didn't help that it was pouring with rain.

There was a Babel of bewildered men, women and children. The wretched little booking office and the baggage room, which was not much larger, were crowded thick with emigrants and were heavy and rank with the atmosphere of dripping clothes... A bearded, mildewed little man, whom I take to have been an emigrant agent, was all over the place, his mouth full of brimstone, blustering and interfering. It was plain that the whole system, if system there was, had utterly broken down under the strain of so many passengers.

Stevenson himself would cross the continent by emigrant train to California. He was appalled by much of what he saw. 'Equality,' he commented, 'though conceived very largely in America, does not descend so low as down to an emigrant.'

In 1879 there was no Statue of Liberty and no reception for immigrants on Ellis Island, which opened thirteen years later and became for millions of Europe's displaced people their introduction to the United States of America. It was memorably described by Henry James.

> That terrible Ellis Island, the first harbour of refuge and stage of patience for the million or so immigrants annually knocking at our official door. Before this door, which opens to them there only with a hundred forms and ceremonies, grindings and grumbling of the key, they stand appealing and waiting, marshaled, herded, divided, sub-divided, sorted, sifted, searched, fumigated...

The first immigrant to be received by the Ellis Island centre was a young Irish girl called Annie Moore. Over the next half century or so thousands of Scots, and millions from all over Europe, would follow. Immigration through Ellis Island reached a peak in the early twentieth century, with over a million entering in 1907 alone. Scottish shipping lines and Scottish-built ships delivered not just emigrant Scots for processing at Ellis Island. As RL Stevenson recorded, emigrants from other parts of northern Europe came by way of Scotland and Scottish ships.

The inspection process was not easily forgotten. There were

checks on physical and mental health. Doctors were on the look out for cholera, diptheria, tuberculosis, epilepsy, trachoma, as well as less threatening ailments, and signs of disability and mental impairment. The sick were sent initially to the Ellis Island hospital, which often meant that families were separated. Those who could not be cured, sufferers from trachoma for example, were excluded. Social and economic factors were also considered. The inspectors had to be convinced that immigrants were fit to work and support their families; those deemed to be likely to become a 'public charge' were rejected. From 1917 there was a literacy test. Further into the twentieth century there were increasing pressures to limit immigration, particularly from non-European countries, and a growing fear of potentially subversive aliens with socialist or anarchist leanings. In 1886 the poet Emma Lazarus celebrated the Statue of Liberty with words that became indelibly imprinted on the image of the USA:

Give me your tired, your poor,
Your huddled masses yearning to breathe free.

The words were not taken literally.

Ellis Island is now a museum and runs an extremely valuable Oral History Project. This records the experience of Mary Dunn, who in 1923 at the age of eighteen left Stirling for Pennsylvania. Her encounter with Ellis Island shattered her vision of the USA as 'the land of opportunity'. 'They really treated you like they didn't want you – these people that were examining you.' The Scots, however, had an advantage. Most spoke English, even if not as their first language. Many had connections or family already in the USA. Through most of the nineteenth and twentieth centuries, Scots and the descendants of Scots were also entering the US across the Canadian border, some of them illegally, attracted by the opportunities for work and higher wages that rapid industrialization brought. The perception of the US as a land of opportunity, for sojourners who stayed temporarily as well as for immigrants, persisted right through the twentieth century and continues to do so. My own parents, who grew up in Edinburgh, lived and worked in the US for thirteen years.

When the poet Thomas Campbell wrote, 'If I were not a Scotsman, I should like to be an American', he was expressing what many Scots felt. He himself never went to America, but his father Alexander had spent some time in Virginia and been involved in the tobacco trade. Thomas was born in Greenock in 1777, when the American revolutionary war was changing everything for Scots in America. Growing up on the Clyde, he could not escape a vivid sense of the transatlantic world, so much so that he wrote about it in *Gertrude of Wyoming* (set in Pennsylvania's Wyoming valley, not what later became a state). That vivid sense spread throughout Scotland, and propelled thousands to try their luck across the ocean, and in some measure affected the lives of just about all those who did not leave.

In an article entitled 'Notes of an Emigrant' published in *Hogg's Instructor* in 1861, the impact and implications of migration are recognised. People were not only on the move to an unprecedented extent, they were travelling further and with more reverberating consequences. 'Emigration is one of the grandest phenomena of this wonderful transitive age, and although making less noise, and awakening less interest than the revolutions of nations, it is nevertheless, one of the most revolutionary elements in the world.' This was written in the year of London's Great Exhibition, at the height of Victorian confidence. Many emigrants would scarcely have recognised the movement in which they were caught up as 'wonderful', but for every individual who left the old country to start again in the new, it was a kind of revolution.

CHAPTER TWO

Take Courage and Come to this Country

You would do well to advise all poor people whom you wish well to take courage and come to this country.
ALEXANDER MACALESTER, 1736

IN MARCH 1772 the governor of North Carolina, Josiah Martin, wrote a letter to the Secretary of State for the Colonies. Part of Martin's task was to encourage people to settle in the colony and develop its resources. He was pleased with the way things were going.

> Near a thousand people have arrived in Cape Fear River from the Scottish Isles since the month of November with a view to settling in this province whose prosperity and strength will receive great augmentation by the accession of such a number of hardy, laborious and thrifty people.

In a few years this flow of immigration would be abruptly suspended, but at this time North Carolina was the destination of large numbers of Scots. They had been making their way there for over forty years.

The union of the Scottish and English parliaments in 1707 had brought the far shore of the Atlantic Ocean rather closer to Scotland. Although Scots had for decades been aware of a new world and its commercial potential, it was only when the Treaty of Union ended exclusion from trade with the Americas that Scots could exploit this. In the eighteenth century America became indelibly imprinted on Scottish consciousness. Scotland was a poor country. The New World offered possibilities of becoming, if not rich, at least comfortable. Individuals were tempted, and so was Scotland as a nation.

Britain's thirteen American colonies lay strung along the eastern seaboard, from Maine in the north to Georgia in the south. In the seventeenth century there were French, Spanish and Dutch interests in the New World that threatened the British presence, but one by one these were dealt with. The Dutch, who in 1626 had purchased Manhattan Island from the Native Americans and called it New Amsterdam, were the first to go. The British defeat of Holland in 1664 meant that the Dutch lost their colony. The Spanish and French were harder to dislodge. The defeat of Spain in 1748 brought some stability to the southern frontier. The defeat of France in 1763 meant the end of French claims to North America and a new chapter in the way the colonies defined themselves. By this time the pioneering phase was well over in the longest-settled areas such as Virginia and parts of New England, and major cities had grown up, chief of them Philadelphia, the child of William Penn who had been granted a large tract of land in 1681. Many Scots would disembark at Philadelphia. Some, including a number who were particularly influential in politics and education, established themselves there.

By the time the Virginia Convention made its declaration of self-government, in March 1775, there were Scots in most, probably all, of the Thirteen Colonies. They had settled in significant numbers in New York and the Carolinas. They dominated the tobacco trade in Virginia and Maryland. They were seeping westward across the Appalachians in spite of efforts to contain settlement. They came as farmers, predominantly, whatever their occupation had been in the old country, but they also brought valued skills. Scots ministers and masons, weavers and woodcutters, tobacco traders and teachers, and of course soldiers, contributed to the viability and growing confidence of the American colonies. And Ulster Scots had in their thousands continued their move westwards and populated some of the colonies' wildest frontiers.

New York was still Dutch New Amsterdam when Scots turned their attention to commercial possibilities along the Hudson River. As well as the Dutch, there were in the eastern settlements Germans, Scandinavians and of course English. There is evidence of a small number of Scottish settlers, a few in Long Island, some further north, some in Virginia, the first British colony. But the story really begins in New Jersey, in the 1680s. New Jersey, which the British also took over from the Dutch, was in 1676 divided into East and West Jersey. The land was in the gift of the Duke of York, for whom a colony and the island of Manhattan had already been named: New Amsterdam was now New York. East Jersey eventually went to a group of Quaker proprietors, which included six Scots, the most prominent of whom were the Earl of Perth and Robert Barclay of Urie, in Aberdeenshire. Barclay was an associate of William Penn, who was busy establishing a powerful foothold in the colonies. Although the Quaker connection was clearly of great importance, Barclay and his fellow Scots were keen to found a distinctively Scottish colony which would provide a refuge for dissenters, and establish plantations and commercial outlets to trade direct with Scotland. It would thus bring some national as well as individual benefit.

Part of the attraction was the fact that Scots owned the land on which the newcomers were to settle. In the colonial decades especially, Scots were known for their tendency to stick together and support each other. They preferred to go where their fellow-countrymen had gone before, especially if those countrymen were sending home favourable reports, as did Peter Watson from Selkirk in 1684: 'Poor men such as myself may live better here than in Scotland if they will but work', he wrote to his cousin John Watson.

Barclay became governor of the new colony. He set out to recruit his countrymen, issuing a pamphlet addressed to 'all tradesmen, servants and others who are willing to Transport themselves into the Provinces of New-East-Jersey in America, a great part of which belongs to Scotsmen'. Settlers were to be granted land as tenants, which would become theirs after fourteen years, on payment of a quit-rent. They were also given stock, though they were required to repay half the increase in their herds during the second seven years. Barclay despatched agents to Aberdeen, Edinburgh and other parts of Scotland, with the result that between 1683 and 1685 around 700 emigrants left east coast ports for East Jersey. Many came as indentured servants. The focus of the settlement was the town of Perth Amboy on the Raritan River; the Earl of Perth was a leading proprietor. Here the proprietors took to themselves the best lots, those with a river frontage, which had practical as well as salubrious advantages, as the river was the trading highway.

Within a few years the six original proprietors had all died or moved on, but others from Scotland became involved. John Johnstone, for example, was an Edinburgh apothecary born in the Borders. In East New Jersey he extended his original land holding of 1685 and became a prominent figure in the area, eventually becoming mayor of New York. Andrew Hamilton was another influential land holder. When in 1702 East Jersey moved from proprietary rule to form part of the colony of New Jersey, Hamilton became its first governor. Scots continued to prosper economically, with the Perth Amboy merchants building increasingly effective networks. With commercial and landowning status came political clout.

The New Jersey Scottish communities attracted more Scots to them, through family and commercial connections. The Scots tended to stick together, and this kind of consolidation heightened their identity. They wanted to deal with ministers, teachers, doctors, lawyers who were their countrymen, and if they came from the same area or if there were some family connection, so much the better. William Trent, born in Inverness of English Quaker parents, emigrated to New Jersey where he became chief justice and founder of the city of Trenton. Other members of the Trent family, James and Maurice, were in Philadelphia where they were involved in a scheme which brought children from Scotland to be sold as indentured servants. By the mid-eighteenth century Scots in the central part of New Jersey comprised about twenty per cent of the total population. Their trading connections reached to the key centres of New York and Philadelphia, their commercial links with Scotland maintained initially with the east coast. An influx of Ulster Scots strengthened connections with Belfast, and gradually Glasgow entered the picture as a key commercial player in the American colonies.

Inevitably, however, the Scottish situation in the colonies was precarious, even though James VII and II had sanctioned the East Jersey colony. His reign came to an abrupt end in 1689, and seven years later another Navigation Act excluded all but native-born Englishmen from public office in the colonies, which brought Andrew Hamilton's governorship to an end. His successor Jeremiah Basse was not a supporter of the Scots. In the aftermath of the failed Scottish attempt to establish an independent colony in Darien, in what is now Panama, which the English did their best to scupper, Scots in the colonies were required to give a pledge of good behaviour. It was perhaps pragmatism as much as anything that brought a reinterpretation of the new act and allowed Scots, including Andrew Hamilton, to return to office. He was reinstated as governor but strong anti-Scottish feeling remained and contributed to the ending of proprietary rule.

One of those with interests in Perth Amboy was Lord Neil Campbell, brother of the 9th Earl of Argyll whose involvement in the Duke of Monmouth's 1685 attempt to overthrow James VII and II led to his execution. Circumstances being somewhat awkward for Neil Campbell, he was forced to sell up and reconsider his options. He estimated that it had cost him £1,100 to buy American land, transport 22 men and three boys to work it, and provide for their needs, including tools and having houses built. Eight thousand acres had been surveyed and laid out, most of it with a river frontage and including 2,000 acres of meadow land. Campbell had been earlier involved with the Carolina Company, whose subscribers had been mainly Covenanters. They planned to establish a Scottish colony in South Carolina, free from religious persecution, which would trade with the Spanish and Native Americans with goods brought from Scotland. The plan received high-level encouragement; it would get rid of potential troublemakers.

The resulting settlement on the Ashleigh River, named Stuart's Town, was established in 1684 at Port Royal in the southeastern corner of the colony, under the leadership of Henry Erskine, Lord Cardross. Attempts to run it as a distinctive Scottish colony fell foul of both the Spanish, who claimed the settlement's territory, and the English. Part of the agreement with the South Carolina proprietors was that the Scots would police the frontier against Spanish attack. The venture was promoted by Sir John Cochrane of Ochiltree and Sir George Campbell of Cessnock who hoped to recruit a thousand initial settlers. In July 1684 the *Carolina Merchant* sailed from Gourock in Ayrshire with 140 passengers from the southwest of Scotland. Within two years Stuart's Town had been overrun by the Spanish. Hindsight suggests a rehearsal of the later and much better-known debacle at Darien, where English intransigence and Spanish hostility brought catastrophe to an infant Scottish colony.

Stuart's Town was abandoned and although the Scottish presence in New Jersey remained, its identity as a distinctively Scottish colony dissipated. But the potential of Scots to create buffer settlements on the frontier was not forgotten. Fifty years after the Stuart's Town venture James Oglethorpe, first governor of the colony of Georgia, was promoting the recruitment of Highlanders 'of Gentlemen's families and of good reputation, industrious, laborious, brave and speaking the Highland language' to combine development of the land with defence against the Spanish and French. In 1735 Lieutenant Hugh Mackay and Captain George Dunbar got together a group mainly from Inverness-shire. Around 150 men and 50 women and children embarked on the *Prince of Wales*, the passage of most paid by Georgia's trustees. Among them were John Mackintosh of Borlum and many of his people.

They crossed the Atlantic to Savannah and then headed south to enter the Altamaha River, where they established the township of Darien (known also as New Inverness) on the north bank. On arrival they were issued with rations and weapons and given 50-acre land grants. Among them were some indentured servants, who received twenty acres for themselves when their period of service was completed. The Darien settlers initially fulfilled their obligations as soldiers, in particular against the Spanish at the Battle of Bloody Marsh in 1742. But Hugh Mackay had struggled to raise sufficient numbers, and criticised the indenture system which he felt inhibited potential emigrants. He wrote to the trustees that clan chiefs were reluctant to allow their people to go. He was also angered by what he saw as a campaign of misinformation, 'carried on in the Vilest Manner, that is by underhand Agents instilling terrible apprehensions in the people's minds'. But in Sutherland, Mackay territory, his own family responded, including a brother and two nephews. He was confident, he wrote to the trustees, that in three years there would be 'more Mackays in America than in the Highlands'.

More Scots came to Georgia, settling mainly in the area around the Altamaha, which became McIntosh County, and on some of the offshore islands. Endeavours to cultivate the land met with mixed success. There was criticism when some of the settlers substituted cattle raising for crops, supplying beef and dairy products to the troops. In 1748 the war with Spain came to an end, and disbanded full-time soldiers were also offered grants of land, which many took up. Land purchased from native tribes accentuated the need for settlement. A colony without colonisers was not viable. Until 1749 Georgia banned slavery, and there were those who condemned the employment of blacks because they undercut white labour. (With bitter irony the black population was free but, in some quarters, unemployable.) The higher cost of agriculture was a disadvantage in relation to the other colonies. But some of the settlers and their descendants did very well, extending their land holdings significantly. By the second half of the century, cattle, rice and timber were all important products.

Pioneers on the colonial frontiers had to be able to deal with all kinds of disruptions and difficulties. As well as the practicalities of getting established, usually with very little help except from fellow settlers, were the hazards of an alien environment and more than one potential enemy. Native tribes erupted as pressure on them increased to vacate desirable land. Until 1763 the French challenged British colonial claims and Spain and then Mexico remained a potential threat until the twentieth century. Whether local skirmish or full-scale war, conflict disrupted the frontier and the lives of those trying to make their homes there. With the end of the French and Indian War the pace of settlement accelerated and this inevitably displaced and disturbed the Native Americans. The activities of John Stuart from Inverness, who in 1763 was appointed superintendent of Indian affairs for the southern colonies, were an attempt to hold the frontier against the rising tide of westward migrants. The peace concluded with France gave Britain jurisdiction over all the territory west of the Appalachian mountains to the Mississippi, which was of course occupied by Native American tribes, including those who had already been pushed west. Stuart's brief was to maintain peaceful relations with them and define a limit to colonisation. Potential settlers, some of whom had already been promised land grants, were resentful and it was impossible to prevent the steady leakage through the mountains. In the north Stuart's counterpart, Sir William Johnson, had a similar challenge on his hands.

The peace with France also gave Florida to Britain and the first governor to be appointed was James Grant of Ballindalloch. He had served in the war. He was keen to promote the settlement of Florida and a number of Scots were involved in emigration schemes. One was Sir Archibald Grant of Monymusk in Aberdeenshire, who acquired 20,000 acres which he planned to settle. Another was Lord Adam Gordon, son of the Duke of Gordon. As these names suggest, it was the titled and influential who were able to get their hands on land, and generally they did so without actually crossing the Atlantic. An East Florida Society set up in London had several Scottish members. A particularly exploitative and disastrous venture was that set in train by Scot Dr Andrew Turnbull, who recruited eight shiploads of people from Italy, Greece and Minorca to settle his 20,000-acre Florida land grant, which he called New Smyrna in honour of his Greek wife. The land was a hell of swamps infested with snakes and mosquitoes. In order to prevent the settlers from attempting to escape, overseers treated them savagely. They were chained and flogged, some to death. After two years half of the settlers had died.

Settlement was the key to consolidating British hold on the colonies, and a condition of these allocations of large tracts of land was that they should be populated. The land speculators saw them as a source of revenue. Very often they failed on both counts: not enough people and not enough money.

From East Florida eyes turned west. Traders were often the first to penetrate new areas of wilderness, using rivers and Indian trails before there was any thought of roads. One such was Scot William Dunbar who left Philadelphia and headed west with goods to trade with the Indians. Eventually he made his way down the Ohio River and took up a land grant near the confluence of the Mississippi and the Iberville Rivers. He brought slaves from Jamaica to grow rice, indigo, tobacco and cotton. He ran his workforce with savage punishments. Flogging was common, with hanging for the worst offenders, but he considered himself a good master. In his journal he commented on runaways, who were tracked down and flogged: 'Poor ignorant devils, for what do they run away? They are well clothed, work easy, and have all kinds of plantation produce at no allowance.'

The frontier had inevitably been moving westward almost from the time of earliest settlement. Alongside the opportunism of traders and land speculators was the seductive belief that there was unlimited and better land just over the next hill or across the next river. In the early eighteenth century, before Scots from Scotland were arriving in large numbers, Ulster Scots were in the vanguard of the moving frontier and, like the Highlanders, were seen as a useful buffer against what lay beyond. In the 1720s and '30s their destination was mainly Pennsylvania, a vast territory stretching from the Delaware River in the east to beyond the Allegheny Mountains in the west. Some of the early emigrants had joined the settlement in East New Jersey, but most of those who came later disembarked at New Castle or Philadelphia on the Delaware. From there they made their way west, where many settled in and around a township named Donegal on the Susquehanna River. 'This is a bonny country,' wrote James Murray from County Tyrone, in a letter printed in the *Pennsylvania Gazette* in October 1737. And in his autobiography John Craig described Pennsylvania as 'a large land of Liberty and Plenty'.

Further south the frontier was also on the move, and Ulster Scots were a part of that expansion, too. But the south was equally a draw for those arriving direct from Scotland. Orcadian James Gordon and his Yorkshire associate Jonas Brown acquired land on Broad River, about 180 miles northwest of Savannah, Georgia, and duly picked up emigrants in Whitby and Kirkwall. Around 80

English and Scottish settlers embarked on the *Marlborough* in 1774. The following year the *Marlborough* made a second voyage with about the same number. James Gordon himself joined the settlement but it didn't take hold before it was disrupted by war. Gordon moved on to South California and eventually back to Britain. Another Orcadian, William Manson who was master of the *Marlborough*, acquired a 300-acre plantation near Savannah and a 3,000-acre grant in the ceded lands further west.

The *Georgia Packet* left Newcastle and like the *Marlborough* picked up emigrants in Kirkwall. There were about a hundred in all, including Manson and his family. They had a terrible 82-day voyage during which there was an outbreak of smallpox. Their inland settlement on a tributary of the Little River, called Friendsborough, was established as a centre of trades and crafts intended to service the surrounding agricultural area. Manson had brought out tailors and shoemakers, smiths and carpenters, to fulfil this aim, but the project was impeded by the Revolutionary War. Manson refused to take the oath of loyalty to the patriots and returned to Orkney. He later went to Jamaica where he became a naval storekeeper. His claim for compensation from the British government took sixteen years to yield about fifteen per cent of what he had asked for.

By the middle of the eighteenth century the colony that was emerging as the most attractive to Highland Scots was North Carolina. Its first governor was a Scot, William Drummond; from 1734 the governor was Gabriel Johnston from Annandale, who had been professor of oriental languages at the University of St Andrews. Navigational markers on the Cape Fear River made it possible to sail fifteen miles inland to what became the port of Wilmington, and the Cape Fear land office was opened in 1724. The Wilmington route was taken by many Scots, who then continued upriver by long boat or lighter for a further hundred miles to what began as a small trading centre called Cross Creek.

The journey could take a week. The first Highlanders may have arrived in Cape Fear in 1729, by which time there were around 36,000 settlers in the whole of the colony. Several Scottish land holders can be identified in the 1730s. It is estimated that between 1739 and 1776 around 50,000 Highlanders settled in North Carolina, at first coming mainly from Argyll.

From 1732 there was a fairly steady stream of Highlanders taking advantage of the colony's policy of offering 50 acres per person, which meant that a large family with retainers could acquire a holding of several hundred acres. In 1732 James Innes from Caithness took up 325 acres in Bladen County. The following year Hugh Campbell and William Forbes are recorded as having substantial holdings on the Cape Fear River, but the first major organised emigration took place in 1739. Gabriel Johnston actively encouraged the emigration of Protestant Highlanders, sending letters to key families in Argyll which played on the growing concern about escalating rents and the undermining of the tacksman's role as intermediary between laird and smaller tenants. He offered various enticements, including exemption from taxes for ten years and providing financial support for poorer families.

Neil MacNeill, a tacksman on the island of Jura, was concerned about rising rents and diminishing resources. Resettlement in North California seemed an attractive prospect, and he initiated an exodus of around 350 people from Jura, the neighbouring islands of Islay and Colonsay, and Kintyre on the mainland. They sailed from Campbeltown to Wilmington on the *Thistle*, and continued up the Cape Fear River to Cross Creek. The more productive bottom lands had already been taken, mainly by English settlers, so the Scots took up grants in the less fertile pine-studded sandhills. A second small town grew alongside Cross Creek which was called Campbelltown. The two became Fayetteville after the Revolutionary War.

The Argyll settlers cleared the land and grew corn, rye, sweet potatoes, flax and cotton. They raised cattle, sheep and horses. They gathered fruit in the wild: exotic mulberries, persimmons and figs as well as more familiar brambles, raspberries and plums. They hunted deer and bear, turkeys, pheasants, wild geese and ducks. And they made productive use of the pine trees. As well as providing material for houses, barns, river boats and furniture there was a lucrative market for turpentine, resin, tar and charcoal. These were shipped downriver and exported out of Wilmington, where the settlers acquired tools and household goods, foodstuffs they could not provide for themselves, and gunpowder.

The first homes were log cabins, perhaps two rooms and an attic, with unglazed windows closed by wooden shutters. Around 1710, Thomas Nairne, who had emigrated to the colonies in the late seventeenth century, published a pamphlet in which he described what was involved for those intending 'to make a Plantation' in Carolina. He assumes settlers of some substance: the biggest outlay is the cost of two slaves at £40 each.

> The first thing to be done is after cutting down a few trees to splitt Pallisadoes or Clapboards and therefore make small houses or hutts to shelter the slaves after that while some Servants are clearing the Land others are employed in Squaring or Sawing Wall plates Posts Rafters Boards and Shingles for a small house for the family which usually serves for a Kitchin afterwards when they are in circumstances to build a larger.

While this is going on the family are expected to reside with a neighbour 'till a suitable dwelling house and conveniencys are provided fitt for them to live decently'. Nairne calculates that in the first year 'each labouring person' should be able to clear three acres ready for planting. By the third winter, 'Persons of any substance provide Brick lime or other Materials in Order to build a good house'. Along with all this advice he includes a warning:

> People who design to make their Fortunes in New Countrys
> should consider beforehand what Method or Course of Life
> they propose to follow when they arrive here & not flatter
> themselves with vain fancys as if Riches were to be got with-
> out Industry or taking suitable Methods to attain them.

Most of the Cross Creek settlers could not have aspired to
plantations on the scale implied here or to employ others to carry
out the labour. In fact, when Janet Schaw visited North Carolina
in 1774 she commented on the ethic of sturdy independence that
she saw being displayed: a boy was taught 'to glory in the stroke
he could give with his Ax, in the trees he felled, and the deer he
shot... and to guard his habitation from Indian inroads was justly
his pride'.

Breaking the ground for cultivation was equally seen as a kind
of heroic endeavour, although Janet Schaw was scathing about the
methods employed. The habit of leaving the stumps of cleared trees
in the ground meant that it was difficult to use a plough, so the
soil was dug and hoed by hand. Schaw felt that her brother's North
Carolina plantation would have been worth twice as much if he
had replaced 'American methods' of cultivation with 'the style of
the East Lothian farmer', neglecting to note that the East Lothian
environment was very different from the Carolinas. There were by
then well-established plantations available for those who could
afford them. When Allan McDonald arrived he was able to buy a
475-acre plantation with a house, barn, storehouse, stables, a grist
mill, and three established orchards. He was a man of substance:
he brought with him eight indentured servants.

As communities and their amenities grew, more substantial
homes became possible. Essential to the success of any settlement
was the construction of grist mills, saw mills, forges and tanneries.
Equally important were churches and schools, and the ministers
and teachers to go with them. For most Scottish settlement

communities the latter were a priority. In 1773 a pamphlet was published in Glasgow under the name 'Scotus Americanus' of Islay, who travelled in North Carolina. Highly critical of Highland landlords, he gave a glowing account of settlement in the Cape Fear valley.

> the banks of the river from Wilmington to far above Cross Creek, were agreeably adorned with fine seats, villas, and pleasant farmhouses, at moderate distances, on either side, which afforded a most enchanting scene of the ease and happiness which the present settlers enjoy.

Slaves, 'young healthy negroes', were available to do the hard graft while the river provided 'an easy conveyance of their commodities to market'. There were opportunities not just for those intending to farm. Professionals were needed, and 'tradesmen, mechanics, and labourers of all sorts'. They were advised to 'hasten across the Atlantic' rather than 'remain in a starving and grovelling condition at home'. In North Carolina, the pamphlet claimed, there was space for liberal sentiments to flourish and talents to find an outlet. 'Here each may sit safe, and at ease, under his own fig-tree, indulging himself in the natural bent of his genius, in patronising the useful arts of life, and in practising the virtues of humanity.'

Nearly forty years after Neil MacNeill brought people out to Cape Fear, an unidentified letter-writer commented that 'the people of Argyle... live as healthily... as in Scotland, witness some of the first Settlers yet alive above 80 years of age'. He reassured his correspondent, George Mackay of Mudal, that there was still land available in North Carolina and the possibility of doing well. Between 1733 and 1775 over a thousand individual land grants and land purchases were recorded as going to people from the Scottish Highlands. The vanguard wrote to family and friends at home and a network of contacts spread an encouraging message.

Here was a country where people could own land and property without fear of tyrannical landlords and punishing taxes. More families came from the Argyll mainland and the inner Hebridean islands. Mull, Jura, Islay, the tiny island of Gigha, furnished significant numbers. When Alexander MacAlester wrote home in 1736 recommending emigration he added that the Carolina back country 'will soon be a new Scotland'. 'They are plentiful in the Carolinas,' went the words of a nineteenth-century song, 'The Warrior Race That Was Once in the Glens'.

The early 1770s brought famine to the Highlands, which in turn put more pressure on landlords. While many, fearing for their rents, tried to inhibit emigration, others, for just the same reasons, were beginning to see the potential of changes in land use. The first evictions of people to make way for sheep began to take place, and departures for North America increased. Significant numbers began to arrive from Skye. In 1788 the *Fame* of Greenock picked up 250 Skye emigrants bound for Wilmington, and two years later another 200 from Skye arrived in North Carolina. Governor Martin wrote in 1772 that in the preceding six months nearly a thousand people had come to the Cape Fear River 'from the Scottish Isles'. He added that the province's 'prosperity and strength will receive great augmentation by the accession of such a number of hardy, laborious and thrifty people'. They joined Gaelic-speaking communities which had retained features of their old lives. Janet Schaw was impressed by the Highland communities she found:

> There is now a numerous body of the sons and grandsons of the first Scotch highland settlers, besides the later emigrants who retain that enthusiastic love for the country from which they are descended, which indeed scarce a highlander ever loses, that they will support its dignity at every risk.

She noted with approval that Highland 'gentlemen', among them former army officers, 'still retain their influence among the people'.

When Lady Liston, wife of Sir Robert Liston who from 1796 to 1800 was British minister in Washington, visited a Highland settlement near Fayetteville she commented in her diary, 'The Gallic language is still prevalent amongst them, their Negroes speak it, and they have a clergyman who preaches in it.' Over fifty years later Gaelic was still spoken, and some churches continued Gaelic services until well into the twentieth century. Fayetteville had a Gaelic printing press in the first half of the nineteenth century, and for a time the post office had to be staffed by a Gaelic speaker as there were so many customers who spoke no other language. Today there are a number of families in Cumberland County who trace a direct descent from eighteenth-century Highland settlers.

The survival of the Highland character of these communities was boosted by the new arrivals who brought their language and traditions with them. Highlanders continued to arrive by the traditional route through Wilmington, but there was also a drift of Scots south from Pennsylvania. They came down the Great Wagon Road, the main inland artery to the south. This former Indian trail was rough and rutted, hard going for the wagons and those on foot and horseback who travelled it, but it was the link, some 800 miles long, between Philadelphia and Augusta in Georgia. At the same time, many of Scottish origin were steadily moving on from the Cape Fear valley, some filtering across the border into South Carolina, others heading west across the Allegheny Mountains, joining the uncontainable westward flow.

One Scot with an eye to the western frontier was James Hogg from East Lothian. His brother Robert arrived in North Carolina in 1756 and became a partner of Samuel Campbell, a Wilmington merchant. Business prospered. Goods were imported from Britain and sold on to the Scottish communities. He purchased 12,000 acres in the interior near Hillsboro on the Great Wagon Road, with the hope that James would join him. Hillsboro has been described by historian Bernard Bailyn as 'the epicentre of backcountry Scottish settlement'. James Hogg's plan to bring 200 emigrants to North Carolina on the *Bachelor* ran into difficulties – the story is told in Chapter One – but he eventually got there and opened stores in Cross Creek and Hillsboro, where he traded imported goods for local produce. He became a prominent figure. Like so many others with some disposable cash or the means to borrow – both incomers and those who never left the old country – he speculated in land, but he also invested in Carolina's infrastructure. He put money into canals and was a key player in the founding of the University of North Carolina at Chapel Hill near Hillsboro, chartered in 1789. He was also involved in a curious episode which fizzled out when the Thirteen Colonies declared their independence. With others he launched an opportunistic attempt to establish a fourteenth colony in Kentucky, called Transylvania, with the aim of legitimising settlement that had already begun.

The project got under way with the formation, mainly by Scots, of the Louisa Company, later the Transylvania Company. Through frontiersman Daniel Boone, it negotiated a deal with the Cherokees: in exchange for £10,000 worth of trade goods, seventeen million acres were acquired in a transaction which was not legal. The land lay between the Kentucky and Ohio Rivers, and was reached via the Wilderness Road, hacked out by Daniel Boone and his axemen to provide a route through the Cumberland Gap. The town of Boonesborough was built on the Kentucky River, near Lexington. A Transylvania colonial government was proclaimed and Hogg was sent as delegate to the Second Continental Congress in Philadelphia with a remit to gain official acceptance of the newly declared colony. But there was a hitch. Thomas Jefferson, leading thinker in the movement towards independent union, was committed to opening up the west for free settlement, in defiance of the British policy of containment. Twenty or so years later, with independence achieved, the Transylvania Company received 400,000 acres of its original territory. Part of it became the town of Henderson.

The timing may not have been right, but looking beyond the Alleghenies was smart. The creation of the United States of America heralded a massive shift westward whose progress would dominate the history of the US for more than a century. For the speculators the challenge was to take up good land before it attracted general attention. That Kentucky was the next step was demonstrated by the fact that it was the first new state (along with Vermont, originally part of New York) to join the original thirteen after independence. James Hogg was canny in a number of ways, as his commercial success and manoeuvrings during the Revolutionary War indicate. His brother Robert declared himself a Loyalist and left North Carolina.

Most of those who left Scotland were looking for land to farm, but by the early eighteenth century commercial activities had created towns of increasing importance. Philadelphia, for example, was a commercial hub and a magnet for professional men. Ships came up the Delaware River, and goods and people moved in and out of the city. Scottish merchants were prominent: James Craig, William McIlwaine, Alexander Leith, John Ross were just some of those based there. The McCall family from Dumfriesshire came to Philadelphia via Glasgow and the tobacco trade. Samuel and George McCall were brothers at either end of the business. Samuel's sons became involved, and a McCall daughter, Catherine, married John Inglis, a Philadelphia merchant from a Midlothian family. Thomas Leiper, from Strathaven in Lanarkshire, only eighteen when he left Scotland, was another who became a leading Philadelphia man of business.

The Scottish networks tied together merchants and ship masters and entrepreneurs, and their families, on both sides of the Atlantic. Their activities were not always above reproach. Peter Williamson was kidnapped from Aberdeen at the age of thirteen, brought to Philadelphia and sold to a Delaware farmer, only to be kidnapped again by Cherokees. He eventually returned to Scotland, exchanged for a French prisoner in 1758. He accused Aberdeen magistrates of being involved in the kidnapping and was hounded out of Aberdeen. He set up a coffee house in Edinburgh where he began a penny post, and in 1733 he published the city's first street directory. Thus, Aberdeen, Edinburgh, Philadelphia, Scots, Americans, Cherokees and French all had a role in a story that was well-known at the time.

Such stories took their place alongside accounts of American opportunity. It was a place to make money, a place of safety, and a place where people could be their own masters. But it was also full of danger and the risks were high. Rivals, potential enemies and all the hazards of the wilderness were not far away. If it took courage to leave Scotland, it took even more to make a new life in a country which, to those who set foot on it for the first time, could be both surprisingly familiar and disturbingly strange.

CHAPTER THREE

The Most Plentiful Country in the World

My situation in this Colony is tolerable & we live in the most plentiful Country in the world, for all the necessaries of life.
RODERICK GORDON, 1734

NORTH CAROLINA SAW the most robust transplantation of Highland communities to the Thirteen Colonies. Canada, British North America as it was until the Dominion was created in 1867, received many more and their legacy has survived with some vigour. One of the most distinctively Highland areas was Glengarry County in Upper Canada (Ontario), originally settled by Loyalists who trekked north from New York's Mohawk Valley after the American defeat of King George. The Mohawk Valley was one of several parts of the colony of New York which attracted Scots. They established themselves commercially in New York City, with varying success, but many of those involved in trade and the professions were also on the lookout for land. Land was seen as the surest route to financial security as well as offering the opportunity for a lifestyle much harder to achieve at home.

John Lindsay's American career began in Philadelphia where he arrived in 1729, but he moved his trading activities to New York. He acquired land grants to the south of the Mohawk River, a major tributary of the Hudson, which he planned to settle with families from Scotland. Although his project didn't come to much – he seems to have settled only half-a-dozen families on his land – the Mohawk Valley later became a focus of Scottish settlement.

An early attempt at organised settlement in New York was that undertaken by Lachlan Campbell from the island of Islay. In 1738 he brought 83 Islay families to Lake George, south of Lake Champlain. Each family was to get 200 acres and be exempted from taxes, paying a quit-rent of 1s 9d per hundred acres. The deal gave Campbell himself a thousand acres for each family settled. It illustrates how the system encouraged land speculators, except that in this case it did not work out. More shiploads of Islay emigrants followed, but the government did not honour Campbell's claim and there followed conflicting accounts of how and why the deal collapsed, Campbell protesting that he had been cheated by the government, the authorities arguing that the families themselves refused to accept Campbell as their laird. They hadn't left their island in order to transplant the old feudal ways they thought they had abandoned. Some of the intending emigrants went back to Scotland, others made their own way in New York and other colonies. Campbell himself returned to Scotland and served under the Duke of Cumberland in the campaign of 1745–46 which crushed the Jacobites. In 1747 he returned to America and died soon after. Eventually his sons were granted land holdings of 47,500 acres north of Albany, the Argyll Patent as it became known, and some of the other original emigrants also received land.

In the same year as Lachlan Campbell brought his first Islay families to Lake George, Ulsterman William Johnson arrived in the Mohawk Valley. Within ten years he was vigorously involved in trade and land deals, and came to preside over a huge tract of land. In 1755 he became a baronet, and the following year was appointed superintendent of the Northern Indian Department and colonel of the Iroquois Confederacy of Six Nations. He brought in large numbers of Ulster Scots, New Englanders and Highlanders as settlers. The latter included soldiers disbanded at the end of the French and Indian War. Johnson himself occupied a fine house, Johnson Hall, maintained a lavish lifestyle, and added to his land holdings through negotiations with the Iroquois. His close relations with the Iroquois (he was living with the sister of an Iroquois chief) certainly helped him to success in pushing the area of settlement west to the Ohio River and concluding the Treaty of Fort Stanwyx in 1768. This allowed the Iroquois to retain lands to the north and west, in exchange for ceding the territory of Indiana. Pressure on Native American tribes from land speculators was increasing all the time and was not contained by formal treaties or attempts to control settlement and trade, but Johnson managed to strike a balance of sorts, in the process benefiting his own position.

Johnson's success in consolidating his land holdings depended on his ability to recruit settlers, at which he proved very effective. The Highland settlement grew. The disbanded soldiers, mainly Fraser Highlanders, were joined by others from Glen Urquhart and Strathglass, Inverness-shire: Fraser country. In 1773 the *Pearl* sailed from Fort William at the head of Loch Linnhe to New York. On board were about 400 emigrants, many from the Glengarry area north of Fort William, led by three brothers, Allan, Alexander and John MacDonnell. The MacDonnell brothers were tacksmen and Catholics who saw little future for themselves in a remote area of the West Highlands where the old life was under threat. They too made their homes in the Mohawk Valley, after an Atlantic crossing that took seven weeks, during which there was an outbreak of smallpox that killed 25 children.

Thanks in part to the activities of Sir William Johnson, large tracts of the colony of New York were being opened to settlement. Three million acres became available between the Mohawk and Susquehanna Rivers. Land due north of Albany on both banks of the Hudson was opened up, and also west of the upper reaches of the Connecticut River (which would become Vermont). Daniel MacLeod from the island of Arran chartered the *Charming Sally* of Philadelphia to bring emigrants to a land grant on the western shore of Lake Champlain. The ship was wrecked and although there were survivors none reached Lake Champlain. Between 1774 and 1776 thirteen vessels arrived at New York from Scotland. In 1774 the *Nancy* carried mainly Gaelic-speaking emigrants from Caithness and Sutherland. After thirteen overcrowded, undernourished, stormy weeks at sea, during which a third of the passengers died, the *Nancy* disembarked the survivors at New York. They were, according to the *New-York Journal*, 'weak and emaciated, thinly clad, some of them sickly, most of them without money, and none knowing where to go'. Their destination was the north of the colony, where Lord Dunmore had 51,000 acres awaiting settlement. In the same year John Cumming from Strathspey brought 172 emigrants on the *George* for settlement south of Albany. Over half of them were called Grant or Cumming, prominent Strathspey names. Cumming paid their passage from Greenock, and became a leading member of the new community.

The following year the first shots were fired in the Thirteen Colonies' bid for independence. In 1776 Cumming joined the Loyalists and after twice being captured by the Patriots he was eventually exchanged for a prisoner held by the British. He and his family got back to Britain, although most of the people he had helped to settle remained. Like Cumming, many of the Highlanders in New York signed up for the king, most notably those in the Mohawk Valley. Their families had little choice but to leave, during and after the war, as did those who survived the conflict. Most of them headed north, crossing the border into what was now defined as British North America, where they started again. In 1777 John MacDonnell led the Glengarry people to safety. They gave their second North American settlement, in Upper Canada, the name Glengarry County. The previous year John Johnson, the son of Sir William, who died in 1774, had escorted another 250 Mohawk settlers to the same area. He named his destination Williamstown after his father and the house that he built for himself now contains the town's public library. His father's estate, when confiscated by New York State in 1779, had grown to 200,000 acres.

The Mohawk Valley was not entirely abandoned by Scots. Not all were Highlanders or Catholic or Loyalist, and many stayed. Some of them would migrate west and south, following the new frontiers and the creation of new states. Pockets of Scottish settlement had been established in the 1760s and 1770s, like the Scots American Company of Farmers at Ryegate, and many individuals from Scotland were helping to build communities. Peter Middleton, for example, a graduate of Edinburgh and St Andrews Universities, settled in New York in 1730 and served as surgeon general of the provincial forces in the French and Indian War. He was allocated a 5,000-acre land grant and became a trustee of the Argyll Patent. In 1767 he founded a medical school. Although a Loyalist who escaped to Bermuda during the Revolutionary War, he returned to New York, where he died.

Professionals and skilled tradespeople came independently to America out of a sense of adventure and ambition as much as being driven by unfavourable circumstances. Walter and Thomas Buchanan, uncle and nephew, were members of the notable Glasgow Buchanan family which had extensive American trading interests. Based in New York City, they used their family connections to develop businesses as shipowners and merchants, exporting raw cotton to Glasgow, for the hungry cotton spinning mills, and shipping out emigrants. Nimble footwork enabled them to survive the Revolution.

The Buchanans relied on their old country connections. Scots tended to retain their links with home and with fellow emigrant Scots, for social and cultural as well as business reasons. Some returned to Scotland, either because their stay in the colonies was intended as temporary or because they gave up the attempt at settlement. Captain Duncan MacVicar, born in Craignish, Argyll, served in the 77th Regiment and took part in the debacle at Fort Ticonderoga in which the French under General Montcalm defeated the British. However, the British won the war and in 1765 Captain

MacVicar was awarded a grant of land in what is now Vermont. He and his family, including his three-year-old daughter Anne, who would later write her *Memoirs of an American Lady* (1808) as Anne Grant, made their home there for ten years but then returned to Scotland. Anne Grant's memoirs paint an almost idyllic picture of colonial life, especially in Albany on the Hudson which had attracted Scots as far back as the 1670s, when Robert Livingston based a Scottish-Dutch commercial network there. The name itself derived from James, Duke of Albany, the Scottish title of the future James VII.

Anne Grant described the genteel existence of the settlement's upper middle class. Albany, she wrote, was 'semi-rural', with a spaciousness that allowed large gardens, trees, and cows grazing on the common pasture. She stayed in a house which fronted the river and was shaded by elms and sycamores. It was a two-storeyed brick house with an attic, and a parlour and kitchen in a separate building at the back. The lifestyle was peaceful and pleasing, although Anne was troubled by the fact that it was sustained by slavery. 'One must have lived among those placid and humane people to be sensible that servitude, hopeless, endless servitude, could exist with so little servility and fear on the one side, and so little harshness or even sternness of authority on the other', she wrote, and went on to say that the settlers 'imagined' biblical justification for keeping 'this hapless race condemned to perpetual slavery'. She was also uneasy at the exploitation of the Native Americans, for whom she clearly had respect.

Albany was a hub that provided a link between the river highway to New York City, a hinterland east and west, and the northern lakes. Anne Grant's account of its well-established polite society gives us a picture of one aspect of Scottish colonial experience, while at the same time highlighting its anomalies. Even as a child she was aware that this comfortable existence was built on a shaky foundation. The British had defeated the French and appeared to have secured the colonies for the crown, but their neighbours were Indians, members of the Five Nations whom she described as 'too sagacious to be deceived, and too powerful to be eradicated', and their servants were slaves. These anomalies were perhaps why the MacVicar family did not remain.

Mrs Grant never lost her American connection. After the death of her husband, minister in the Highland parish of Laggan, she lived in Edinburgh. She published several books, which brought her considerable notice on the other side of the Atlantic, and welcomed many visiting Americans to her home.

For Scots with any awareness of the Clyde's relationship with the New World, the burgeoning American cities held a special resonance. So many of them – New York, Philadelphia, Norfolk, Wilmington, Charleston – grew as Glasgow grew and shared the same sense of challenge and potential. In some respects Glasgow was a frontier city, characterised by industrial and maritime pioneers. It was a city of crossroads and transitions. And there was one commodity above all that cemented the connection between the Clyde and the colonies: tobacco. Tobacco, and all its associated trade, took hundreds of Scots across the Atlantic and ensured that thousands more had a perception of American possibilities, even if they never themselves set foot on the continent.

There is evidence that tobacco was being imported to Scotland from the New World as early as the middle of the seventeenth century. The activity was illegal. In 1696 a report by Edward Randolph spoke of 'Scotsmen and others' in Virginia and Maryland with 'great stocks lying by them to purchase tobacco... The vessel lying in some obscure creek 40 or 50 miles from the Collector's office is presently loaded and sails away undisturbed.' From 1738 to 1744 Scotland's share of the tobacco trade was between ten and twenty per cent. By 1758 it was 30 per cent, and Glasgow had become the most important market for tobacco. Scottish merchants were also shipping tobacco to Liverpool and Bristol. In 1774, on the eve of the disturbances that led to war, 36 Glasgow firms brought 31,090 hogsheads of tobacco from America to Greenock and Port Glasgow. Most of it was shipped out again to other European ports, although Scots themselves were enthusiastic smokers and snuff-takers. The wealth of artefacts associated with these activities bears witness to that: pipes, snuff mills, snuff mulls for the pocket and for the table, survive in large quantities. The ram's horn snuff mull has become an almost iconic object associated with Scottish regiments and societies in many parts of the world. Tobacco, like sugar, lastingly imprinted Scottish life. The consequences are still with us.

The wide bay of the Chesapeake was the gateway to the tobacco plantations. There were Scots merchants, factors and planters noticeably present in the area before the end of the seventeenth century. Ninian Bell, banished from Scotland after the defeat at Dunbar, arrived in Maryland in 1652. He settled on land between the Potomac and Patuxent Rivers and called his estate Fife's Largo. Tobacco was one of the first commercial crops to be developed by settlers along the rivers of tidewater Virginia and Maryland, the James, the Potomac, the Rappahannock, although it was a demanding crop to grow. The young plants had to be nursed and protected from weeds and disease. And the crop was greedy of the soil's nutrients. After three years the soil was exhausted and new land had to be cleared. The harvested leaves were stored and cured, then packed into hogsheads for transportation downriver. The work was done increasingly by slaves, although indentured labour was vital, especially in the early years. Without slave labour Glasgow's extraordinary Atlantic success would not have been possible.

The Scottish involvement in tobacco grew from the activities of smugglers before the Union of 1707 to total dominance of the trade in the 1770s. The key players were a relatively small number of families, many of them connected, whose legacy can be seen in

Glasgow street names: Glassford, Buchanan, Ingram are among the better known, but on the south side of the Clyde you can also find Oswald, Dunlop and Wardrop Streets. Names like Virginia, Washington and Jamaica are also reminders of Glasgow's transatlantic connections. These were the men, most of whom never set foot in the colonies and were rarely to be seen on docksides downriver, who became the icons of success in tobacco, the 'tobacco lords' as they were described. They were able to put their profits into land and status, and also to foster the Clyde valley's industrial output generally. Iron manufacture, coal mining and textiles particularly attracted the tobacco lords. Some set up businesses to supply the goods they needed to trade for tobacco. They built fine houses: William Cunninghame's in Queen Street, Alexander Speirs' in Virginia Street, for example. Those who could developed estates on land outside Glasgow. John Glassford acquired the estate of Dougalston in Dunbartonshire; William Cunninghame's estate was at Lainshaw in Ayrshire. On the other side of the Atlantic, Norfolk, Virginia became virtually a Scottish town, with Scots also prominent in other centres of the tobacco trade: Alexandria, Dumfries, Falmouth, Richmond in Virginia; Port Tobacco, Baltimore and Bladensburg in Maryland. John Campbell wrote from Bladensburg in 1772 that 'a man of slender fortune can live here much more easy and to his satisfaction than he can in Britain'.

The tobacco merchants were kenspeckle figures in Glasgow's social, economic and political life, but their profits depended on the activities of the planters, factors and storekeepers on the other side of the Atlantic, and the shipmasters and crews who brought the precious weed to the Clyde. Scottish success in a highly competitive trade was the result of an intricate network of mutually-supportive connections and the development of a distinctive system of trade. The shorter passage from the Chesapeake to the Clyde also gave them an advantage over those trading to English ports. The foundations were laid by men who went out to the colonies and through a combination of opportunism, hard work and building on connections established themselves as traders. John Graham grew up in Dumfriesshire and went to Virginia in around 1739, where he helped to found Dumfries on the Potomac as a centre of the tobacco trade. John Carlyle from Annan was by 1749 running his own business in Alexandria, also on the Potomac, trading grain, beef and timber to the West Indies and bringing back rum, sugar and slaves which supplied the plantations. Thomas Leiper from Lanarkshire went to Maryland and then to Philadelphia. His success as a tobacco exporter brought him to prominence as one of Philadelphia's leading businessmen. He fought for the Patriots in the Revolutionary War, became a director of the Bank of the United States, and founder of Philadelphia's Franklin Institute.

Early successes encouraged Scots to try their luck in tobacco in the hope of returning to Scotland after a few years with money in their pockets. There was fierce competition for colonial jobs. It helped if you knew the right people, or at least had letters of introduction from people with connections. Sometimes, with a job as factor or store keeper for one of the tobacco companies, it was possible to carry on some independent trading, but generally fortunes were not made by the middlemen. They were expected to work hard and often had to make do with rudimentary accommodation.

Those who achieved most financially tended to have their fingers in several pies. Neil Jamieson is a good example. As chief colonial representative of John Glassford & Co he arrived in Virginia in 1760 and took charge of the company's tobacco stores. Based in Norfolk, he also engaged in commercial enterprises on his own account, trading with the Caribbean, the Azores and the Mediterranean, and was involved in shipbuilding and coastal shipping. He dealt in sugar, timber, wine, salt and slaves, shipping the latter from the Caribbean to the Carolinas. He became a partner in the Glassford company and also in a Virginia-based distillery.

Never one to miss an opportunity, he was quick to offer to supply the British army when the Revolutionary War forced him to abandon Virginia for New York. But, like many Scots who were caught by the outbreak of war, his losses were huge.

William Allason from Glasgow was a store keeper on the Potomac in the late 1740s and in 1757 became the representative of Alexander Walker & Co, based in Norfolk. He went into business independently in Falmouth as William Allason & Co, and traded in tobacco, slaves, grain and rum, dealing with a number of Glasgow-based firms. He had his own plantation to which he retreated during the war, and managed to trade with both the British and the Americans. He emerged unscathed and remained in the new state of Virginia as a wealthy member of the landed gentry until his death in 1800. Another Norfolk-based independent merchant was James Parker from Port Glasgow, though as a Loyalist he was hit hard by the Revolutionary War. In a letter, his wife reported how they and other members of the Scottish community were struggling to maintain themselves.

The trading system favoured by the Scots meant that the factors bought the planters' crops outright, thus taking the risk of storing, transporting and selling the tobacco on. The system involved providing extended credit to the planters for the goods they purchased, locking them into a relationship from which they could not escape. Although it diminished the risk for the planters, it put them in a position where they could not bargain. When times were good Scots could offer better prices, but often the planters had to accept low prices for their crops or find themselves peremptorily being asked to pay their debts. If there was a squeeze on credit generated on the other side of the Atlantic – which occurred strikingly in 1772 – they felt the impact. As a result, complaints against the Scottish operators were loud. Sometimes complaints erupted into physical abuse. The tone of anti-Scottish feeling is well illustrated in the *Virginia Gazette* of 11 October 1771:

The Scotch Nation about fifty years ago, being informed of this valuable Country, and of the weak and blind Side of its Inhabitants, chose, some of them, to quit their Packs and leave their poor Fare, and Barren Country, and make an Experiment in the Tobacco Trade; which, by a little Industry, and the mechanick Turn of Mind and the artful Craftiness and Cunning natural to that Nation, they soon not only raised great Estates for themselves, but found a Plan to enrich their Country, and raise Glasgow, from being a poor, small, petty Port, to one of the richest Towns and trading Ports in his Majesty's Dominions, and all by Fawning, Flattery, and outwitting the indolent and thoughtless Planters.

As the rumblings of war grew louder, attacks on Scots intensified. 'Everything is in the greatest confusion,' wrote 'A Gentleman in Virginia' in a letter printed in the *Caledonian Mercury*, November 1774, and went on, 'A Scotchman is in danger of his life (at least being tarred and feathered) if he says a word that does not please them'. There were around 2,000 tobacco factors in Virginia at this time, and most of them were Scots.

The Revolutionary War hit both planters and merchants hard. Those with foresight were able to ship out their cargoes and sell them at a higher price as demand exceeded supply. But many who did not support the patriot cause lost crops, goods and cash. Land was confiscated by the new state authorities. Debts became almost impossible to recover. Most Scottish factors were forced to depart in short order. Inevitably some companies did not survive the war, although the tobacco trade did not cease altogether and after the war it recovered quite quickly. Profits continued to roll into Glasgow, but the days of Scottish dominance were over and the special relationship between the Clyde and the Chesapeake was never re-established.

That special relationship has tended to overshadow other aspects of Scottish activity and settlement in Virginia and Maryland. Tobacco and commercial interests were powerful magnets that attracted not only those directly involved. As 'Scotus Americanus' pointed out, there was a need for all kinds of skills, not only to service the growing communities but to develop the colonies' industrial base. Hugh Orr from Lochwinnoch provides an example of the role Scots played in the move away from dependency on the mother country. A gun and lock smith, he emigrated to Massachusetts in 1737 and started a business in Bridgewater making scythes and axes, essential tools which had initially come from Britain. Orr was creative and adaptable. He invented a machine for dressing flax, and when war came, turned to arms manufacture. Peacetime found him producing spinning and carding machines for the growing New England textile industry.

There was scope for teachers, ministers, doctors and lawyers. Scots preferred their professionals to come from the old country, and the new country provided a refuge for a wide range of individuals who found themselves on the margins. Among these were Episcopalians, under pressure from the Presbyterian Church of Scotland. James Blair had been Episcopalian minister in the village of Cranston, Midlothian, and went to Virginia in 1685, where he represented the Bishop of London – Virginia was in the bishop's diocese. He soon became a highly influential and rather contentious figure in political, religious and educational circles, helping numerous Scottish Episcopalians to colonial posts. It was largely through his efforts that the College of William and Mary was founded in Williamsburg in 1693. He became its first president, which he remained until his death in 1743.

Episcopalians were attracted by America because it offered them freedom of worship. Presbyterian ministers came because there were communities who needed them. By 1760 there were around 200 Presbyterian church ministers in the American colonies. Of these 55 were Ulster Scots, who were particularly active in the founding and sustaining of Presbyterian congregations, and 26 were from Scotland. The Presbytery of Philadelphia had been set up in 1706 by an Ulster Scot called Francis Makemie, a graduate of Glasgow University. He arrived in the colonies in 1683 and immediately ran into trouble with the authorities by preaching in Anglican New York. In 1706 Makemie acted as moderator at the first recorded American ordination of a Presbyterian minister, a man called John Boyd, at Freehold, New Jersey.

In a letter of August 1716 to the principal of Glasgow University, the Reverend James Anderson, who had arrived in Delaware in 1709, gave a picture of the colonial Presbyterian Church:

> In this country there are since I came here settled three other Presbyterian ministers, two of which are from your city of Glasgow. There are, in all, of ministers who meet in Presbytery once a year, sometimes in Philadelphia, sometimes here in Newcastle, seventeen; and two probationers from the west of Ireland, whom we have under trial for ordination; twelve of which have had the most and best of their education at your famous University of Glasgow... We make it our business to follow the Directory of the Church of Scotland, which, as well we may, we owe as our mother church.

Of necessity American Presbyterian congregations looked to Scotland to provide ministers and the education of ministers, but demand exceeded supply. There were appeals for Presbyterian ministers to go to congregations across the Atlantic. In New York in 1724 John Nicol was asking for both ministers and funds from Scotland. Generally the congregations themselves had to raise the money to bring ministers to America.

Ministers also arrived as missionaries. The Society for the Propagation of Christian Knowledge was founded in Edinburgh in 1709 with a primary aim of operating in the Scottish Highlands.

But later their concerns spread to the American Indian. By the time the General Assembly of the Church of Scotland had authorised colonial missionary activity in 1762, there had already been some success in educating and converting members of eastern tribes. In at least one case a minister, Reverend John MacLeod in Georgia in 1735, served both Gaelic-speaking Highlanders and Indians. The conversion of Native Americans was seen as a means of integrating them into the social and economic habits and methods of colonial society, but it was rare for them to be accepted as equals.

Alongside the Presbyterian presence was the role of Scots as educators. The value Scots placed on education travelled with them. In the colonial context a school was almost as much of a priority as a minister; often minister and teacher were one and the same. The needs of both church and community were exemplified in the activities of William Tennent, a graduate of the University of Edinburgh who emigrated in 1718. Interestingly, Tennent, Presbyterian in background, had turned to the Anglican church but reverted to Presbyterianism when he arrived in the colonies. In 1735 he opened a college at Neshaminy in the north of Pennsylvania to prepare young men for the ministry. Tennent was an advocate of a revivalist, more liberal Presbyterianism which did not find favour with the more conservative strand of the church; nevertheless, several other 'log colleges', as they were called, were opened. The College of New Jersey, which became Princeton University, was inspired by the broad-based log college approach.

It is not surprising that Scottish and Scottish-trained doctors were so prominent in colonial America. Edinburgh University's Faculty of Medicine was established in 1726 and rapidly became a world centre for medical training. From 1748 Glasgow University was also providing medical training. Historian William Brock estimates that probably all the American colonies had Scottish doctors, but most were to be found in Virginia, the destination of at least 45. Nineteen went to Maryland and the same number to

South Carolina. Fifteen went to North Carolina. The Scottish influence on medicine was considerable, not only through Scottish doctors but through American-born men who went to Scotland, mainly Edinburgh, for their training. The first American to graduate in medicine at Edinburgh was John Moultrie from South Carolina, whose father was himself a Scottish doctor. Scottish medical training influenced the medical schools that were founded in the colonies. The first of these was in Philadelphia in 1764, modelled on the Edinburgh pattern and with the majority of its professors educated there. The medical school which opened four years later in New York was also strongly influenced by the Edinburgh model.

There was scope, too, for colonial administrators. The colonies generally had a high proportion of Scottish governors and other officials. Robert Dinwiddie from near Glasgow was surveyor-general of the southern colonies, which gave him control of customs from Philadelphia to Jamaica. He was lieutenant-governor of Virginia from 1751 to 1757. He had arrived there via business activities in Glasgow and Bermuda, where he was collector of customs. He was in an advantageous position to involve himself in land deals beyond the Appalachians, not yet opened up for settlement.

The last royal governor of Virginia was John Murray, 4th Earl of Dunmore, appointed in 1771 having already been governor of New York. He built Fort Dunmore on what is now the site of Pittsburgh and led a campaign against the Shawnees, who were being pushed, like all the native tribes, steadily further west as new settlers clamoured for land. The Shawnees were persuaded to support the British against the patriots. Lord Dunmore had the task of dissolving the provincial assembly of Virginia because it defied British control. When war broke out he made an ineffective attempt to govern from a warship anchored offshore. After the war he became governor of the Bahamas.

Scotland's traditional emphasis on education meant it produced more literate, numerate and professionally qualified men than the home economy could absorb. North America became a safety valve for Scottish aspirations as well as for Scottish grievances. It wasn't the only part of the world where surplus Scots found a role – India was also an attractive prospect – but America was the nearest, and by the middle of the eighteenth century it had well-established Scottish communities and a strong network of Scottish connections. India was a place to work for a number of years with the hope of making sufficient money to return in comfort to Scotland rather than a permanent destination. For a new life, rather than the means to sustain an old one, America beckoned. It was portrayed over and over again as an environment of plenty where a family had time to enjoy the fruits of their labours.

Alexander Thomson abandoned farming near Paisley to settle in Pennsylvania with his wife and twelve children. In a letter of 1773 he evokes an idyllic scene: 'While I and my sons are clearing ground, and go for a while to walk, or rest ourselves in the forest among the tall oaks on a summer day, the sight of the heavens and the smell of the air give me a pleasure which I cannot tell you how great it is.' Janet Schaw on her visit to the colonies in the 1770s was often critical, but she concluded that 'nature holds out to [the settlers] every thing that can contribute to conveniency, or tempt to luxury'. She went on to say that the settlers did not make the most of these advantages and made brisk suggestions as to how they might do better. Alexander Thomson was not just impressed by the climate and environment. He also emphasised the more democratic nature of colonial society. 'With respect to our laws they are made by those who are, not nominally only, but really our representatives; for without any bribes or pensions, they are chosen by ourselves, and every freeholder has a vote.'

At around the same time as Janet Schaw was visiting, William Mylne was also in the colonies. Mylne, the builder of Edinburgh's North Bridge, had left the city under a cloud. The unfinished bridge had collapsed in August 1769, killing five people, and he had had to finance the rebuilding out of his own pocket. Debt drove him to America, where he arrived in the autumn of 1773. Although he hoped to acquire a plantation and slaves to work it, he was forced to struggle for survival in a cabin at Stephen's Creek, near Augusta, Georgia. There he lived alone, growing vegetables, hunting and fishing. But the prospect of making a go of pioneer life was daunting. 'It is impossible for me to do anything in these woods by myself,' he wrote. 'There are trees to cut down, roots to grub up, the ground to plow, corn, indigo, tobacco, to plant. At present a great part of my time is lost in providing victuals for myself, this I mostly do by my gun and fishing.' He asks for news from home, and clothes, books, magazines and a recipe for curing fish. In spite of his difficulties, he managed remarkably well, although with little chance of expanding beyond subsistence farming.

After around a hundred years of growing involvement in North America, Scots had made an imprint on each of the Thirteen Colonies. Scottish ships plied in and out of most colonial ports. Scots were likely to have a foothold in commercial centres of any importance, and most communities of any size had their share of Scottish lawyers, doctors, ministers and teachers. Significant numbers, including many of the colonies' most prominent men, had been taught and trained by Scots, and a steady stream of non-Scots sought an education in Glasgow or Edinburgh. The Presbyterian church flourished, although not without internal strife. Above all, increasing numbers of the aspirational, the anxious and the dispossessed were leaving Scotland to start afresh along America's vast frontier. The message coming back to those at home, in Highland and Lowland Scotland and in the Ulster counties where so many identified themselves as of Scottish Presbyterian descent, was that America was indeed a land of plenty. It was that perception of bounty that ensured that sooner or later the colonies would bite the hand that attempted to control them.

CHAPTER FOUR

American in My Principles

*I am an American in my principles and wish
we would let them alone to govern or misgovern
themselves as they think proper.*
DAVID HUME, 1776

ON THE EVE of the revolt of the American colonies, Janet Schaw
was on her brother Robert's plantation at Wilmington, North
Carolina. She did not like everything she saw and heard. There
was, she said, 'a most disgusting equality' with little distinction
between a 'gentleman' and a 'clown'. She commented severely on
the anti-government protests that in 1775 were increasing in
vehemence, and briskly stated her opinion that 'two regiments'
of the British army would quickly sort things out in North
Carolina.

She was not alone in her views. William Mylne had been in
Georgia for six months when he wrote in a letter to a friend in
Scotland in May 1774, 'We are still in suspense whether there is to
be a war or not.' The following spring he abandoned his attempt
at settlement and set off to make his way north and east by slow
stages, which took him through South and North Carolina, Virginia
and Maryland. Everywhere troops were mustering and drilling.

In the back parts the[y] have several companies whose exer-
cise is shooting with rifled guns at a dollar fixed to a tree at
the distance of 120 paces, these are the most dangerous, being
accustomed to fighting amongst the trees with Indians they
are very dexterous... In Maryland they muster every where,

I could get no sleep for some time in Annapolis for the noise
of their drums and fifes...

Nevertheless, his view was that 'in case they come to blows... one
third would run away, one third be killed, the other hanged'. In
spite of the evident fighting skills he witnessed, and the growing
level of disturbance, he did not take rebel abilities seriously.

Trouble had been brewing for some time. British victory in the
French and Indian War brought security to the Thirteen Colonies
and encouraged territorial and commercial confidence. Colonial
soldiers, who were not professionals, had proved themselves as
frontier fighters. Settlers were accustomed to carrying arms, and
in the back country, where the formalities of law and order were
thin on the ground, they were used not only to protect themselves
from Native, French and Spanish incursions but also to enact
summary justice and deal with disputes for themselves. Large
numbers of Ulster Scots had settled in the back country, and they
brought with them their own traditions of self-protection and family
feuding which centuries of border warfare in both Scotland and
Ireland had fostered. The Presbyterian Ulstermen had little reason
to favour the British government, and most were energetic
supporters of separation. They were likely participants in the back
country target practice witnessed by William Mylne.

Britain had fought an expensive war which had inevitably
encouraged a spirit of independence. The British government
response was to try to exert tighter control of a potentially volatile
situation. In 1765 the Stamp Act was passed, through which it
was hoped to raise revenue to pay for the war by taxing all
documents, contracts and newspapers. It provoked demonstrations
and riots in the colonies and had to be repealed the following year.
A leader of disturbances in Boston was one Ebenezer MacIntosh, a
shoemaker and clearly of Scottish descent. The government tried
again, with a tax on imported goods – glass, paint, paper, tea –

which affected almost everyone in the colonies. The Scottish tobacco trade, of course, depended on imports as trade goods. There was more protest and this, too, was repealed, except for the tax on tea. The response was a boycott. In Charleston tea was left to rot on the quay. From Philadelphia and New York it was sent back to Britain. In Boston in 1773, 300 chests of tea were dumped overboard – the celebrated Boston tea party. Three years earlier edgy British troops had fired on a provocative Boston crowd, full of resentment against the tax. The sense of injustice went deep. Colonials were being asked to pay for a British war, albeit one that protected them, while colonial profits were going to the mother country in whose government the colonies could not participate.

Scottish settlers, merchants and soldiers were caught up in the building tension, while emigrants from Scotland continued to arrive. It was not a good time to start a new life. In the summer of 1775 the *Edinburgh Advertiser* was reporting that hundreds were disembarking with nowhere to go and little means of supporting themselves. 'Several emigrants from Scotland have of late arrived here,' commented the *Advertiser* of 25 July. 'I wonder that any persons that could make shift to live at home would come to this infatuated continent till matters are once settled, when there will be room enough for thousands to sit down upon *estates* already cleared.' Many of the new arrivals were attempting to return to Scotland, though most did not have the means to pay their passage. The message going back to Scotland was that intending emigrants should be deterred from coming to a country where 'anarchy and confusion' prevailed.

In July 1776 the Continental Congress, set up two years before in defiance of the British government, convened in Philadelphia and adopted a statement divorcing the American colonies from Britain: the Declaration of Independence. It was drafted by Thomas Jefferson, but others influenced its content, in particular Benjamin Franklin and John Adams. They were not Scots, but the impact of

Scottish thinkers and teachers helped to shape their thoughts and their language. Franklin had twice visited Scotland, in 1759 and 1771, a time when Scotland was electric with intellectual exchange and practical innovation. That was what attracted Franklin and why he was eager to meet Scottish luminaries such as David Hume, Lord Kames, William Robertson, Adam Smith and others. He saw at first hand some of the practical results of the Enlightenment belief in the possibilities of improvement. He visited Lord Kames's estate at Blairdrummond, near Stirling, where he was impressed by the programme of land reclamation and the introduction of improved crops and breeds. Here was evidence of humankind's ability to take control of the future. Franklin was so impressed by the people he met and the things he saw that he felt that 'did not strong Connections draw me elsewhere, I believe Scotland would be the Country, I should chuse to spend the Remainder of my Days in'.

Back in America, he corresponded with many of his new acquaintances, who themselves took a keen interest in transatlantic developments. David Hume's essays on political and moral philosophy were widely read in the colonies, and he himself was sympathetic to the Americans. He predicted revolution, although he died in 1776 before the full consequences were apparent. William Robertson, a Church of Scotland minister and principal of Edinburgh University from 1762 to 1793, set out to write the first history of America, but was interrupted by the war which he condemned. Adam Smith was very influential. Americans were also familiar with the work of Kames; we know that he was read by Jefferson, John Adams and James Madison, a key figure in the drafting of the American Constitution. Kames himself was in favour of a 'consolidating union' between Britain and America.

Ideas emanating from Scotland had an impact on Thomas Jefferson. As a boy he was taught by a Scottish clergyman, William Douglas. His tutor at the College of William and Mary was William

Small, a graduate of Aberdeen's Marischal College. Small would later become president of the College of Philadelphia, whose first provost had been another Scot, William Smith, who had come from Aberdeen in 1751. Scots were prominent in education throughout the colonies, acting as private tutors, founding schools and colleges and shaping the curriculum. This ensured that American education was developing along lines that differed from those pursued by English institutions. The Scottish approach was more broadly based, more practical in its stress on training the mind. Many of the Scottish teachers who made their way to America were grounded in the ideas of Thomas Reid, professor of moral philosophy at Glasgow University who had also taught at Aberdeen, and founder of the 'common sense' school of philosophy which highlighted the existence of objective reality. This pragmatism seemed suited to a pioneer country which, while eager to educate its young, was acutely aware of the need for practical skills.

Thomas Reid's thinking had been influenced by an earlier professor of moral philosophy at Glasgow, Francis Hutcheson. Hutcheson, an Ulster Presbyterian whose grandfather had come from Ayrshire, had taught that the study of philosophy provided guidelines for how life should be conducted. It was not just an intellectual pursuit. Hutcheson's ideas, like Reid's, were channelled into the colonies by the many Scots who had been exposed to them, and their impact on those who would shape events in America was striking. His *System of Moral Philosophy* has been identified as a key influence, not least because it highlighted circumstances in which it was justifiable for a colony to break away from the mother country. 'If the mother country attempts anything oppressive toward a colony, and the colony be able to subsist as a sovereign state by itself... the colony is not bound to remain subject any longer,' he wrote. Not only that, he believed that it would be unnatural for a society to continue to be governed by 'a distant body of men who know not sufficiently [its] circumstances and experiences'. He also articulated notions of democracy that fed colonial demands for liberty: 'civil power can scarcely be constituted justly in any other way than by the consent of the people'. One phrase of his in particular has an echo in the Declaration of Independence which included 'the pursuit of happiness' as an inalienable right: 'That action is best, which procures the greatest happiness for the greatest numbers.'

The origins of American ideas of independence and democracy were not exclusively Scottish, of course. The English philosopher John Locke, who died (in 1704) before the Scottish Enlightenment was underway, was deeply influential on the generation of writers and thinkers that followed him and has always been identified as a key source of American thinking. But the impact of the Scots is clear and direct, and men such as Franklin and Jefferson acknowledged their debt. The approach to education adopted by William Small at the College of William and Mary emphasised the teaching of ethics and of rhetoric, the earliest incarnation of literary studies. Jefferson paid tribute to him in his *Autobiography*:

> It was my good fortune, and what possibly fixed the destinies of my life, that Dr William Small of Scotland was then Professor of Mathematics, a man profound in all the usual branches of science, with the happy talent of communication, correct and gentlemanly manners, and an enlarged and liberal mind.

Jefferson was generally well disposed towards teachers from Scotland and encouraged their recruitment. From Scotland, he said, 'we are surest of having sober attentive men'. But the Scottish influence was not only distilled through Franklin and Jefferson. Three of the 56 signatories of the Declaration of Independence were taught by Francis Alison, who had been a pupil of Francis Hutcheson at the University of Glasgow and arrived in America in

1735. At the College of Philadelphia he lectured on Hutcheson. Two other signatories were born in Scotland (nine signatories were of Scottish descent). John Witherspoon and James Wilson were prominent participants in the professional and educational worlds, and had a significant input to the documents that defined the emerging republic.

John Witherspoon from East Lothian was minister of the Laigh Kirk in Paisley when in 1766 he was approached by the College of New Jersey, later Princeton University, with an invitation to become its sixth president. After some deliberation he accepted, and sailed for Philadelphia in 1768. His impact on American education was profound. He, too, considered philosophy and rhetoric the foundation of study, and stressed the importance of writing skills. Benjamin Rush, an American who studied medicine at Edinburgh and played a key role in developing medical training in the colonies, commented in his autobiography that Witherspoon 'gave a new turn to education, and spread taste and correctness in literature throughout the United States'.

Witherspoon's American activities were many-stranded. He was involved in land speculation and settlement schemes in New York State and Nova Scotia, and he contributed publicly to the cause of American independence. In May 1776 he preached a sermon which included 'An Address to the natives of Scotland residing in America', which was later published. Witherspoon was provoked by the widespread attacks on Scots in the colonies, who were commonly considered to be pro-government. It didn't help that the figure most associated with a repressive colonial policy was Lord Bute, a Scot who was head of the British government for a short period but influential for much longer. He was particularly close to George III, to whom he had been tutor. Bute and fellow Scots in London were popularly seen as being dangerously big for their boots. In Britain, as in the colonies, there were outbursts of anti-Scottish invective. There were plenty of Scots who believed their commercial and land-owning future depended on the colonies remaining British, but Witherspoon argued: 'There are many natives of Scotland in this country, whose opposition to the unjust claims of Great Britain has been as early and uniform, founded upon as rational and liberal principles, and therefore likely to be as lasting, as that of any set of men whatever.' His own position was unequivocal: 'I willingly embrace the opportunity of declaring my opinion without any hesitation that the cause in which America is now in arms is the cause of justice and liberty.'

The vehemence of anti-Scottish feeling is expressed in a response to Witherspoon by Ezra Stiles of Yale University, who wrote, 'The Policy of Scotland & all the governmental Ideas of the Body of that People, are abhorrent to all Ideas of civil Liberty & are full of rigorous tyrannical Superiorities & Subordinations.' And he added, 'Let us boldly say, for History will say it, that the whole of this War is so far chargeable to the Scotch Councils, & to the Scotch as a Nation (for they have nationally come into it) as had it not been for them, this Quarrel had never happened.'

Underlying much of the animosity against the Scots was resentment of their commercial success and the grip of the tobacco merchants, whose interests lay with supporting the government. When Virginia and other colonies demanded a pledge of loyalty from merchants, storekeepers and others, large numbers of Scots were among those who chose to leave, abandoning their assets to be taken over by the colonial authorities. The *Scots Magazine* reported that Scottish houses in Virginia had been destroyed 'and all their goods and effects distributed among the populace'. Some Scottish families were making their way to the West Indies 'having been driven from Virginia for their joining with the friends of government'.

Witherspoon's thinking fuelled ideas of independence and he himself was unequivocal in stating his views. Like many other Scots who were products of a Presbyterian environment and a Scottish liberal education he was prepared to burn his boats. James Wilson, twenty years younger, was another. Born near St Andrews, he had attended the universities of St Andrews and Glasgow. He emigrated in 1765 at the age of 23 and studied law in Philadelphia. He would eventually become the first professor of law at the College (later University) of Pennsylvania and Associate Justice of the US Supreme Court. He signed the Declaration of Independence and helped to draft the constitution of the United States.

There were other signatories of Scottish and Ulster Scottish descent. Philip Livingston, for example, was the grandson of Robert Livingston from Ancrum in the Borders. Thomas McKean's family had left Argyll for Ulster in the mid-seventeenth century. George Ross was the son of a Scots minister and uncle of Betsy Ross, who sewed the original stars-and-stripes. The Scottish supporters of independence were mainly Presbyterian in background. Episcopalians, like William Smith, for example, and Catholics were more likely to remain loyal to King George. Smith's counterpart William Small was a Presbyterian and a Patriot, although he eventually returned to Britain.

But perhaps more important than the Scottish credentials of key figures in framing and carrying out the American rebellion was the fact that so many Scottish ideas were current in the colonies. Scottish Enlightenment thinking travelled with individuals who crossed the Atlantic and in publications which, directly and indirectly, were available in America. Many Americans went, like Benjamin Rush, to Edinburgh or Glasgow for their education and brought back innovatory ideas which were applied to colonial institutions. Even those who did no more than practise their Scottish university training, like the many physicians, ministers and teachers, were imprinting what Robert Louis Stevenson described as 'a strong Scotch accent of the mind' on communities with evolving identities. It wasn't just accidents of emigration that made Scots so influential, but that fact that Scotland attracted the attention of many leading colonial figures and produced ideas that filtered through to colonial communities.

Some of these leading figures, including James Wilson and William Smith, were members of the Philadelphia St Andrews Society. The first St Andrews Society in the colonies was founded in Charleston in 1729. The Philadelphia Society came eighteen years later, set up by a gathering of Scots in the city's Tun Tavern on Chestnut Street with the aim of providing assistance to Scots in need. A plaque put up near the site of the tavern reads:

Here, in 1747, at the Tun Tavern 25 Gentlemen of Philadelphia from that part of Great Britain called Scotland formed the Saint Andrew's Society of Philadelphia. Since that time, Scotsmen of honour and integrity have contributed toward a charitable design to provide for the relief of distressed Scots after their arrival in Philadelphia.

The members were lawyers, ministers, medical men and merchants. They met regularly to consider requests for help and the allocation of funds, which were generous by the standards of the times. They also enjoyed convivial evenings, and it is tempting to speculate that these may have echoed the gatherings in Edinburgh at which leading figures of the Enlightenment enjoyed vigorous debate and unrestrained consumption of claret. Any discussion in the 1770s of issues of the day must have been spirited – James Wilson and William Smith did not agree on the matter of independence, for example.

Five members of the Society were signatories of the Declaration of Independence. The Society's minute book records the escalation of events with its entry on 31 August 1776: 'the President and Vice-President judg'd proper to put off this Meeting, owing to a number of the Members being out of Town, or more particularly on account of the convulsed and unsettled State of the Times'.

When the Declaration of Independence emerged there had already been a year of sporadic fighting and the convulsions were intensifying. The centre of sedition was Virginia. It was at the Virginia Convention in March 1775 that Patrick Henry, whose people came from Aberdeen, made his bold and inflammatory 'give me liberty or give me death' speech. The previous year he had announced, 'I am not a Virginian, but an American', thus embracing an overarching identity that could express a confederation of states. But the opening shots were fired in April 1775 at Lexington, Massachusetts, and there followed the first moves in a campaign that the British had little reason to believe would be other than short-lived.

Attempting to deal with these anti-British eruptions was Lord Dunmore, governor of Virginia. He tried to enlist support for the government by offering to free slaves and indentured servants in return for service with the British, a move which did not endear him to plantation owners. He twice dissolved the obstreperous provincial assembly, but his efforts to remain in control were in vain. He was forced to retreat to Norfolk on the coast, the focus of much Scottish trade, which was devastated by British and Patriot troops. For a while he struggled to govern from the safety of a warship, but when the British fleet withdrew to New York it carried him and numerous Scots who were abandoning the smouldering ruins of their trade. There was little Dunmore could do to salvage the situation and in 1776 he returned to Britain.

Many Scots hoped to keep their heads down and ride out the storm, and a few succeeded, but most could not escape a choice between loyalty to the British crown and actively supporting the Patriot cause. They soon realised that the former involved either joining in combat or leaving the country. Some faced an even starker choice. Scottish merchant James Dunlop chose the Patriot cause in the face of hanging. Another had to choose between execution and setting fire to his own vessel, which had carried a prohibited cargo.

For those in debt to Scottish firms it was an opportunity to clean the slate. James Parker, a Scot based in Norfolk, commented: 'Generally speaking the more a man is in debt the greater Patriot he is, in short the meaning of words like Tyrant is greatly altered and calling a man a patriot here is saying he is in bad circumstances.'

Although many Loyalists had been Jacobites, there were supporters of Prince Charles Edward who became American Patriots. Prominent among them was Hugh Mercer, born in Pitsligo, Aberdeenshire, in 1725. He served as a surgeon in the Jacobite army and became a fugitive in 1746 after Culloden, managing to escape from Leith for Philadelphia, where he became a member of the St Andrews Society, which still possesses his sword. Alongside other former Jacobites he served with distinction in the French and Indian War. A friendship developed with George Washington, a fellow officer, and when the revolutionary war broke out he joined the Patriots, serving as a general. He was fatally wounded at the Battle of Princeton in 1777, where the Americans had a minor success before their major setback at Brandywine nine months later.

Washington needed skilled and dependable soldiers, but his campaign relied also on knowledge of the terrain. In 1777 he appointed Robert Erskine as his army's geographer and surveyor general. Dunfermline-born Erskine was a surveyor and engineer who had arrived in America in 1771 at the age of 36, to take on management of the American Iron Works. Although he died suddenly in 1780, his work for the Continental Army resulted in maps of New York, New Jersey and Connecticut, and of the road to Yorktown where the final episode of the war was played out.

In the early stages of the war the Highland Scots who had settled in North Carolina's Cross Creek area prepared to take up arms for King George. They were recruited by General Donald MacDonald of the British army, whose cousin Allan MacDonald of Kingsburgh was the husband of Flora who had thirty years earlier helped to rescue Charles Edward Stewart from another British army. Allan became General MacDonald's second-in-command. Allan and Flora MacDonald were people of substance and authority in the clan. They had come from Skye to North Carolina in 1774, so hardly had time to establish themselves before hostilities erupted. After staying in a temporary home on a plantation owned by relatives, they purchased a plantation and house of their own. They had been there less than a year when the call to arms came. Most of the North Carolina Highlanders were Loyalists, prepared to fight for a royal family that in 1745 the Jacobites among them had been ready to supplant. But this was not so much a change of allegiance as a commitment to the authority of king and clan and all that that implied. They had fought for king – albeit Stewart rather than Hanoverian – and clan at Culloden, not a republic. There were those who were scornful of 'tattered Scotch Highlanders' and their adherence to old-fashioned 'feudal notions', as one Philadelphian put it, which kept them 'wholly at the beck of their chiefs'. But 'feudal notions' were not the only reasons for opposing the new republicanism.

General MacDonald's plan was to march his Highlanders to the sea to rendezvous with regular troops expected to arrive at the mouth of the Cape Fear River. There were 1,400 men under his command, inadequately armed. Two thousand American Patriots led by Colonel James Moore set out to intercept them. On 27 February 1776 the two forces were 25 miles northwest of Wilmington, on opposite sides of Moore's Creek, which the Loyalists had to cross to make their way to the coast. The American troops removed the decking planks of the only bridge, and smeared the remaining timbers with grease. When the Loyalists attempted to make their way across the greasy remnants of the bridge they were easily picked off; the vast majority turned and fled. Thirty Loyalists were killed and 850 captured, among them Allan MacDonald, who had taken over command when General

MacDonald became ill. After a period of imprisonment in North Carolina and Philadelphia he eventually rejoined his wife, who had returned to their home in Skye. But most of the Highlanders who survived the war did not get back to Scotland, although many thousands left the American colonies. With American victory in 1783 around 30,000 Loyalists were evacuated from New York to Nova Scotia and New Brunswick, and had little option but to have a second try at making their homes in North America.

Alexander Morrison was also taken prisoner after Moore's Creek. Seven years later he was claiming compensation from the British government, describing how 'the modern way of improveing Estates in Scotland' had forced him to leave Scotland 'with 300 of his Neighbours' and settle in North Carolina. He spent his own money in supplying Loyalist troops, which resulted in persecution from 'an Enemy wanton in Cruelty and Barbarity who for five years sweapt away all the Produce of his Plantation leaving only a bare Subsistence for his Family'. As a prisoner he was 'for more than a year dragd from Gaol to Gaol & marched more than 1,000 miles before he was admitted to parole in 1777'. The following year he was exchanged but was captured again as he was trying to make his way back to North Carolina. Even allowing for some exaggeration to strengthen his claim, his account gives us a glimpse of an experience of war which was shared by many in his position. Communities in the back country were already vulnerable, contending with frontier conditions and poor communications when war erupted. Some never recovered, whichever side they supported.

For many Patriots, Scots became symbols of all that they most detested about government from Britain. For them, a Scot was by definition the enemy. A captured officer of Fraser's Highlanders wrote in the *Scots Magazine* of how he and his men had been abused by local people as they were marched inland by their captors. They were easy targets for the resentment that had existed long before hostilities broke out. As so often, the turmoil and anxiety of war merely heightened simmering tensions.

The battle at Moore's Creek proved for large numbers of North Carolina Scots the end of their American adventure. For those who stayed in the fight, activities were limited to minor skirmishes and guerrilla raids until the British turned their attention to the southern states later in the war. Following Moore's Creek, Cape Fear merchants were arrested and stores closed. Scottish communities, especially those who were openly Loyalist, were no longer viable, but not everyone was able or willing to leave. Alexander Morrison managed to return to Britain after four years of confusion. Families deprived of their menfolk struggled on if they could. Some settlers withdrew deeper into the back country in the hope of sitting out the hostilities, but there were few who were able to escape the war and its immediate consequences.

Loyalist regiments were recruited throughout the colonies. The Royal Highland Emigrants (84th Foot), as the name implies, was formed mainly of Highlanders already settled in North America, though it included some new arrivals who were virtually forced to enlist. In September 1775 the *Glasgow Packet* was intercepted and men on board required to volunteer, while their families were taken on to Halifax. This wasn't an isolated occurrence. New Jersey, Maryland, Virginia and Pennsylvania all fielded Loyalist regiments. From the Mohawk Valley came two battalions of the King's Royal Regiment of New York, and the men who formed Butler's Rangers, organised in 1777 by Major John Butler. The Caledonian Volunteers from Pennsylvania indicates Scottish origins. Not all Loyalists were Scots, of course, but substantial numbers were.

The war was fought at sea as well as on land, and it was in that arena that probably the best-known Scottish fighter for American independence distinguished himself. John Paul Jones was born at Kirkbean on the Solway coast in 1747 and went to sea at an early age. He made a number of transatlantic voyages, and for five years was mate on a slave ship. In 1773 he inherited property in Virginia, and when war broke out became an officer in the American navy. He was soon a byword in Britain through his raids on the coast and his victory in an engagement with the British off Flamborough Head. The *Pennsylvania Gazette* of 20 January 1780 greeted his exploits with rhapsodic enthusiasm:

> The gallant adventurer John Paul Jones... has entered the Humber, and would have burnt Hull, had not his orders been to the contrary. He has had it in his power to burn Leith, and many other towns upon the coast, and to light up a flame, that, like the Aurora borealis of their skies, would have made the night luminous.

If the threat of a raid on Leith brought the American war to Scotland's doorstep, the daring reality of a raid on the Solway home of Lord Selkirk, close to John Paul's birthplace (he took the name Jones later), brought the war across Scotland's threshold. Although after American independence he moved on, becoming commander of Russia's Black Sea fleet, John Paul Jones achieved heroic status in the United States. He died in Paris in 1792. Over a hundred years later his remains were returned to the USA.

During the winter of 1777–78 it looked as if the Americans, demoralised after their defeat at Brandywine, could not succeed. The British had captured Philadelphia and the Continental Army, now under the command of a member of the Virginia gentry called George Washington, was underfed, under-equipped, and leaking soldiers who lost heart and headed for home. But the Patriots had a crucial advantage, which Moore's Creek illustrated. As William Mylne commented, these were men used to fighting an elusive enemy in rough terrain which they knew well. Guerrilla tactics were their speciality. British troops, trained to fight pitched battles in open country, were forced to adjust their strategy. Their first major setback was the American victory in October 1777 against General Burgoyne at Saratoga, New York, after which the British focused their attention on the south where they hoped to rekindle Loyalist support. At first this seemed effective, and in Georgia and the Carolinas General Cornwallis's army was augmented by new recruits as it worked its way north from Savannah. The objective was Virginia, but to the west were areas settled by Ulster Scots whose allegiance to the American cause was well known (although just as there were Patriot Highlanders, there were Loyalist Ulster Presbyterians). Prominent in this campaign was Major Patrick Ferguson, an Edinburgh-born professional soldier who had seen service in the Caribbean. He attracted attention both for his soldiering and for his development of a breech-loading rifle that was lighter and faster to load and fire than the muzzle-loading muskets used by the infantry. He arrived in New York in May 1777, in charge of an experimental company of light infantry armed with Ferguson rifles.

Ferguson took part in the capture of Charleston and then made his way northwest with his American Volunteers, recruiting as he went. It was the autumn of 1780. Gathering to meet him were men from the back country of Georgia, the Carolinas and what would become Tennessee, including large numbers of Ulster Scots. At King's Mountain on the border between North and South Carolina, Major Ferguson's troops were surrounded and attacked by a force of 3,000 under the command of Colonel William Campbell. Ferguson, his right arm crippled by an earlier wound, had two horses shot from under him before he was brought down. A witness estimated that 'almost fifty rifles must have been levelled at him at the same time'. When his demoralised troops tried to surrender they were slaughtered by Patriots inflamed by the memory of recent defeats in the area, although Colonel Campbell tried to restrain them. It is probable that throughout the campaign, in skirmishes as well as major battles, men of Scottish origins found themselves facing each other.

Hostilities were not confined to formal encounters. In the confusion of guerrilla warfare old scores were settled and communities and families divided. Divisions and differences endemic in the old countries erupted in the new. Back country Scots continued the fight for King George, mainly as bands of a few hundred led by men such as Archibald McDougald, Duncan Ray and Hector McNeill, until their defeat in 1781 by General Rutherford at Big Raft Swamp. There were some very bloody encounters. By the time peace was restored, about half the Highland Scots who had settled in North Carolina had left. But that meant that half remained, although perhaps not where they had originally settled. Officially they had to take an oath of loyalty to the new republic, as did Duncan Blue who in 1769 had arrived in Cape Fear country from Knapdale, Argyll. Many must have avoided this by slipping away into frontier territory.

The British army raised sixteen regiments in Scotland in response to the war, although they were not all sent to America. The regiments that fought there suffered huge casualties as well as losses from disease, capture and desertion. Recruits were enticed with promises of New World benefits – many would have known that Scots who fought in the previous American war had been awarded land. Highland recruits in particular may already have had connections in North America. The Revolutionary War both strengthened and undermined those connections. There were more Scots on American soil, but they were engaged in a divisive struggle that forced a choice of allegiance on those caught up in it.

The slaughter on King's Mountain did not halt the progress of Cornwallis, who carried on into Virginia and captured Richmond before establishing his army at Yorktown on Chesapeake Bay. But the Americans persisted, and with the help of their French allies isolated the British and cut them off from supplies. In October 1781 Cornwallis surrendered. When nearly two years later peace was concluded in Paris, one of the chief negotiators was Benjamin Franklin. There was now in theory a union of thirteen states which had to be forged into a real and governable confederation. Scots were again influential in what transpired.

Alexander Hamilton, whose grandfather was from Ayrshire, was born in the West Indies in 1757 and arrived in the American colonies in 1772. He joined the Continental Army and at the age of twenty became Washington's aide-de-camp. After the war he studied law and became a member of Congress, the first stage along the road to his becoming a skilled and canny statesman, although not so canny that he was able to avoid confrontation with rival Aaron Burr in a duel that killed him. But by that time he had made his contribution to the infant republic's political future. He was prominent among the 54 members of the Constitutional Convention whose task it was to draft a constitution for the United States of America. Faced with the challenge of balancing the hard-won liberty of the new nation, the interests and identities of the thirteen states, and the individual freedoms in the name of which the war had been fought, Hamilton favoured a strong centralising government. He wanted a president and senate elected for life.

What emerged was inevitably a compromise, but a compromise that directly reflected some Scottish ideas, perhaps not surprising as twelve members of the Convention were of Scottish descent and others were the product of an education that had a strong Scottish flavour. Key to the successful achievement of compromise was James Wilson. He argued for a blend of federal authority and democratic principle, which at the same time protected the interests of those who he and others believed to be essential to the future of the new republic. He insisted that government authority depended on the consent of the people – but democratic rights extended only to male property owners. Slaves, indentured servants, women and all others without property were not included in the process. Some of the material which was being used to construct a new style of government had been around for a long time.

If Alexander Hamilton represented the new generation of American political players, Wilson, fifteen years older and equally ambitious, was a direct link with the ideas and experiences that had led to the Declaration of Independence. He was also, of course, a direct link with Scotland. A powerful ally in these debates was James Madison, a former student of John Witherspoon at the College of New Jersey, who introduced him to the work of David Hume. In his essay 'The Idea of a Perfect Commonwealth' Hume had discussed how centralised power might be contained and guarded from corruption. He believed that a degree of dispersal would prevent the forming of over-powerful alliances. Madison interpreted this in the American context in his own 'Notes on the Confederacy'. James Wilson and James Madison were the principal authors of the American Constitution.

In the years leading up to the Revolutionary War and during the war itself Scotland took considerable interest in events in the colonies. Much of this was driven by a keen awareness of the importance of transatlantic trade, to individuals and to the Scottish economy. The proliferation of family connections with the colonies meant that there were also strong personal ties. News took a long time to cross the Atlantic (it was two months, for example, before Patrick Ferguson's family learned of his death) but it was eagerly sought, and newspapers and magazines gave America significant space. The *Scots Magazine* had a regular 'Plantation News' feature, and in an issue of 1775 reminded readers that 'the American dispute has been an object of our particular attention ever since its beginning'. When war broke out, all over Scotland the rebels were condemned. The motion passed by Kirkcaldy Burgh Council sums up the sentiments, 'expressing abhorrence of that rebellious spirit which has prompted [George III's] subjects in America to take arms in opposition to his Majesty's Government'. Many would remember the last rebellion against the king of thirty years earlier and the panic it had caused. The American colonies were 3,000 miles away, but people in Scotland were well aware of what the repercussions could be.

There were also, of course, expressions of support for the Patriot cause. Several prominent Presbyterian ministers made no secret of their pro-American views. The Reverend John Erskine, for a time minister in Kirkintilloch, wrote a pamphlet published in 1769 but reprinted in 1776, entitled 'Shall I go to war with my American brethren?'. In two further pamphlets he took issue with government colonial policy. He corresponded with several Americans, sent them books and was keenly interested in developments there. David Erskine, 11th Earl of Buchan, was vigorously pro-American and greeted the Declaration of Independence with enthusiasm. He, too, had met Benjamin Franklin in Edinburgh, and he corresponded with George Washington. He considered emigrating to what he called 'this new sanctuary of truth and freedom'.

The new republic lost many Scots in the course of its violent birth, both as casualties and as defectors. But its gains were also significant. Now, as well as land and opportunity, the United States offered political space where every (male) freehold property owner could vote. For many potential emigrants this strengthened the pull of the New World, although those who were reluctant to sever their ties to Britain would opt for British North America rather than the US.

The impact in Scotland was much more than a persuasive factor in emigration. American success was an inspiration, as the French Revolution would be a few years later, to a growing radicalism. It provided a tangible example of the possibilities of democracy in a climate where growing numbers were expressing their discontent at their exclusion from the political process. Many joined a radical organisation called Friends of the People, seen by the government as seditious. For some of those caught up in the radical disturbances of the 1790s, the US did indeed become a sanctuary.

In January 1793 Thomas Muir, an Edinburgh lawyer and leader of the movement for political reform, was arrested. He was tried and sentenced to transportation to Botany Bay. Accounts of this and subsequent trials were published and distributed in the US, where they were followed with keen interest. Muir himself became an iconic figure for Americans, a radical martyr, although he was never in America. In 1796 he escaped from Botany Bay with the help of an American ship dispatched for the purpose, and settled in France.

Other radical refugees did find a home there. Grant Thorburn, for example, joined the Friends of the People and paid for his involvement with imprisonment. In 1794 he made his way to the US. Another political refugee was James Tytler, editor of the second edition of the *Encyclopaedia Britannica* and also of the *Historical Register*, which promoted reform. After a stay in Ireland, he found a home in Salem, Massachusetts. John Craig Millar also joined the Friends of the People, as a consequence of which, as described by Mrs Archibald Fletcher in her *Autobiography*, he 'lost his professional employment, and though a most able and honourable man, was so disgusted with the state of public affairs in Scotland that he determined to seek peace and freedom in the United States of America'. His father John Millar, professor of law at Glasgow University, was also a radical. There were those who continued to see the former American colonies as a repository for undesirables. For a significant number the new republic was a beacon. Although not all the thousands who headed westwards over the next century felt, like David Hume, American in their principles, most believed that the United States of America offered something that Scotland did not.

CHAPTER FIVE

Ideas of Living More Comfortably

The People have got Ideas of living more comfortably,
and believe it easier to effect elsewhere than at home,
and in the present state of the Highlands it certainly is so.
GEORGE DEMPSTER, 1784

THOMAS HAMILTON FROM Glasgow sailed to New York nearly fifty years after the conclusion of the peace that secured the future of the United States of America. At first he was impressed. The American packet *New York* was well-appointed, the accommodation 'admirable' and the passengers well looked after. His first sight of America was favourable, 'one of the most beautiful prospects I have ever seen... New York on its island, with its vast forest of shipping, looming in the distance'.

Hamilton would soon get better acquainted with New York, which he found packed with 'business and bustle, and crowded with a population devoting their whole energies to the arts of money-getting'. This obsession with making money coloured everything about New York and the social intercourse of New Yorkers. Everyone was identified in terms of their economic worth. Hamilton found this disconcerting, and commented somewhat acidly:

> In a population wholly devoted to money-getting, the respect paid to wealth is so pervadingly diffused, that it rarely occurred to anyone, that it was impossible I should feel the slightest interest in the private circumstances of the gentlemen with whom I might chance to form a transient acquaintance.

Hamilton, born in 1789, was the son of William Hamilton, professor of anatomy at the University of Glasgow. Though Thomas attended the university he did not take a degree, but entered a Glasgow merchant's warehouse. Growing up in Glasgow he could not have avoided an awareness of the city's transatlantic connections, but his involvement in commerce didn't last long and in 1810 he acquired a commission in the army. He saw service in the Peninsular War, and then was posted to Nova Scotia and New Brunswick during the War of 1812 when the US threatened British North America. Eighteen years later he returned to America, this time intending to write about his travels, having already published a novel and a book about the Peninsular campaign. He journeyed through New England, then south to Philadelphia, Baltimore and Washington, and across the Allegheny Mountains to the Ohio River and eventually to New Orleans. He followed routes that had been taken by many of his countrymen.

The relationship between Scotland and the new republic would never regain quite the same closeness it had before 1775. The Loyalists who had moved north were now encouraging friends and relatives to join them in their new settlements in territory that remained British. Although the Clyde ports did not cease transatlantic trade during the war, it was costly to keep it going as merchant shipping required protection from American privateers. With the end of the war Glasgow merchants were much concerned with the recovery of debts in the former colonies, and large numbers of displaced Scots who had lost property and goods attempted to claim compensation. This proved hugely problematic. It took nearly thirty years of investigation and negotiation before a substantial amount of the American money owed to Glasgow traders was recovered. Most individuals did not get what they asked.

The years following the end of the war were uncertain for the Clyde's transatlantic trade, with confidence fluctuating. It was a struggle to reinvigorate commercial activity, but eventually it climbed almost to pre-war levels. Tobacco exports from Virginia and Maryland soon rose again, but Glasgow would never again be the tobacco centre of Europe. The tobacco lords' pre-eminence in the city's mercantile life was over. Scottish exports, however, were still leaving the Clyde for America, which remained an important market and strengthened Scotland's manufacturing base. In 1785 one Port Glasgow firm, Smith, Huie, & Alexander, was optimistically claiming: 'Glasgow will have a large share of the American trade in future. There have been more orders lodged this year for goods to go out to America than Great Britain could execute in three years.' An expanding export was cotton cloth, produced in mills in central and west Scotland. The raw cotton came from the US and the Caribbean. It was rapidly accelerated textile production that marked the first phase of Scotland's industrial revolution; by 1800 Scotland's textile industries were employing nearly 260,000 people. This level of activity depended on overseas markets.

The Scots who had remained in Virginia and Maryland were vital contacts for re-establishing trade. But many had died in the war and many had left, devastated by personal and financial losses. One of those with heavy losses was Alexander Campbell, father of Thomas the poet, who had been a merchant in Falmouth, Virginia. Some of the Scottish enclaves survived, in North Carolina for example, and although much depleted retained a sense of their origins. This was reinforced by new arrivals to Highland communities in North and South Carolina. In 1788 the *Fame* of Greenock carried 250 emigrants from Skye to Wilmington. Two years later another 200 arrived. In 1791 a group of Highlanders from Appin also arrived in North Carolina, and there were further migrations from the same area early the following century. In 1783 the first Scotch Fair was held at Laurel Hill in the Cape Fear area, featuring wine, whisky, food, horse racing and betting booths. Ninety years later it was still going, although the

Reverend AN Ferguson petitioned to have the fair abolished. It didn't celebrate Presbyterian values of sober piety and respect for law and order.

Although there were a few collective emigrations from the Highlands, the story of the Scots who went to the United States becomes increasingly a tale of individuals and families rather than of communities. In 1830 Thomas Hamilton met a 'Scotch baker' in Mobile, Alabama who had left Hamilton in Lanarkshire for New York, where he worked as a journeyman before eventually settling in Mobile. There his family joined him. He had a successful business, owned two slaves and had been able to send $100 back home to his mother. In spite of this he did not recommend emigration to anyone who could survive in Scotland, as it was 'a sore trial'. He missed the Clyde, but appreciated being able to make a decent living relieved of economic anxiety. Hamilton recounts this with the comment, 'My countrymen are accused of cherishing a certain indestructible sentiment of affinity.' The tendency of transatlantic Scots to seek each other out was often remarked on.

In New York State, as in the Carolinas, there was still a Scottish presence, although many had left. In 1790 Charles Williamson went to New York as an agent for a large tract of land in the west of the state which had been purchased by a syndicate headed by Sir William Pulteney. Williamson, from Edinburgh, had become acquainted with America when he joined the army. His ship was captured by a French privateer during the revolutionary war and he was landed in Boston as a prisoner. He married a Boston girl and returned to Scotland in 1781, but he had clearly seen enough of America to whet his interest and to suggest opportunities. On the Pulteney estate he got to work surveying, making roads, building bridges and schools. He founded the town of Bath, while not far away his assistant, Dugald Cameron, founded the town of Cameron, and built himself a fine house suited to the lavish lifestyle he favoured. Williamson was elected to the state legislature. But the syndicate was not pleased at the dearth of profit and in 1800 his appointment was revoked. After a spell back in Scotland, he died in New Orleans in 1808 on his way to Jamaica to take up a government position.

White settlement had been edging west for years before the revolutionary war; now westward expansion was official. John McMillan from Campbeltown, born in 1794, arrived in New York with five sons and three daughters and made his way to Shap's Landing, Illinois, via Pittsburgh and Cincinnatti. The main route through the Alleghenies, the Cumberland Gap, was well established, and Tennessee and Kentucky quickly joined the original thirteen states. In 1750 the Shenandoah Valley had been the frontier. Half a century later it was, briefly, Ohio. In 1790 there were around 4,300 whites settled north of the Ohio River and east of the Mississippi, in tiny scattered settlements and isolated log cabins. According to Eneas Mackenzie, Ohio in the 1780s was 'a wilderness frequented only by savages'. By the turn of the century the territory contained 45,000 settlers. In 1803 Ohio became a state. The McMillan family followed the river routes that were familiar to the increasing numbers who were heading west.

By 1810 Ohio had a flourishing textile industry producing two million yards of woollen, linen and cotton cloth. Whisky and sugar production also thrived. Boats plied the Ohio River laden with goods manufactured in the state. But the wilderness was still not far away, as anyone who had crossed the mountains and travelled the rivers to reach Ohio was aware. It was a striking feature of the young nation that wilderness could co-exist with the burgeoning industry vital for its economic survival. Throughout the nineteenth century the slow labour of the pioneer settler breaking virgin ground contrasted vividly with the speed of the transformation brought by the extraction and processing of the country's resources.

Until 1803 heading west meant crossing the Appalachians into the Mississippi valley, a vast area watered by the many mighty tributaries of the Mississippi. It was not, of course, empty. Settlement of the eastern seaboard had only been possible because the original population had been displaced. Native Americans had no rights under the new republic's constitution and the only way they could resist the appropriation of the land they had traditionally occupied was through warfare or by negotiating treaties that offered them some protection. But treaty after treaty proved worthless as the inexorable pressure of immigration pushed European incomers west. As the frontier moved west, so did the Indians. Most of the tribes had supported the British in the revolutionary war, as Britain had tried to contain settlement. But peace brought a renewal of the pressure. The first president's secretary of war, Henry Knox (of Scottish descent) stated that, 'The Indians being the prior occupants, possess the right of the soil', and Jefferson, then secretary of state, was insistent that those who lived within existing state boundaries should not be encroached on.

By 1800, when Jefferson himself became president, there were 700,000 white settlers beyond the line the British had tried to draw in 1763. The agenda changed. The frontier could not be held back and Indians would have to make way for settlers who would plough up the land for cotton and grain, plant cities, dig canals to link the river systems, and eventually build railroads which would help to move the frontier yet further west. Jefferson's successful negotiation of the Louisiana Purchase, the acquisition in 1803 of territory that had been French, doubled the size of the US and instantly expanded the nation's aspirations. Jefferson proposed removing Native Americans from the areas that were most useful and under most pressure. They would be encouraged to give up their traditional dependence on hunting and small-scale farming and to adapt to the agricultural and industrial activities of the incomers. Existing treaties that got in the way of this policy were ignored.

Land hunger had driven settlers west in colonial times in spite of attempts to hold them back; now land hunger was a tool for the nation's expansion. A Tennessee lad called Andrew Jackson had enlisted with the patriot army to fight the British. He was the son of Ulster Scots who had emigrated from Belfast and settled in the Carolinas. After the war he became a major-general in the Tennessee state militia. Land speculators were not known for being generous to Indians who got in the way of land deals. Jackson was a leading figure in the War of 1812, which was fought not just to consolidate US borders but to expand, north, south and into the territory of Native Americans who were resisting dispossession.

One of these was Tecumseh, a Shawnee chief who tried to unite the tribes against the takeover of their land. Andrew Jackson relentlessly fought this resistance, most notably in 1814 at the Battle of Horseshoe Bend where his troops, with the help of Cherokees who were promised government support, killed 800 of a thousand-strong band of Creeks. As a land speculator himself, Jackson was a direct beneficiary of removing such obstruction. During the next ten years he negotiated treaties which displaced Native Americans from large areas of Alabama, Florida and Tennessee, and from smaller chunks of Georgia, Mississippi, Kentucky and North Carolina. His advantageous position allowed him to negotiate land deals for himself and appoint his friends and relatives as Indian agents and traders, land agents and surveyors. After his campaign against the Seminoles in Florida, which resulted in the American acquisition of Florida from the Spanish in 1819, he became governor of the territory. Nine years later he was elected president.

Several Scottish Americans allied themselves with the Creeks and other tribes who defied Jackson and the loss of tribal lands. Alexander McGillivray was the son of Lachlan McGillivray, a Scots trader from Strathglass near Inverness, who around 1738 had arrived in Charleston. His mother was Sehoy Marchand, part Creek, part Spanish, part French. Lachlan, one of those who settled in Darien, Georgia, later became a trader and penetrated deep into the hinterland exchanging rum, gunpowder and textiles with the

Native Americans for beaver pelts and deer hides. His standing with the Creeks was considerable and he helped to maintain their support for the British. He remained a Loyalist and returned to Scotland after the revolutionary war. His son Alexander grew up among the Creeks, although he was educated by a Presbyterian minister in Charleston. In 1783 Alexander McGillivray was elected chief of the Creek nation, and in this capacity went to New York in 1790 to President Washington. The resulting treaty guaranteed Creek entitlement to the territory they then occupied. To protect Creek interests McGillivray did not confine himself to talking to the Americans. He looked also for support from the British, the French and the Spanish. It was this that led to the alleged comment by General Robertson: 'The Spaniards are devils, but the biggest devil among them is the half Spaniard, half Frenchman, half Scotsman, and altogether Creek scoundrel, McGillivray.'

McGillivray, who died in Florida in 1793, had bought time for the Creeks but their hold on their land could not last. The next generation faced the onslaught of Andrew Jackson. Among them was William Weatherford, son of a Scot and a younger Sehoy, and Lachlan McGillivray's step-grandson. He, too, became a leader of the Creeks, and was forced to surrender to Jackson at Horseshoe Bend, with the words: 'My people are all gone. I can do no more than weep over the misfortunes of my nation.' He was talking about the Creek people, but the words could equally have applied to the Highlanders who were at that time being cleared in increasing numbers to make way for sheep.

Another Highland Creek was William McIntosh, whose grandfather had left Inverness for Georgia in 1736, and whose father, Captain William McIntosh, had enlisted the Creeks to fight for the British. The younger William accepted the inevitability of American incursion, and in 1825 was killed by his own people after he had signed away a large part of their territory.

By the time Jackson became president in 1828, the United States controlled a vast area stretching from the east coast to the Rocky Mountains. The nation needed people, and people obliged by pouring in, mainly from northern Europe at this stage, but this would soon change. Among them were many Scots, who tended to go where they already had connections. In 1842 Allan and Joan Pinkerton left Glasgow for Illinois where they had friends, and joined a settlement of Scots at Dundee, fifty miles northeast of Chicago. Six years later William and Margaret Carnegie from Dunfermline travelled to Pittsburgh where Margaret's sister and her husband were already living.

Newcomers, as well as the long established, joined the movement west. By the 1800s their transatlantic voyage was most likely to begin in the Clyde, though Liverpool was also a point of departure. By the 1850s steamships were regularly crossing the Atlantic, which made the voyage easier and faster. The Atlantic world was shrinking. The Cunard Shipping Company was started in 1840, backed by George and James Burns and David and Charles MacIver of Glasgow. Samuel Cunard himself was born in Nova Scotia. The Cunard ships sailed from Liverpool to Halifax and Boston. The *City of Glasgow*, built on the Clyde by Tod and McGregor for the Glasgow and New York Steamship Company, made the journey in a record twelve days and five hours. By 1856 the Scottish Anchor Line was running a regular service from the Clyde to New York and soon dominated the transatlantic passenger trade. Scottish ships were taking not only Scots to America, but thousands of other north Europeans, Germans, Scandinavians, Russians, who crossed the North Sea to Leith and then crossed Scotland to the Clyde.

In 1819 Thomas Dudgeon became president of a society of 'very poor and destitute farmers' in Easter Ross who appealed for aid to emigrate. He himself spent nine years in New York and Pennsylvania. His verdict was that 'The States may be said in general to hold out the fairest prospects of any country in the world to the sober and industrious, and the worst to the dissipated and idle.' In other words, there were opportunities but the streets were not paved with gold. Also in 1819 Eneas Mackenzie published his account of the United States, also emphasising that there were rewards for those prepared to work hard. He addresses his book to:

the industrious labourer, the mechanic, the farmer, the man of moderate capital, and the father of a family who feels solicitous about settling his children; in short all those who are prepared to encounter the numerous privations and inconveniences of emigration, in order to enjoy the great and acknowledged advantages which America offers to adventurers.

He was not impressed by New York, where he found people bad-mannered and indifferent, a consequence, he believed, of the American brand of populist democracy. Shopkeepers, for example, 'stand with their hats on, or sit or lie along their counters, smoking segars, and spitting in every direction'. For someone used to British deference this was hard to take.

Mackenzie's purpose was to provide guidance for the intending emigrant. He prefers the hard-working New Englanders to the southerners. He is impressed by the range of trades and skills to be found in cities such as Philadelphia and Cincinnati as well as by the hard graft of pioneering farmers in newly settled areas such as Illinois, which became a state in 1818. Further west lay Michigan and Missouri, territories since 1805 and 1812 respectively, and beckoning the prospective settler. He advises that those planning to go west should take passage to Philadelphia – he recommends American ships – and from there head across the mountains for Pittsburgh, 'the gate of the western empire... the connecting link between *new* and *old* America'. Those who could afford it could ride; the poorest could walk and have their baggage carried 'by the regular stage-waggons'. They should take their own food and be aware that the inns were 'extravagant'. Those who purchased their own wagons should make sure that they were robust and the horses in good condition. They should carry any tools necessary for repairs.

From Pittsburgh the journey continued by river boat, down the Monongahela to the Ohio River which was the major north–south waterway before reaching the Mississippi. For the river journey Mackenzie suggests warm clothing and the following essentials: nails, hammer, hatchet, tinder-box, box for fire, gridiron, iron pot, coffee pot, coffee mill, tea pot, plates, spoon, knives, forks, mugs, candles, coffee, tea, sugar, spirits, meat, potatoes, bread, pen and ink, paper, medicine, and a gun. The final stages of the journey were again by wagon, which could be purchased or hired. A wagon and two horses could accommodate seven people and cover about twenty miles a day.

Even those familiar with the Clyde must have been awed by the extent and magnitude of the American river systems and by the emptiness of much of the territory they flowed through. When Thomas Hamilton went west he crossed the Alleghenies to Wheeling on the Ohio and then sailed downriver on a 1,500 mile journey to New Orleans. Between Wheeling and Cincinnati he passed the scattered log huts of 'stray settlers'. Then the steamboat joined the Mississippi which took him through 'dreamy and pestilential solitudes, untrodden save by the foot of the Indian'. Alligators lurked in the river and vultures haunted the river banks.

It was like nothing Hamilton had encountered before: 'the giant river rolling onward the vast volume of its dark and turbid waters through the wilderness, form the features of one of the most dismal and impressive landscapes on which the eye of man ever rested'. Here and there were the cabins of 'ill-looking' squatters who supplied the steamboats with wood. 'Many', according to Hamilton, 'have fled for crimes, to a region where the arm of the law cannot reach them. Others are men of broken characters, hopes, and fortunes, who fly not from justice, but contempt.'

The frontier was unforgiving. It could bring out the worst as well as the best in those who tried to make their homes there, and provided a refuge for all manner of outcasts. This had been the character of the frontier from the start and it did not change as it moved west. Hamilton was scathing not just about the squatters. His fellow passengers spent their time 'gambling and drinking, and wrangling and swearing... [with] an utter disregard for all the decent courtesies of society'. Like Mackenzie, he was not impressed by American manners. Further down the Mississippi, wilderness gave way to plantations of sugar, cotton and rice, 'with the houses of their owners, and the little adjoining hamlets inhabited by slaves'. In New Orleans he commented on the slave auctions, which were occurring almost every day. Slave-owning was another sign of depravity, in Hamilton's eyes, and an affront to democracy.

At around the same time, William Grahame from Glasgow made a similar trip down the Ohio River. He had sailed from Liverpool to Philadelphia on the *Monongahela* in October 1831, a voyage which he found comfortable and well-provisioned. Four meals a day were served. Dinner consisted of soup, roast meat, vegetables, rice and potatoes, and tarts and dumplings. He makes no mention of steerage passengers, who were almost certainly on board. He disembarked in Baltimore and proceeded up the Delaware by steamship to Philadelphia before heading west. He travelled through Kentucky on his way to Cincinnati and was:

> a good deal disappointed with the western country. I thought
> no Englishman or Scotsman could be happy in it, and that
> to be so would be a hard task for a man who had enjoyed
> the comforts of even a small competency.

At Cincinnati he boarded the steamer *Mohawk* for St Louis. He, too, describes 'a wilderness of forests, flats and swamps' with log huts plastered with mud and roofed with rough planks. The trees were felled by cutting round the bark and leaving them to die. On his travels Grahame encountered a number of Scots, including Robert McGregor from Perth, who had for seven years been a riverboat captain and:

> prefers this country to Scotland where, though fond of life in the country he would not live for the best farm in it. He hated America for several years but is now reconciled, and plans to delight in it. He recommends marrying an American wife and says Scots women are scarce ever broken into Yankee ways.

Unlike Hamilton, Grahame intended to stay in America, although when he eventually found land to buy it was near Toronto rather than in the US.

During the first half of the nineteenth century the trans-Appalachian west was increasingly the destination of Scottish emigrants and it has been suggested that by the middle of the century over a quarter of the Scots who arrived in the US pushed on to Ohio, Indiana, Wisconsin and Illinois. For most the aspiration was to farm their own land, although some hoped for employment appropriate to the skills they brought with them. There were continued efforts to recruit settlers, with agents representing the shipping companies and state governments touring Scotland to sign up potential emigrants. In 1822 Nahum Ward went to Scotland on behalf of the Ohio state authorities promising cheap fertile land, free education and a freely elected government. The price of the passage from Greenock to Marieta, Ohio was £9.

There was a steady flow of pro-US propaganda, but not all the comment was favourable. An anonymous *Emigrant's Guide*, published in 1816, reckoned British North America was a better bet than the United States. The US, in the writer's view, had been oversold:

America has been considered by those who have been dazzled

by the infatuating sounds of democracy, independence, liberty, and equality, as the only happy spot upon earth; where all the necessaries, comforts, and luxuries of life, flow spontaneously, or are to be obtained without that perseverance and industry which are required for their attainment in other civilised nations... Thousands have inconsiderately emigrated to the new world.

The Yankees were dishonourable knaves and the southerners 'luxurious, indolent, and proud', and he warned those contemplating leaving Scotland to 'balance well between the reality of comforts which they now enjoy, and the uncertainty of remote ones they may never possess: nor suffer themselves to be misled by the phantoms of ideal happiness emanating from democratic equality'.

For some Scots who commented on the US, democracy was either a myth or seriously overrated. Thomas Hamilton was critical both of the US constitution and of the administrative system. Government was 'abjectly dependent on the people', the press too influential, and American statesmen given to 'interminable drivellings of an insatiable vanity'. Democracy seemed to coarsen thought and manners. Eneas Mackenzie shared this scepticism. Democracy was fine in principle, but American practice was two centuries behind American theory. The US had become 'the receptacle for speculators and fortune-hunters, for adventurers and base and demoralised characters of every shade and description', a situation which did not encourage a positive democratic outcome. And how could a nation describe itself as a democracy when a large proportion of its population was deprived of freedom as well as the vote?

Yet Scots still found plenty to admire and good reasons to go there, as visitors, sojourners and settlers. In the first half of the nineteenth century there was a steady stream of guides and manuals for emigrants, as well as accounts written by Scots who had travelled in the United States. With the end of the Napoleonic Wars and again in the 1840s when potato blight brought famine to Scotland there was a surge in the numbers of those seeking to emigrate. American interest in Scotland was also considerable. Scottish journals such as the *Edinburgh Review* and *Blackwood's Magazine* crossed the Atlantic. Editions of Burns had been published in the colonies since 1788; his democratic credentials made him popular not just with exiled Scots. The novels of Sir Walter Scott were avidly read and profoundly influential. The economic ties remained important on both sides of the Atlantic and the intellectual ties were still vibrant.

John Galt visited the United States in 1825, on his way to Upper Canada on behalf of the Canada Company. He sailed to New York, then travelled up the Hudson by steamboat. When in New York he met Grant Thorburn from Dalkeith, whose radical activities had enforced his emigration to New York in 1794. Now he was running a successful business as a seed merchant. Thorburn would become the model for the hero of Galt's 1830 novel *Lawrie Todd*. Galt did not spend long in the US but interestingly, at a time when American fiction had not yet come of age, he wrote a novel about pioneer life in New York State. The novel had an enthusiastic readership.

Forced to leave Scotland after getting embroiled in radical politics, Lawrie Todd and his brother, with a single kist containing their belongings, travel steerage on the *Providence* from Leith. The crossing to New York takes eight weeks. The steerage accommodation has headroom of 4 feet stacked with two tiers of berths. There is a ration of two bottles of water a day, one of which is for making porridge. Lawrie arrives in a New York that is a collection of ramshackle timber buildings, yet he quickly finds his feet. New York turns out to be 'full of Scotchmen' and he is soon plugged in to a network of his countrymen. After a time as a seed merchant, he tries farming in New Jersey, but the land he buys is exhausted and he loses money. He is forced to sell up and head north where he starts again as a pioneer settler on a 50-acre lot.

He takes the steamship up the Hudson River to Albany, then travels by wagon west to Schenectady and on up the Mohawk River. Lawrie's travelling companions are a family from Paisley, who have brought 'all their gear and chattels', which include hampers packed with crockery as well as furniture: 'everything, in short, that a plain mechanical family requires, even to a bairn's chair with a hole in the bottom, and its appurtenance in wood'. Much of the crockery is smashed in the course of the journey and the furniture has to be disposed of in Schenectady.

The last stage of the journey follows a 'mere blazed line of what was to be a road; stumps and cradle heaps, mud-holes and miry swails, succeeded one another'. All around settlers are busy felling trees, logging and burning:

> Hundreds on hundreds of vast and ponderous trees covering
> the ground for acres, like the mighty slain on a field of battle,
> all to be removed, yea, obliterated, before the solitary settler
> can raise a meal of potatoes, seemingly offer the most hope-
> less task which the industry of man can struggle with.

The scattered villages are composed of shanties and log cabins. Lawrie Todd and his family build their own shanty, which is flooded out. They build another which perishes in a forest fire. This house, too, is rebuilt and eventually Lawrie sets up a store. In the course of his American adventure he loses two wives and two children. His comment on his pioneer efforts is: 'The discomforts of the first few years of a new settlement are unspeakable.'

Lawrie Todd illustrates the emigrant experience, but it also highlights the contrast between the new and old worlds. When Lawrie eventually returns to Scotland he does so in style, in a comfortable cabin on a ship that takes only three weeks to reach Glasgow. His American sojourn allows Lawrie to see Scotland with different and inevitably critical eyes. The steamboat from Greenock up the Clyde to Glasgow cannot compare with 'the floating palaces on the North River' and the 'polluting coal smoke' is obnoxious. Lawrie feels that America has outstripped Europe in terms of progress and improvement. But he finds the lack of trees a relief. The countryside is tamer, more civilised, and the roads are better. And Glasgow 'holds a prouder head than New York' in spite of the smoke, which indicates Glasgow's status as 'a great place of manufactures, where kettles do the work of men, and iron wheels make cotton cloth better than malcontent weavers'.

The sheer scale of America inevitably features in the commentaries of travellers and settlers. Perhaps just as inevitable are the remarks on Americans themselves, who are repeatedly described as rough, crude and brash, often drunk and foul-mouthed. New Englanders are characterised as cold and calculating, southerners as idle and intemperate. But none of this proved a deterrent to immigration. The commentators, of course, are largely middle-class, their sensibilities likely to be offended by deficient table manners and lack of deference. For those leaving Scotland because their means of earning a livelihood were disappearing, this was hardly going to stand in their way. Indeed, vanishing signifiers of class distinction could be an added attraction.

Mountains and rivers marked the main continental barriers, physical and psychological. The movement west was as much about a perception of independence and self-sufficiency as about the actual filling up of space. The frontier always attracted misfits and mavericks who from choice or necessity operated at the edge of the law. Among these there were Scots and Ulster Scots, often the products of a frontier tradition. They provided many of North America's trailblazers, official and unofficial. By the time Jefferson concluded the Louisiana Purchase the Appalachian barrier was well breached and the Ohio River was becoming a highway for migration. Now Jefferson could look further west. He put into action a plan to explore beyond the Mississippi, and in 1804 an expedition led by Meriwether Lewis and William Clark, an Ulster Scot, set off into country that was almost entirely unknown to Europeans. A few adventurers, Indian traders and outcasts had pushed into trans-Mississippi territory, but with little understanding that two-thirds of the continent lay before them.

Lewis and Clark set off from St Louis in May 1804 and made their way up the Missouri to the Continental Divide. They crossed the Rockies and continued down the Columbia River to the Pacific coast, which they reached in November the following year. 'In those tremendous mountains,' wrote Clark in a letter to his brother, 'we suffered everything which hunger cold and fatigue could impose.' They travelled by boat, on foot and on horseback, and relied on Native American help and information. Jefferson had hoped for a commercially viable water route to the Pacific, which would enable trade with Asia. That did not exist, and the land routes to Oregon that opened up thirty years later lay further south, but the achievement of Lewis and Clark opened the door to a new wave of pioneers. Mountain men, trappers and traders, often travelling alone, were soon reaching into the wilderness.

Another Ulster Scot, John Colter from Virginia, was one of the first. He had joined Lewis and Clark in Kentucky but on the return journey decided to strike off with two trappers, Joseph Dixon and Forest Hancock, into the upper reaches of the Missouri. Colton was described by another trapper as being naturally suited to 'the hardy indurance of fatigue, privation, and perils', and he could expect to find plenty of all of these. Trapping by whites had been outlawed in 1802. Fur traders were required to have a licence which allowed them to barter with Indians, not to trap themselves. This remained the case over the next few decades when fur trading in the northwest expanded in response to demand in the east and Europe, but there was no way such a restriction could be policed. It wasn't just renegade individuals who ignored the rules. In 1809

William Clark joined the St Louis Missouri Fur Company, which was set up to hunt (in other words trap) furs as well as trade for them. As one historian of the American West, David Lavender, put it: 'Winking at inconvenient statutes is an old American custom.'

The story of John Colter's sojourn in the mountains contains all the ingredients of Wild West adventure. Often alone, facing savage terrain, hunger, extreme cold and hostile tribes, he spent the next two years in the mountains. Then in the autumn of 1808 he was captured by Blackfeet angry at white intrusion. He was stripped and ordered to run for his freedom, with no expectation that he would succeed. But amazingly he did, outrunning his pursuers through rock and cactus, killing the only one who gained on him, and diving into the icy Madison River where he hid in an air pocket under floating brushwood until his pursuers gave up. He then walked, unprotected from the night's freezing temperatures and the day's baking sun, the two hundred miles to Fort Raymond on the Bighorn, keeping himself alive by eating roots and bark.

Soon after this adventure John Colter abandoned the mountains, but there were plenty more who followed. It was the mountain men whose accumulating knowledge of a vast area of wilderness enabled the first routes to be mapped out for serious migration to the west. But they were there not for the benefit of the nation but to make money out of furs. The Montreal-based and largely Scottish North West Company had spearheaded exploration further north, particularly with the epic journeys of Alexander Mackenzie from Stornoway who reached the Pacific coast in 1793, and Simon Fraser, also a Scot, who while Colter was trapping in the mountains to the south was making his way down the river named for him. The North West Company had outposts in the Columbia River area. In 1810 the Montreal company would be challenged by an American company founded by John Jacob Astor. The rivalry between British and American fur traders and the environment in which they operated is vividly evoked in Margaret Elphinstone's novel *Voyageurs* (2003), an absorbing story of early nineteenth-century frontier experience and its consequences.

Astor organised two expeditions to the Pacific, one overland and one by sea, and manned them with Scots, several poached from the rival company. Alexander MacKay had accompanied Alexander Mackenzie, the first to cross the continent. Donald MacKenzie, from Cromarty in Ross-shire, attracted the notice of Washington Irving who was sponsored by Astor to write about his activities in the northwest. Irving described Mackenzie as having 'a frame seasoned to toils and hardship, a spirit not to be intimidated', with a reputation as 'a remarkable shot'. Duncan MacDougall, David Stuart and his nephew Robert were all Highlanders. Ramsay Crooks was from Greenock, and with his partner Robert McClellan, formerly a scout with the American army, had been trading along the Missouri for several years. They all joined the Astor enterprise. Crooks would become general manager of Astor's American Fur Company running their western operations, and later president. But before that he and his comrades endured all the hardships of the mountains and near-starvation in their journey through the Rockies to the coast. There they found that the sea-going expedition, which had left New York in September 1810 and included MacDougall and the two Stuarts, had successfully sailed round the Horn to the mouth of the Columbia River. Several lives were lost before they were able to make landfall and begin the task of felling trees and building the fort that would be called Astoria.

That summer the Astorians were visited by David Thompson of the North West Company, who had made his way downriver in the last phase of his own epic explorations. On his way he had put up a sign where the Snake River meets the Columbia:

Know hereby that this country is claimed for Great Britain as part of its territories and that the N.W. Company of Merchants from Canada... do hereby intend to erect a factory in this place.

Fort Astoria was forced to sell out to the North West Company during the War of 1812. The Scots in charge had little difficulty in reverting to their former loyalties. The Nor'Westers, and later the Hudson's Bay Company with which it amalgamated in 1821, set up several posts in Oregon Territory. The best known was Fort Vancouver, established in 1825 and presided over by Dr John McLoughlin, who was born in Quebec but studied medicine at Edinburgh University. The leading fur traders in the area were of Scottish origins. Finan MacDonald, known as 'Buffalo' because of his enormous strength, was from Perthshire. James MacMillan from Loch Arkaig west of Fort William accompanied David Thompson in his explorations of the Columbia River, and later was with the Bay Company's overseas governor, George Simpson, when he made his first trip across the Rockies. In 1828 Simpson, from Dornoch in Easter Ross, made his way down the Columbia River. 'As we wafted along under sail,' wrote Archibald MacDonald who accompanied him, 'the Highland bagpipes in the governor's canoe were echoed by the bugle in mine'. MacDonald, from Glencoe, had been based in Oregon since 1821.

Kenneth Mackenzie, a relative of Alexander, in 1818 emigrated from Ross-shire to work for the North West Company before going south to St Louis in 1822. He joined the Columbia Fur Company, which amalgamated with the American Fur Company in 1827. Based at Fort Union, he opened up trading posts in the remote upper Missouri country and did good business until in 1834 he chanced his luck with an illicit distillery. After a spell in Europe he returned to the US and founded a successful – and legal – liquor business, and made a great deal of money from land speculation and the railroad. Robert Campbell arrived in the US from Ulster in 1824, aged twenty, and after several years as a fur trapper served as Indian commissioner and built Fort Laramie in Wyoming.

In 1846 the competition between the American companies and the Hudson's Bay Company, a majority of whose employees were from Scotland, came to an end. American settlement in the area was already under way when Oregon Territory was ceded to the United States. The Bay Company pulled out of its Oregon trading posts. John McLoughlin, who had aggravated his bosses by assisting Americans on the Oregon trail, stayed in the US and founded Oregon City. James Douglas, a Scottish protégé of McLoughlin's at Fort Vancouver, went on to Vancouver Island to run the Bay Company's new post at Victoria and eventually become the first governor of British Columbia.

Angus MacDonald, from Torridon in the West Highlands, was posted by the Hudson's Bay Company to Fort Hall, Washington Territory, in 1840. There he married Catherine of the Nez Perce. A Gaelic speaker, he could also speak English, French and several native languages. He was, said a fellow fur trader, 'excessively fond of the life of the aborigine and would rather live in a tent, or lodge, than in a house built in accordance with civilised plans'. Angus MacDonald was one of many Scots who not only respected the aboriginal way of life but recognised how well adapted it was to the environment which sustained it. He made a striking figure, tall, dark and bearded, dressed in deerskin with a black silk handkerchief round his neck, and fond of singing Gaelic songs. In 1846 MacDonald took up ranching in Montana, retaining his close involvement with the Nez Perce and recognising the affinity between their displacement as white settlement encroached and the clearances that had displaced so many of his own people.

It was beaver that was the main interest of the fur trappers and traders, beaver pelts to supply the apparently insatiable demand for beaver hats. The fur traders and mountain men were not keen on settlement, because it threatened both their livelihood and their independence. Yet inadvertently their path finding made the next phase of the frontier possible, and gradually the Hudson's Bay Company softened its resistance to settlement. In 1839 it set up a subsidiary, the Puget Sound Agricultural Company, whose objective was to grow produce to supply Bay Company trading posts. In 1841 they recruited 21 families from the Red River settlement (now Winnipeg) which had been founded by Lord Selkirk 30 years earlier. Scottish Highlanders, mainly from Sutherland, were the first settlers. Families from Red River also moved south to found Scotch Grove, Iowa, where the museum contains two quern stones originally brought from Sutherland.

For the fur traders the wilderness was a means to an end. For a few, the far west spelt simply adventure – although the seeking out of adventure was not simple. One particularly eccentric adventurer was Sir William Drummond Stewart of Murthly Castle in Perthshire. He made his first expedition west in the 1830s after serving in the British Army during the Napoleonic Wars. Following in the trail of the fur trappers, he hung out at the annual rendezvous where trappers and supply trains from the east got together. He commissioned the Baltimore artist Alfred Jacob Miller to make a record of Native Americans they encountered, and collected specimens of plants and wildlife which were sent back to Perthshire. Murthly Castle became well known for its American trees and the herd of buffalo grazing its parkland. Miller's pictures adorned its walls. Stewart made his last American trip in 1843, before returning to Scotland to take up his responsibilities as laird of Murthly. He wrote two novels based on his wilderness experiences, *Altowan, or Incidents of Life and Adventures in the Rocky Mountains* (1846) and *Edward Warren* (1854).

By the 1840s wagon trains were rolling across the plains and through the Rockies, their destination Oregon and California. As Bernard De Voto, a prominent historian of the West, put it: 'The common man moved westward. A thirsty land swallowed him insatiably. There is no comprehending the frenzy of the American folk-migration.'

Tabitha Moffat Brown joined this migration at the age of 66. Of Scottish descent, she was the daughter of Dr Joseph Moffat, a physician in Massachusetts. She married the Reverend Clark Brown, an Episcopal minister, and they lived in Maryland. When he died in 1817, she taught in schools in Virginia and Missouri. It was from Missouri that in 1846 she set off for Oregon, with her son and daughter and their families. Until Fort Hall on the Snake River they had a 'pleasing and prosperous journey', but there they were persuaded to take what was promised as a short cut. There followed a nightmare of desert and mountains, Native attacks and supplies running out, with the approaching winter bringing 'mud, snow, hail, and rain'. Tabitha Brown lost everything but her horse. At one point she found herself benighted with one exhausted companion:

Worse than alone, in a savage wilderness, without food, without fire, cold and shivering wolves fighting and howling all around me. Dark clouds hid the stars. All as solitary as death.

Miraculously, she made it through to the Willamette valley settlements and with extraordinary determination established herself as a teacher and ran a boarding house. By 1854, when she wrote a letter to her brother and sister-in-law in Ohio describing her experiences, she owned nine town lots in Forest Grove with her own 'nicely furnished white frame house' on one of them.

The excitement generated by a young republican nation, the opportunities to own land and have a vote, the promises of financial gain, were a heady mix for men and women who felt that the old country denied them a great deal and offered them very little. Tabitha Brown in her seventies achieved financial security and a white frame house after extraordinary hardship, but for many of those who left Scotland, and for their descendants, the 'ideas of living more comfortably' mentioned by George Dempster proved to be an illusion, at least in the short term. In 1818 James McCowan in Richmond, Virginia wrote a letter home to his family in Perthshire: 'there is some that likes it [America] and some don't, and some does well and some does not'. The barriers to success were probably fewer, but the challenges, especially for the pioneer, were beyond what most at home could imagine.

CHAPTER SIX

Within the Reach of All

*Here the field was open and everyone was striving
for what seemed to be within the reach of all
– a foremost rank in his own sphere.*

JD BORTHWICK, 1857

HECTOR CRAIG FROM Paisley arrived in New York in 1790. He
founded the town of Craigsville, where he set up grist, paper and
saw mills and was soon presiding over a thriving community. He
was elected to Congress in 1823. In 1830 he became surveyor of
the Port of New York and later New York Surveyor of Customs.
He was appointed US Commissioner of Insolvency. John Regan
from Ayr settled in Illinois about 50 years after Craig's arrival. He
became a newspaperman and eventually the proprietor of the
Knoxville Journal. These men exemplified the belief that the United
States offered opportunities denied by Europe. There would be
tales of more spectacular success, but for most people contemplating
emigration, it was the examples of modest achievement that held
out the greatest hope. There were some, certainly, who set their
sights on making a fortune, especially when gold entered the picture
in the late 1840s, but most aspired to the means of leading an
ordinary decent life.

Although the streets of New York or Pittsburgh could be as crowded
and noxious as those of Glasgow or Dundee, there was a whole
continent to the west that would surely never be filled, where there
would always be land for those enterprising enough to make something
of it. John Regan captured something of the intoxication of vast
empty space when he described his journey across the Illinois plains.

Before us lay one vast plane of verdure and flowers, without house or home, or anything to break in upon the uniformity of the scene, except the shadow of a passing cloud. To the right and left long points of timber, like capes and head-lands, stretched in the blue distance, the light breeze of the morning brushing along the young grass and the blue and pink flowers – the strong sunlight pouring down everywhere.

This was space which invited ordinary people to build new lives and communities. It also offered possibilities for breaking out of the limits of narrow thinking as well as breaking away from poverty and oppression. It was space for experiment.

One experiment was the settlement of New Harmony in Indiana, founded by Robert Owen in 1825. Owen, born in Wales, had taken over management of the model manufacturing community of New Lanark 25 miles from Glasgow, set up by his father-in-law David Dale, who aimed to improve both efficiency and the lives of working people. Owen, too, believed that a decent social environment and good working conditions were beneficial for people and profits. Housing, schools and nurseries were provided for those who worked in the New Lanark cotton mills. New Harmony was an attempt to run a community along co-operative lines, and Owen attracted people who reacted against the raw individualism fostered by the US. One of them was Hew Ainslie from Ayrshire, who had studied law at Glasgow University and emigrated in 1822.

Also influenced by Owen's ideas was Frances Wright, the daughter of a Dundee merchant. She grew up mixing with an intellectual elite in Glasgow and London, to become a feminist and radical. She saw the United States as offering an escape from the stifling conformities of Europe. In her commonplace book she wrote, 'if wisdom and virtue are ever to be found more widely spread among a people, it must be among one possessed of Freedom'. In 1818 she and her sister Camilla sailed for New York on the American packet *Amity*. The voyage was not a pleasant one. Both sisters were very seasick and Frances Wright's suggested remedies sound worse than the condition they were intended to cure: 'For the first two or three days after every attack of retching drink gruel or water, and when the stomach is cleansed thoroughly up and down take a mouthful of something highly seasoned with salt or pepper.' She recommended pills of rhubarb and aloe. The experience perhaps intensified her reaction at the sight of New York harbour: 'I thought it was for the first time in my life that I had drawn a clear breath.' For a year and a half Frances and Camilla travelled extensively before returning to England. An old Glasgow friend Robina Millar remarked that the sisters had come back 'wholly American in all their sentiments & feelings'. America, a 'great and growing country', provided 'natural, moral & political features' which could engage Frances's 'capacious – her magnificent mind'.

In 1824 the Wright sisters returned to the US, again sailing into New York harbour. By this time Fanny, as she was generally known, was a published author who had written in praise of the republic. The tone of her *Views of Society and Manners in America* (1821) is positive: 'What country before was ever rid of so many evils?' She believed the United States to be without industrial squalour and disease-ridden slums. There were no spurious class divisions and no corruption. Democracy worked: 'the wheel of government, moved by the united impetus of the whole people, turns noiseless and unimpeded'. Her enthusiasm seemed unalloyed:

> Truly I am grateful to this nation; the study of their history and institutions, and the consideration of the peace and happiness which they enjoy, has thawed my heart and filled it with hopes which I had not thought it could know again.

There was, however, slavery, and on her second visit it was slavery and how to end it that occupied most of her thoughts.

Fanny and Camilla decided to visit the place where Owen was embarking on his experiment. This involved crossing the Alleghenies in March, two weeks of hard travel with the weather still severe, and continuing by steamboat on the Ohio River. Owen had purchased the existing community of Harmonie, founded by a group of German immigrants from Württemberg. (They left to found another community in Pennsylvania, which they called Economy.) At Harmonie the Wrights met Owen's son William and Donald MacDonald, who were among the advanced contingent of Owenites. On a second visit, they met Robert Owen himself and saw the beginnings of the new community. Owen's intention was to change society 'from an ignorant, selfish system to an enlightened social system which shall gradually unite all interests into one, and remove all causes for contest between individuals'. Fanny Wright was inspired.

Her response to New Harmony and her own observations of slavery led her to found a settlement herself, with the intention of providing a haven for freed slaves. The place she selected was in Tennessee, on the Wolf River about fifteen miles from Memphis, then just a trading post. She called it Nashoba, the Chickasaw name for the river, and settled the first black family on the 320 acres she had acquired. The plan was to have black and white living together, those who had known only slavery learning how to be their own masters, and former slave owners learning to respect black labour. But both New Harmony and Nashoba faced huge problems. Many of those who signed up for New Harmony did not have the necessary skills to maintain the trades that provided its economic base, and there was friction about how the community should be run. From the start Nashoba had financial difficulties and Fanny Wright had to make strenuous efforts to raise funds. She was well connected and knew many influential people, but most believed that her experiment could not possibly succeed. It did not help that one of Fanny's associates at Nashoba, James Richardson, also a Scot, openly lived with a black woman and declared his belief in free love.

The Nashoba experiment collapsed, and in 1827 Robert Owen's sons, William and Robert Dale Owen declared that New Harmony's 'bold and hazardous attempt' at communal living was 'premature'. Many of its residents had given up and left. But it was not the end of Fanny Wright's career. She continued her campaign against slavery, she wrote, above all she lectured, often to packed audiences. Her radicalism, her call for the United States to return to its true revolutionary values, her condemnation of organised religion and conventional morality, her feminism, shocked many and provoked some violent criticism, but this did not silence her. And she had plenty of admirers. Walt Whitman commented: 'She was a brilliant woman, of beauty and estate, who was never satisfied unless she was busy doing good – public good, private good.'

Frances Wright believed that the United States was a nation that could and should nurture freedom for all peoples and both sexes. It is unlikely that she would have found so strong a voice in Scotland, or in England. It is unlikely, too, that the Scottish-born sons of Robert Owen would have found room to experiment in Britain as they had in the US. There were plenty more who continued to see the US as offering a home for unusual or marginal ideas. A few years after the failure of Nashoba a colony was established near Independence, Missouri by followers of the Church of Christ, or the Church of Jesus Christ of Latter-day Saints as it became later. By 1839 they had shifted to Illinois, and Scots were among those who responded to their call. In 1847 Brigham Young led the Latter-day Saints, the Mormons, west to Salt Lake Valley in what would become the Territory of Utah. In Scotland the Mormons recruited in Glasgow, Edinburgh and Fife, and possibly as many as 5,000 Scots joined the migration to the Utah settlements which would become Salt Lake City, Ogden and Logan.

Scots continued to respond to the US potential as a territory for salvation and for doing good. Slavery was a key issue. Scots had been active in the slave trade and Scottish-owned plantations in the West Indies and southern states depended, like all the others, on slave labour. Richard Oswald from Glasgow acquired an Ayrshire estate with the proceeds of his slave trading activities. But Scots were also at the forefront of the abolition movement: the slave trade in the British Empire was abolished in 1807 and slave owning in 1833. A Scottish Quaker, George Keith, one of the settlers in East New Jersey in the 1680s, published a pamphlet condemning slavery and persuaded the colony's proprietors not to use slave labour. James MacGregor from Perthshire was a Presbyterian minister in Pictou, Nova Scotia, when he urged the end of slavery and spent his own money to free slaves. The Reverend Alexander MacLeod, from Mull, arrived in the US in 1792. He refused to take up the call to a ministry at Coldingham, New York, because church members included slave owners: owning slaves was subsequently banned by the church.

The 1816 *Emigrant's Guide* was scathing about a so-called democracy that fostered the institution of slavery:

> If there be any consistency in the character and principles of democracy, how must it stand impeached by this inhuman practice! Can that be the seat of freedom where a million human beings groan beneath the scourge of slavery?

Many others highlighted this inconsistency. Eneas Mackenzie argued that the institution of slavery undermined the moral and social fabric of the southern states. 'As the negroes perform all the manual labour, their masters are left to saunter away life in sloth, and too often in ignorance.' Most of the 'errors and crimes' of the state of Virginia could be ascribed to 'the system of slavery'. Thomas Hamilton had much to say about both slavery and prejudice in his account of his American travels. Freedom, he argued, was not just about lack of enslavement but equally about lack of prejudice. Black people who had been freed were subject to 'the most grinding and humiliating of all slaveries, that of universal and unconquerable prejudice'. Providing education and equipping them for a trade did not help, as whites would not order a suit from a black tailor or buy food from a black grocer. It was, he said, 'an abuse of language', to call blacks free.

Hand in hand with prejudice went hypocrisy, and Hamilton was particularly uncompromising in his condemnation of Jefferson, a slave owner and begetter:

> The moral character of Jefferson was repulsive. Continually puling about liberty, equality, and the degrading curse of slavery, he brought his own children to the hammer, and made money of his debaucheries. Even at his death, he did not manumit his numerous offspring, but left them, soul and body, to degradation, and the cart-whip.

Plantation owners believed that productivity, and therefore the economy of the southern states, depended on slaves. Hamilton, writing in 1833, saw no social or economic reason why slavery should not be 'instantly abolished' in Maryland, but acknowledged that further south the hot and humid climate meant that it would be impossible to raise crops such as rice and sugar without slave labour, which was nevertheless a curse: 'a curse deeper and more deadly never was inflicted on any community'. Other Scottish voices were uncompromising. An 1840 article in a Gaelic paper stated:

> It is an enormous disgrace to this powerful country in which people are so boastful of their freedom, and so quick to speak against every other country, that they still approve of slavery and bondage in their society, and that men and women

and children are sold in market exactly in the same way as sheep and cattle.

Two prominent Scottish abolitionists were William Steel, from Biggar in Lanarkshire, and James Brownlee from Glasgow. Steel had emigrated to Virginia with his parents in 1817, aged eight. Later he was in Ohio and worked with the underground railroad which smuggled escaped slaves across the border into Canada. James Brownlee was 26 when he emigrated, and like Steel became an active abolitionist in Ohio. He proposed a resolution against the Fugitive Slave Act, passed in 1850, which facilitated the recapture of supposed runaways and in practice meant that any black person, free or otherwise, could be picked up. Brownlee called upon people to 'neither aid nor abet, the capture of a fugitive slave; but, on the contrary, [to] harbour and feed, clothe and assist, and give him a practical godspeed toward liberty'. Glaswegian Allan Pinkerton in Illinois was another Scot who provided a safe house for runaways on the underground railway.

The slavery debate gathered force, with the abolitionist cause receiving a striking boost when in 1852 Harriet Beecher Stowe's *Uncle Tom's Cabin* was published and within eight months sold a million copies. She visited Scotland where she was received with enthusiasm; there was strong support for the abolition of slavery, particularly in Glasgow. But there were those who were critical of her visit, especially when she praised the 'improvements' effected by the Duchess of Sutherland who had initiated clearances and sent many of the dispossessed across the Atlantic. Some felt there were people in Scotland who were worse off than America's slaves.

In order to provide services and develop an industrial base the United States needed skilled workers. In colonial times Scots had provided labour in iron works in New York, New Jersey and Philadelphia, and in the coal mines. The demand for labour increased and the prospect of higher wages continued to attract Scots. As coal mining expanded Scottish colliers were recruited by agents sent from America. Developing towns and cities required buildings and builders and Scots were involved in both design and construction work. John McComb, whose father came from Ayrshire, according to Peter Ross designed 'all the principal buildings put up in New York between 1795 and 1830'. John McArthur from Bladnoch near Wigtown on the Solway Firth emigrated to the US as a child and became a carpenter. By the 1840s he was designing buildings in Philadelphia, and in 1869 he built the city's town hall. A prominent Scottish architect in Philadelphia in the colonial period was Robert Smith from Glasgow. He built Princeton University's Nassau Hall. Scottish masons were also highly regarded and much in demand.

New arrivals had to be prepared to move beyond the eastern seaboard. Eneas Mackenzie, writing in 1818, highlights the range of skilled workers required in Cincinnati, growing fast on the banks of the Ohio River. He lists masons, brick-makers, carpenters, cabinet-makers, coopers, turners, machine-makers, wheelwrights, smiths, nailors, coppersmiths, tinsmiths, silversmiths, gunsmiths, clock and watch makers, glovers, tailors, tanners, saddlers, shoemakers, butchers, bakers, brewers, distillers, cotton spinners, weavers, dyers, printers, book binders, rope makers, tobacconists, soap boilers, candle makers, comb makers and painters. But often skilled workers had to go 'on the tramp', moving from place to place picking up work where they could get it.

The need for labour ebbed and flowed with the economy, but the message generally was that the opportunities were there for those prepared to seek them out and to work hard. Writing in 1876 Alexander Craig said that St Louis needed 'not idle clerks and lazy shopkeepers but hardworking industrious men who mean to succeed'. The pattern continued of Scots providing contacts for each other and supporting new arrivals until they found their feet.

It helped that they were often identified as having the necessary rigour and practical education to respond to the opportunities available.

Scots made a mark as manufacturers. Henry Burden from Dunblane in Stirlingshire went to the US in 1819 aged 28. He began to make agricultural implements in Troy, New York and developed what would become one of the largest ironworks in the US. In 1846 he got together with a group of entrepreneurs in Glasgow to found the Atlantic Steam Ferry Company. Duncan Campbell from Greenock, who arrived in Boston in 1827, invented a leather-stitching machine for making shoes. Thomas Dickson, born in Lauder, Berwickshire, emigrated to Pennsylvania and became head of the Dickson Manufacturing Company at Scranton. He was also president of the Delaware and Hudson Canal Company and set up an iron plant on Lake Champlain. James Oliver from Newcastleton in Roxburghshire left Scotland for New York in 1835 and carried on west to South Bend, Indiana. There he started a foundry business where he developed a new type of plough that cut the first furrows in thousands of acres of prairie. The Oliver plough was produced in great numbers and at the height of its manufacture the factory had a workforce of 2,000. A model of the Oliver plough is displayed in Edinburgh's Museum of Scotland. Scots were prominent in American shipbuilding. Ayrshire-born Henry Eckford left Scotland in 1791 at the age of sixteen. He became a shipbuilder with yards on Long Island, where in 1822 he built the *Robert Fulton*, named for the Scottish builder of America's first steamboat, the *Clermont*. Eckford became Naval Constructor at the Brooklyn Navy Yard. Donald Mackay from Tain, Easter Ross, established shipyards in Boston which built clipper ships. Angus Macpherson from Inverness-shire built the frigate *Ironsides*, the iron-clad ship that played a part in the Civil War. George Dickie from Arbroath went to California where he designed marine engines. Both east coast and west coast shipyards employed large numbers of Scots.

For 200 years waterways defined where colonies were planted and the routes of trade and migration. Areas that could not be reached by water were overlooked. In the 1820s canals began to make connections which changed the balance. The Erie Canal opened in 1823; its chief engineer was a Scot, James Geddes. Ten years later it was possible to travel from New York to New Orleans entirely by water. But by this time another form of transport had arrived which would change the face of America. The United States had begun to construct railroads, and many of the engineers involved were Scots. The first locomotive to be built in the US was the work of a Scot, Peter Cooper. James Kirkwood, born in Edinburgh in 1807, became consultant engineer for several American railroads, and also constructed docks and the Nassau Water Works in Brooklyn. James Laurie was 21 when he arrived in the US in 1832. Before long he was chief engineer for the Norwich and Worcester Railroad. Later he specialised in bridge building, and was responsible for the first wrought-iron bridge in the US, which crossed the Connecticut River at Windsor Locks. Donald McCallum from Renfrewshire emigrated in the same year as Laurie. He went initially to Rochester, New York, and became involved in railroad and bridge construction. In 1855 he became general superintendent of the Erie Railroad, for which the assistant surveyor was James Ferguson from Perthshire. During the Civil War McCallum was director of military railroads for the Union.

The early decades of the nineteenth century saw textile manufacture take the lead in Scottish industry and generate widespread repercussions. Handloom weavers displaced by factory methods emigrated in large numbers. But in the other direction came Americans who were keen to learn from what Scots were achieving. They were looking for skilled labour and were also quite prepared to hijack jealously-guarded techniques. The export of textile machinery and skilled mechanics was forbidden by law. The US textile industry was initially focused around Philadelphia but soon developed in New England. In 1817 Scottish looms were beginning to be introduced in New England mills. Scottish organisation appealed as well as Scottish techniques, with considerable American interest in New Lanark and other model mill towns. The textile town of Lowell in Massachusetts, where water powered mills were set up on the Merrimack River in 1822, was influenced by Scottish examples. The New England mills would employ large numbers of Scots, with agents sent to Scotland to recruit workers, including many women who were an important part of the textile workforce in Scotland. Several Scottish weaving settlements grew up in New England. Recruitment continued after the Civil War.

Two of Scotland's most successful textile-related businesses were the firms of Coats and Clark, both of Paisley. From the 1820s they were producing cotton sewing thread. In 1850 Coats opened a spinning mill at Pawtucket, Rhode Island, and Clark followed with a cotton thread factory at Newark, New Jersey. The Glasgow Linen Company operated a factory at Grafton, Massachusetts, which employed mainly Scots. Other Scottish businesses were transplanted to the US later in the century in order to exploit the potential of the American market. Better wages and working conditions made transatlantic relocation attractive for the workers who went.

The pressure on the United States to build industrial and commercial self-sufficiency kept the gates open to immigrants and ensured that an enticing picture of employment and settlement possibilities was promoted. Some immigrants were more welcome than others. There was a prejudice against the Irish which only grew when the 1840s potato famine encouraged the view that the US was being flooded with Irish paupers. By and large the Scots escaped this negative perception. Although there were Scottish families who arrived in the US with little or nothing, like the Carnegie family, they were generally welcomed by Scots prominent in the professions and as managers. Peter Ross, writing in 1896, claimed that all over the United States:

> the Scot is looked up to with respect. He is regarded as an embodiment of common sense, a natural lover of civil and religious liberty, a firm believer in free institutions, in the rights of man, in fair play, and exemplary in his loyalty to whatever cause he may have adopted.

The Scots were 'model colonisers', ready to take up 'all the duties of citizenship' and 'to promote the general wealth of the country by building up its commerce, by developing its resources, and by adding to its higher aspirations by widening and popularising its educational, artistic, and literary aspirations and opportunities'. On the educational front Scots in the nineteenth century continued to teach at all levels, both formally and informally, still carrying across the Atlantic the traditional Presbyterian belief in education as a route to advancement. A commitment to good works also travelled. The St Andrews Societies, which helped Scots in difficulties, proliferated from their 1729 beginnings in Charleston. As early as 1789 Isabella Graham from Lanarkshire started a fund in New York for helping the impoverished sick and eight years later she helped to found a society for the relief of widows and children, the first of its kind in the US. In 1811 she was presiding over the New York Magdalen Society dedicated to rescuing prostitutes. She also started a school for girls. Joanna Bethune was a product of a school Isabella Graham ran for a time in Edinburgh. Her family emigrated to the US in 1798 and she taught at Graham's New York school. She became much involved with helping orphans and with the Sunday school movement and has been described as the 'mother of American Sabbath Schools'.

Institutions developed in colonial times often maintained links with Scotland and fostered a continuing interest in the Scottish academic and intellectual world. James McCosh from Ayrshire maintained Princeton University's Scottish connection with his twenty-year presidency from 1868. John Greig from Moffat, educated at the University of Edinburgh, practised as a lawyer in New York State. In 1845 he became vice-chancellor of the State University of New York as well as holding a variety of official positions. He also set up a seminary for girls. John Gilchrist, a plantation owner in North Carolina who served in the state legislature, in the early nineteenth century founded with Dr Angus MacLean the Floral College for Women.

Many institutions reflected a distinctively Scottish approach to learning, more generalist than the English and often more concerned with the needs of the wider population. A good example is the Smithsonian Institution founded in Washington in 1846. Its first secretary and director was Joseph Henry, grandson of Scottish immigrants, who moved to the Smithsonian from Princeton University, where he was professor of natural philosophy (physics). Henry's experiments with electro-magnetism laid the foundations for the telegraph, telephone and radio. In his Smithsonian role he promoted the study of American archaeology and anthropology, paralleling work being done by the brothers Daniel and George Wilson in Edinburgh. (Daniel Wilson also emigrated, but to Canada, where he became President of the University of Toronto. George Wilson was keen to collect native North American material as part of his commitment to educating the Scottish public.) Joseph Henry, too, believed both in intellectual enquiry and making its benefits available to all. He developed a network of contacts all over the country who collected material and sent it to Washington. George Wilson did exactly the same thing when he became the first director of Edinburgh's Museum of Science and Art in 1854, encouraging the Scottish diaspora to collect for him. In 1847 Henry wrote: 'The most prominent idea in my mind is that of stimulating the talent of our country to original research.' He wanted that research to lead to the general enlightenment of the nation', and he organised collections of introductory material as a way of encouraging public interest. Their study, he argued, could be 'an inexhaustible source of pleasure and contentment to the most numerous and the most important classes of the community'. The Smithsonian is now one of the most important museum institutions in the world.

The Smithsonian was a symbol of the nation's need to understand its own territory. The expeditions which explored and mapped the west were not only about forging links and charting routes for trade and settlement. They were also about investigating the natural world. In this Scots played a distinctive role. One of the first was Alexander Wilson, the radical weaver forced to leave Scotland in 1794. He worked for a time as a teacher in New Jersey and Pennsylvania, but his real interest was ornithology. He journeyed extensively, collecting bird specimens and making drawings, producing between 1808 and 1814 the seven volumes of his illustrated *American Ornithology*. A friend of Wilson's was George Ord, also a Scot and a naturalist, who accompanied him on one of his collecting trips. Ayrshire-born gardener William Dunlop Brackenridge emigrated in 1837 and was appointed chief botanist with the Pacific expedition led by Captain Charles Wilkes, which in 1841 landed in Washington Territory. Later, he founded a nursery business in Maryland, and became horticultural editor of the *American Farmer*.

It was a Scot, William Maclure, born in Ayr in 1763, who produced the first survey of American geology in 1817. He travelled extensively in Europe but by 1800 was in the US, where he continued his travels, making detailed geological observations as he went. From 1817 to 1840 he was president of Philadelphia's Academy of Natural Sciences, which he had helped to found. He was committed to education, believing that schools were 'the only mode an individual has to benefit or improve mankind', and personally financed a number of radical educational endeavours. These included an involvement in Robert Owen's community at New Harmony, although he had reservations about Owen and the way the community was run. He was also an admirer of what Fanny Wright was attempting at Nashoba.

Scotland was keenly interested in the natural science of America. Outstanding among several Scots who collected American specimens for Scottish institutions was David Douglas, the son of a stone mason, born at Scone near Perth in 1799. He became gardener first to the Earl of Mansfield at Scone Palace, then to Sir Robert Preston at Culross in Fife. From there he went to Glasgow's Botanic Garden to become assistant to the renowned botanist Professor William Hooker. He went to the US on behalf of the Royal Horticultural Society. His first collecting trip in 1823 was not very productive, but two years later he was back on a more extensive expedition which took him round Cape Horn to the mouth of the Columbia River. A third major collecting expedition began in 1829. He travelled in California as well as the northwest, and brought back many plants which are now well-known in Scotland, especially the Douglas fir. The original specimen can still be found in the grounds of Scone Palace. His final trip took him to the Sandwich Islands, now Hawaii, where he died in a grisly accident, killed by a wild bull. He was only 35. It was a terrible end for one of Scotland's and America's most adventurous plant collectors. After his death another Scot, John Jeffrey from Perth, travelled to Oregon to carry on Douglas's work.

David Douglas's short career demonstrates a particular aspect of American opportunity – the scope for adventure, for extending boundaries. America offered wider horizons. These could be intellectual as well as territorial; in Douglas's case they were both. They could also encompass opportunities for public life less trammelled by class and convention than in the old country. Frances Wright and Isabella Graham are good examples. A specifically political role was not open to them, but they had the opportunity to operate effectively and make use of their brains and their skills.

Scottish names feature in most areas of public life, carrying on the colonial tradition. William Lowrie, born in Edinburgh, emigrated to Pennsylvania in 1791. He began his career as a school teacher and finished it as a US Senator. Archibald McBryde from Wigtownshire went to North Carolina as a child. After a period as a lawyer he too became a Senator, in 1813. William Phillips from Paisley emigrated aged fourteen in 1838. In Illinois he became involved in the abolitionist movement. He had a career as a lawyer and newspaper correspondent, and worked in Kansas where he founded the city of Salina in 1858. He commanded the Cherokee Regiment in the Civil War, and was three times elected to Congress.

Before the Revolutionary War Scots had initiated several American newspapers. James Robertson, the son of an Edinburgh printer, went to Boston in the 1750s. Later he and his brother Alexander started the *New York Chronicle* and in 1771 the *Albany Gazette*. They were Loyalists, and with the approach of war their printing press and type were attacked by patriots and burned. Undeterred, they started the *Royal American Gazette* in 1775 and then the *Royal Pennsylvania Gazette*, before lighting out for Nova Scotia and eventually back to Edinburgh. Miller Grieve, also from Edinburgh, was a journalist before becoming a diplomat, working on the *Southern Recorder* in Savannah, Georgia. He became the US minister to Denmark in 1852. He was also involved in the Presbyterian church and in education, and was a keen promoter of railways. James Gordon Bennett was born in Keith, Banffshire and went to the US in 1819. In 1826 he became assistant editor of the *New York Enquirer*, later the *Courier and Enquirer*. In 1835 he was editing the *New York Herald* from a cellar in Wall Street. Thomas Affleck from Dumfries, an agricultural writer, was in 1840 editing the *Western Farmer and Gardener* in Cincinnati. Peter Brown and his wife Marianne Mackenzie arrived in New York in

1837. Brown was a radical Edinburgh town councillor who had for a while been a partner in the Alloa glassworks on the other side of the Firth of Forth. In New York he started the *British Chronicle* aimed at a Scottish readership, though soon after he departed for Toronto, where he and his son George continued their newspaper career, becoming best known for founding the Toronto *Globe*. Other Scottish-interest papers and magazines followed later in the century: the *Scottish-American Journal*, the *Caledonian Advertiser*, the *Caledonian*. There was clearly an identifiable market that was distinctively Scottish.

The majority of Scots, however, were absorbed into the general English-speaking population of the expanding nation, although some maintained a personal Scottish identity and there were Scottish enclaves and place names. In the 1830s Scottish families from Kintyre settled at Argyle, Illinois, and by mid-century there were around 5,000 Scots in the state, with over a hundred townships echoing old country names, Elgin, Inverness and Dundee, for example. One of the earliest settlers in Iowa was Samuel Muir, a graduate of Edinburgh University. In Iowa's Tama County the names of farms reflected the origins of their owners – Kilpatrick, Renton, Craigbrae, Drumgrier – while names such as Scotch Grove also clearly signalled the origins of the first settlers. Parts of North Carolina remained distinctively Highland. Scottish networks and support systems continued to operate. But the pioneer experience, whether in industrial cities like Pittsburgh or later Chicago, or on a frontier homestead, could also fragment cohesion and sever cultural and emotional links with the old country. Most of the Scots who came to the United States after independence came as families or individuals rather than communities. Across the border in Canada emigrant Scots continued to arrive and settle in groups, retaining the same sense of cohesion that had shaped their lives in Scotland. That was less likely to happen in the US.

For the best part of a century the pull west was a dominant

feature of American experience. Scots were among those who carved out the first trails and among the thousands who responded when routes were opened. Part of the movement west was the wholesale shift of Native American tribes who occupied the land white America aspired to. This displacement in which Andrew Jackson had played so major a part in his early career intensified under his presidency. The story of the Cherokees encapsulates the process and also highlights the role of several Scots. Like the other tribes of the southeast, the Creeks, the Choctaws, the Chickasaws and the Seminoles, they had been pushed gradually westward, forced to cede their lands to make way for white settlement.

In the 1830s the leader of the Cherokee nation was John Ross, a Scot with a Cherokee great-grandmother. The southeast tribes had tried to adapt to the incomers' way of life, and the Cherokees in particular lived in permanent settlements, farmed and raised stock, in some cases owned slaves, established mills and forges and owned wagons and ploughs. They set up schools and had their own printing press and newspaper. But they were in the way. One by one the other tribes departed, first the Choctaws in 1831, then the Creeks four years later, and the Chickasaws in 1837. John Ross fought against the threatened removal of the Cherokees but President Jackson refused to accept a decision of the Supreme Court that the Cherokees had a right to stay in their southeastern territory. They were already being harassed by Georgia settlers; now the army was ordered to remove them west of the Mississippi. What followed, in the autumn of 1838, became known as the Trail of Tears. Their possessions loaded onto 645 wagons, most of the people themselves on foot, they were forced to make their way west. About a quarter of them died of disease or starvation. The destination of those who survived was Oklahoma, arid, inhospitable and totally unlike the lands they had left. In spite of this devastating experience, when the Cherokees heard about the effects of potato blight in the Highlands they raised money to send to the victims of famine. 'Have the Scotch no claim upon the Cherokees?' asked John Ross. 'Have they not a very special claim?'

Among those close to the Cherokees and sympathetic to their plight was a 45-year-old Ulster Scot called Sam Houston. His family had settled first in Virginia, then in Tennessee. He had fought under Jackson against the Creeks at Horseshoe Bend, but he was considered a friend by the Cherokees. Davy Crockett was a comrade of Houston's. He, too, was of Scottish descent and had grown up on the frontier. He, too, fought with Jackson at Horseshoe Bend. By 1832 he was in Texas, part of Mexico, which had won independence from Spain in 1821, although with growing numbers of American opportunists and freebooters infiltrating a sparsely populated territory. Among them was Dr James Grant, a Scottish land speculator and gang leader operating below the Rio Grande. Houston got involved in politics and had the task of recruiting a Texan force to support the demand for autonomy. In December 1835 a band of volunteers took over the southern Texas town of San Antonio and established themselves in the Alamo, a former mission. Three months later, Texas declared its independence from Mexico. The commander of the independent republic's armed forces was Sam Houston.

Mexico's response to this pre-emptive move was to send in troops under General Antonio Lopez de Santa Anna. They besieged a garrison of 189 men in the Alamo, a collection of adobe buildings surrounded by a wall. Almost a third of those men were Scots or Ulster Scots. They included Davy Crockett, Jim Bowie, Kentucky frontiersman and inventor of the Bowie knife, and John MacGregor, who played the bagpipes through the attack. The MacGregor clan had a long and distinguished piping tradition as well as a more dubious reputation as cattle thieves. John Lee Hancock's film *The Alamo* includes a brief skirl on the pipes, but more striking is Davy Crockett's performance on the fiddle, which has a distinctly Scottish flavour. There is possibly little truth in the suggestion that the fury of Santa Anna's attack was spurred on by a determination to silence the sound of the pipes; but every man of the besieged was killed. The famous picture by Robert J Onderdonk shows the valiant buckskinned figure of Crockett wielding his musket like a club against the Mexican attack. (The Alamo force was actually commanded by William Travis, a lawyer.) In case we are not sure who the enemy is, one of the Mexican soldiers wears a sombrero. The following month, on 21 April, Houston avenged the Alamo, defeating Santa Anna at the Battle of San Jacinto. Six months later he was elected president of the Republic of Texas.

The independent republic lasted only nine years. In 1845 it became part of the United States. War followed. The US invaded Mexico on a slender pretext, with an eye on the tempting territories of New Mexico and California, also a part of Mexico. Inspired by the notion of 'manifest destiny', that it was the mission of Americans to occupy and 'civilise' the whole continent, there was a rush of public support. 'We must march from Texas straight to the Pacific Ocean, and be bounded only by its roaring wave,' proclaimed the Maryland representative in Congress, as reported in the *Congressional Globe*, and added, 'it is the destiny of the Anglo-Saxon race'. Scots may not have been included among Anglo-Saxons, but they were participants in the war and benefited from its outcome. Ulster Scot Kit Carson, born in Kentucky in 1790, trapper and trader, played an important role in opening up routes to California as a guide for John Frémont. He assisted Frémont in the California campaign, and it was Carson who carried the dispatches east which brought the news that southern California was in American hands. In 1848 the treaty of Guadalupe Hidalgo gave New Mexico and California to the USA. Soon Americans, including many recent immigrants and many Scots, would be pouring into California in their thousands.

The Scottish imprint on the history of Texas was permanent. The city of Houston, near the site of the San Jacinto victory, is an obvious reminder, but over the next few decades, and particularly after the Civil War, Scots would play a key role in developing what Texas became most famous for, cattle ranching. It has been suggested that the tradition of Highland and Border cattle raising, not to mention thieving, was transplanted to the Texas plains. The Scottish imprint on California is less obvious. The Spanish influence in California was extensive, as settlement and Spanish missions in particular had been established since at least the seventeenth century. Inevitably, other Europeans filtered in, first by sea, then overland. Hugo Reid arrived in California by way of South America. He was born in Cardross in Dunbartonshire in 1810, the son of a shopkeeper, and left Scotland at the age of eighteen. At 22 he was trading in Hermosillo, Northern Mexico. Two years later he was in Los Angeles, and eventually settled permanently in California, where he married a widowed Native American, Dona Victoria, which necessitated his conversion to Catholicism. His marriage brought him into close contact with California's Natives, and he became very knowledgeable about their traditions and way of life. He ranched in the San Gabriel Valley, raising cattle and growing vines, and was also involved in sea-going trade, operating a ship called the *Esmeralda* as far afield as the Sandwich Islands. With the outbreak of war with Mexico, his Catholicism and his sympathy for the Indians meant Americans viewed him with suspicion and his ranch was confiscated by the US government.

The overland journey to California was gruelling. In 1846 the Donner and Reed families and members of their party (including the McCutcheon family, from Missouri but clearly of Scottish descent, and Milford Elliot from Illinois, either a Scot or an Ulster Scot) crossed the Wasatch Mountains and Utah's Salt Desert, which they barely survived, into what was still Mexican territory. Already weak and demoralised, they had another desert to cross and then the formidable barrier of the Sierra Nevada to negotiate, on trails that barely existed and were harassed by Indians. In the mountains they were overtaken by winter. The ensuing saga of blizzards, desperate cold, starvation and cannibalism is well known. It was a terrible opening chapter, but only the beginning of a transcontinental flow that in 1849 suddenly accelerated. It was in that year that gold was discovered at Sutter's Mill on the Sacramento River. For decades the green and fertile coastal fringe of California had tempted Americans. Now there was something much more potent.

For Hugo Reid the discovery was opportune. With Jim McKinley, also from Cardross, he opened a store in Monterey to supply gold prospectors. At the same time he was also pursuing his project to record the customs and culture of the local tribes, which he published in the *Los Angeles Star*. He died of tuberculosis in 1852, a year after California achieved statehood.

On the back of gold San Francisco expanded into a major port and provisioning centre, and a thriving environment for banking and business. Scots played their part and Scots, like just about every other nationality, were pulled by the promise of riches and joined the stampede for the gold fields. Some, like William Murray, jumped ship and headed for the mountains. Murray was a seaman on the *Columbia*, a Hudson's Bay Company ship which sailed round Cape Horn between Gravesend and Fort Victoria on Vancouver Island. We don't know what happened to him, but letters to him from his mother in Aberdeen survive. She is concerned that she has heard neither from him or his brother Robert, who has also vanished.

The Donahoe brothers were in the thick of San Francisco enterprise. From a Glasgow Irish family, they left Scotland in the 1830s. Michael, James and Peter all served apprenticeships in a locomotive workshop at Paterson, New Jersey. In 1844, after a spell at the Union Iron Works and then at sea, Michael went to Cincinnati. He joined the First Ohio Volunteers and fought in the Mexican War. When gold was discovered in California he was running an iron foundry on the Rio Grande, repairing US navy vessels, but he abandoned this to join the gold rush. James had gone south to Alabama and then the West Indies, while Peter had sailed in the first steamship to make the voyage round the Horn. After two years in Peru he arrived in San Francisco and was reunited with Michael. The two of them tried their luck at prospecting gold but gave up and started a foundry in San Francisco manufacturing stoves and shovels to supply prospectors. James joined them.

Michael and James both went east within a few years, but Peter remained. He secured the franchise for supplying gas in San Francisco. He started a steamship company that operated between San Francisco and Sacramento, and built steam engines for the navy. He was responsible for a whole string of California firsts: the first quartz mill, the first printing press, the first locomotive. He became president of the Omnibus Railroad Company and a director of the Hibernia Savings and Loan Society and the First National Gold Bank. He built the San Francisco and San Jose railway. The town of Donahoe, in Sonoma County, was named after him. He died a very rich man. So did Michael Donahoe. In Davenport, Ohio he built steam engines and agricultural machinery, and was involved in the Davenport and St Paul Railroad. Later he constructed a new waterworks for the city. Both men were known for their charitable work, which included Peter's funding of the redecoration of St Mary's Church in Glasgow.

One by one, the frontier territories were added to the Union. Statehood did not necessarily bring order and social organisation, but it was often the signal to move on. Scottish names are scattered through every chapter of American frontier history, as outlaws and law makers, as guides and pathfinders, as traders and entrepreneurs, as well as in the roles that Scots are often happier to lay claim to – teachers, ministers, doctors. Scottish individuals and families were part of the flux of population which shaped the still-young nation. When JD Borthwick wrote of aspirations that seemed 'within the reach of all', he was referring specifically to California, and for more than a decade before the Civil War shook the foundations of the United States the Pacific coast, enhanced by the lure of gold in its flanking mountains, epitomised New World potential. To reach it overland meant traversing a vast stretch of apparently useless prairie, empty of anything but buffalo and a few Indians. It was country to be crossed. After the Civil War it became country to settle.

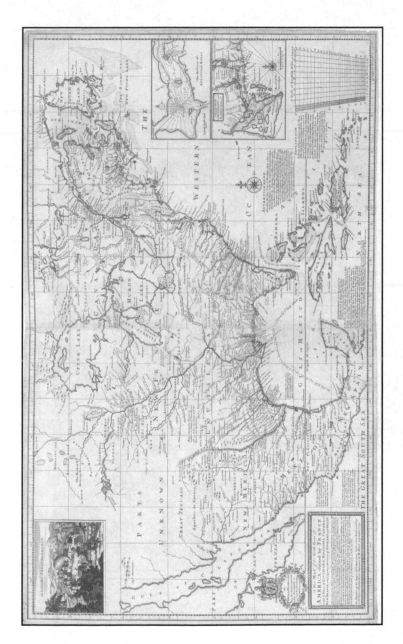

1. Map of 'the north parts of America' dated 1720.
(Trustees of the National Library of Scotland)

The Indian Fort SASQUESAHANOK

2. 'The Indian Fort', detail from the 1720 map. A few maps and images were among the limited sources of information available to early settlers.

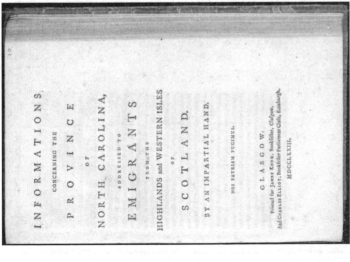

4. Poster in Gaelic promoting Ohio as a destination for emigrants, 1822. Nahum Ward visited Scotland to recruit settlers. (Trustees of the National Library of Scotland)

3. 'Scotus Americanus' recommended that people from 'the Highlands and Western Isles of Scotland' could improve their prospects by settling in North Carolina, 1773. (Trustees of the National Library of Scotland)

5. Letter dated 18 October 1823, from an emigrant from Scotland to relatives at home, describing the death of his mother who 'got sick in the Wagon'. Her funeral was attended by 'above twenty Scotsmen'.
(Trustees of the National Library of Scotland)

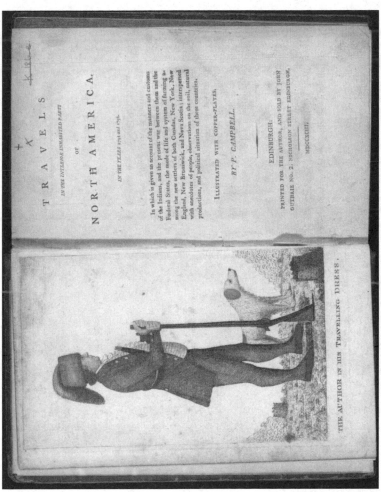

6. Title page and frontispiece from Travels in the Interior Inhabited Parts of North America by Patrick Campbell, published in Edinburgh in 1793. (Trustees of the National Library of Scotland)

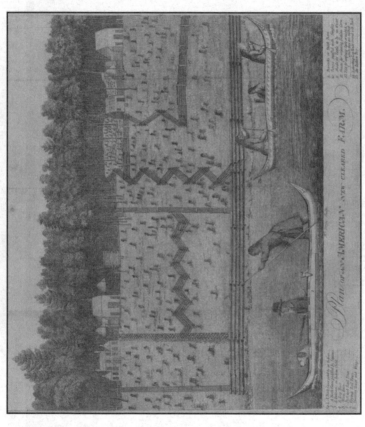

7. An area cleared for farming illustrated in
Travels in the Interior Inhabited Parts of North America
by Patrick Campbell, 1793. The tree stumps are clearly visible.
(Trustees of the National Library of Scotland)

8. The Mohawk River. The valley of the Mohawk was settled by several groups of Scots in the period before the War of Independence. (Library of Congress)

9. The Cumberland Gap, the route west through the Allegheny Mountains taken by many Scots in search of land to settle. (Library of Congress)

10. John Paul Jones, hero of the American War of Independence, was born on the shores of the Solway Firth in 1747. (Library of Congress)

11. Washington Irving, creator of Rip Van Winkle, was born in New York in 1783, the son of a merchant from Orkney. (Library of Congress)

12. Andrew Jackson played a key role in suppressing Native American opposition to settlement west of the Appalachians before becoming president of the United States in 1828. (Library of Congress)

13. John Ross (1790–1866), son of a Scottish trader and a half Cherokee mother, became chief of the Cherokee people. (Library of Congress)

14. *Ironsides*, the iron-clad frigate prominent in the Civil War. It was built by Angus Macpherson from Inverness-shire. (Library of Congress)

15. Allan Pinkerton at Antietam. During the American Civil War Pinkerton, from Glasgow, and his agents spied for President Lincoln. (Library of Congress)

16. Pennsylvania Railway brochure publicising train connections
on both sides of the Atlantic.
(Trustees of the National Library of Scotland)

17. Anchor Line poster advertising the steamship service between Glasgow and New York. (Trustees of the National Library of Scotland)

18. Texas Central Railway brochure advertising 5,000,000 acres of land for settlement in Texas. It is signed Robert M Elgin.
(Trustees of the National Library of Scotland)

20. Andrew Carnegie at St Andrews Golf Course, Westchester County, NY. Carnegie became an icon of Scottish success in the US. (Library of Congress)

19. Robert Louis Stevenson, wife Fanny and stepson Lloyd at Saranac Lake, winter 1887–88, when he was being treated for suspected TB. Nine years earlier he had crossed the continent as 'an amateur emigrant'. (Writers' Museum, Edinburgh)

CHAPTER SEVEN

The Lure of the West

[I] woke up one morning at North Platte... to taste on the platform of the depot that champagne air, otherwise known as the lure of the West.

JOHN CLAY, 1924

FIFTY YEARS BEFORE the publication of his memoirs John Clay, from near Kelso in the Scottish Borders, alighted from the train at North Platte, Nebraska. An ambitious and energetic young man from a prosperous farming family, he responded at once to the lure of the west:

> There was a freedom, a romance, a sort of mystic halo hanging over those green, grassy, swelling divides It was another world; the rough, ready, joyous prospect of a broader field on wind-swept plains blotted out for the time being softer scenes where pleasant meadowlands and fields of golden grain with far-off heather hills lay five thousand miles away.

Clay had been attracted to America because he felt constrained by Scotland, which was, he felt, too limited in opportunity and too class-bound for a man with his ambitions. Clay arrived in the prairie states nine years after the close of the Civil War, in time to participate in the cattle ranching boom and the last phase of the frontier. He became a very successful man.

The United States was still a youthful republic when civil war erupted with devastating effect. Scottish travellers in the US in the first half of the nineteenth century commented on the differences between the northern and southern states, and on the anomalies of slave-owning in a nation that promised freedom. Several predicted confrontation. Scottish voices were prominent in the abolitionist cause but Scots were also slave owners themselves, and saw no other way of sustaining the production of tobacco, cotton and the other crops on which the economy of the southern states depended. White people were just not physically adapted to intensive labour in relentless southern heat. And of course the demand in Scotland, for tobacco and sugar and then for cotton to feed its textile industry, contributed directly to a slave-owning economy.

There were slaves in the colonies before significant numbers of Scots arrived. Those who settled in Virginia, Maryland, the Carolinas, Georgia encountered slavery as an established institution. Scots were involved directly in the slave trade as well as profiting from slave labour on their plantations. By 1800 there were about a million slaves in the US, and a slave in good physical condition might have sold for $350. Sixty years later, with an increasing demand for slave labour to work the expanding cotton plantations, prices had rocketed to around $1,500. Slaves were valuable commodities and slave owners were understandably anxious to ensure their property did not disappear.

Agriculture in the northern states was on a smaller scale and there was less demand for cheap labour than in the south. There, the larger plantations might have over 100 slaves, and their owners were families with political power, well placed to resist any criticism of the system. In the north there were gradual efforts to limit slavery. As early as 1775 Rhode Island had granted freedom to the children of slave mothers. Ten years later the Northwest Ordinance banned slavery north of the Ohio River and east of the Mississippi. In 1808 the importation of slaves was banned, although there was an illegal trade from the West Indies. The Missouri Compromise of 1820 prohibited slavery in Louisiana Purchase territories north of

Missouri's southern border. By 1827 New York State had banned slave owning.

In 1849 the balance between slave and free states was held at fifteen each, but the equilibrium was threatened when California proposed to enter the Union as a free state. The Fugitive Slave Act, which brought in harsher measures against runaways and those who assisted them, was the trade off. The slavery debate intensified, fuelled by Harriet Beecher Stowe's *Uncle Tom's Cabin* and by the Kansas-Nebraska Act of 1854 which ditched the Missouri Compromise and opened more of the west to slavery. In October 1859 John Brown with 21 men attacked the US arsenal at Harper's Ferry on the Potomac. Brown, who was of Ulster Scottish descent, was captured, convicted of murder and treason, and hanged. The following year a Kentucky backwoods lawyer called Abraham Lincoln was elected president and pledged to tackle the slavery issue, stating: 'The house divided against itself cannot stand. I believe this Government cannot endure permanently half slave and half free.' The day after his election South Carolina hauled down the American flag at Charleston and left the Union. Mississippi, Florida, Alabama, Georgia, Louisiana and Texas followed. They would be joined by Virginia, North Carolina, Arkansas, Tennessee, Delaware, Maryland, Kentucky and Missouri. Jefferson Davis became president of the Confederacy, based in Richmond, Virginia. Richmond is only 100 miles from Washington DC, the target of Confederate strategy for most of the war east of the Appalachians.

Inevitably Scots were caught up in the war. On both sides Scots and Ulster Scots were among both leading participants and foot soldiers. Particularly in the south, where Scots and Ulster Scots may have amounted to around a third of the white population, large numbers of Scottish families were broken by four years of appalling destruction. It has been estimated that about 50,000 soldiers in the Union army were born in Scotland. Many more must have been of Scottish descent. There were specifically Scottish units, such as Chicago's Highland Guard led by John McArthur, a boilermaker from Erskine who had emigrated in 1849, and the 79th Highlanders of New York under Colonel James Cameron, who was killed at Bull Run. There were several other Cameron units: the Cameron Guards (3rd Battalion, District of Columbia Infantry), Cameron's Highlanders (65th Illinois), Cameron Rifles (68th New York) – plus two Illinois Scotch Regiments and the Scotch Rifles of the Pennsylvania Reserves. On the Confederate side there were even more. From North Carolina alone there were the Highland Boys of North Carolina, two companies of Highland Rangers, Moore County Scotch Riflemen, Scotch Greys Artillery and the Scotch Tigers, and there were Scottish units from Tennessee, Alabama, Virginia, Louisiana and Mississippi. In addition there were hundreds of Scots scattered through the regiments fielded by every state and also fighting with irregular troops. There can be few Civil War memorials that are without Scottish names.

Angus MacDonald, great grandson of the great Gaelic poet Alasdair maćMhaighstir Alasdair, who had emigrated from the island of Eigg to Wisconsin at the age of 24, joined the 11th Wisconsin Regiment with his cousin. They fought in Alabama and Mississippi. Arthur MacArthur was the son of a Glasgow emigrant who had arrived in Massachusetts in 1825. He joined the Union Army and was a colonel by the age of twenty. Wounded three times, mentioned in dispatches ten times, and decorated, he later fought in the Spanish American War and ultimately became military governor of the Philippines. His son was General Douglas MacArthur. William Duff from Elgin, later US Consul in Glasgow, became staff officer to General Grant. James Geddes from Edinburgh came to Iowa in 1857 aged 28, having fought in the Crimean War. In 1861 he enlisted as a private in the 8th Iowa Volunteers, and fought under General Grant at Vicksburg and then under Sherman. He ended the war as a general. David Morrison from Glasgow joined the 79th Highlanders as a captain; he, too, had served in the British Army, and was promoted to colonel. John A Campbell from Ohio served as brigadier-general, and became the first governor of Wyoming. One of General McClellan's staff officers was James Forsyth, also a Ohio Scot. After the war he was in charge of Fort Riley in Kansas and later fought the Sioux in Wyoming and Montana. Another Ohio Scot, George Crook, had a distinguished career with the Union Army and then went on to fight in the Indian wars of the 1870s.

The war divided families and neighbours. James Campbell in Charleston and his brother Alexander, a stonemason in New York State, fought on opposite sides and were both present at the Union attempt in 1862 to capture Charleston. Ebenezer and Margaret Allison left Scotland in 1856 and settled in Missouri. Ebenezer joined the Union army, but their neighbours supported the south and in his absence harassed and threatened his family and stole their livestock. Missouri and Kansas were deeply and violently divided.

David MacRae, whose book on *The Americans at Home* was published in 1879, believed that most Highlanders in the south were opposed to secession, but followed the lead of North Carolina where there was a distinctive Highland presence. 'Almost every man of them I met,' he wrote, 'had served in the Confederate Army, and had left dead brothers or sons on the battlefield.' Among several senior Confederate officers of Scottish origins were General Joseph E Johnston who led the army in its initial successes, the dashing Jeb Stuart, and the brilliant Thomas 'Stonewall' Jackson. General Jackson had gained his soubriquet at the first Battle of Bull Run, a Confederate victory on Washington's doorstep, but he died two years later at Chancellorsville on the Rappahannock, in spite of outmanoeuvring the much larger Union force.

The Union Army was initially commanded by General George McClellan, of Scottish descent, whose profound reluctance to initiate any kind of action increasingly exasperated President

Lincoln. In early engagements the losses on both sides were grim. At Antietam in Maryland the battle of September 1862 left 12,000 Union and 10,500 Confederate dead. At Gettysburg ten months later the Confederates lost over 20,000, the Union Army over 23,000. By this time McClellan had been relieved of his command, but it was not until March 1864 that General Ulysses S Grant took over, after fighting a successful campaign west of the Alleghenies.

Grant, from Ohio, had fought in the Mexican War but was a reluctant soldier. Disillusioned and resorting to drink, he made a mess of civilian life. 'Yet,' wrote American journalist and historian Herbert Agar, 'when the war came he woke from his slack despondency and became a man of unbending purpose, with a grasp of detail which astonishes military historians.' He was not an abolitionist – his wife owned slaves – and he hated war. He was unpopular, and Lincoln was under considerable pressure to get rid of him. But the day after the Union victory at Gettysburg, 3 July 1863, Grant had achieved the surrender of Vicksburg on the Mississippi. It was a turning point, for Grant's career and for the war, although there was much bloody fighting and ruthless destruction to come.

On 9 April 1864 General Lee surrendered the Army of Northern Virginia to General Grant at Appomattox Court House, near Lynchburg, in the home of a man called McLean who had moved there after the first Battle of Bull Run had been fought in his backyard. A year later Lincoln was shot while attending a performance at Ford's Theatre in Washington. With his death Vice-President Andrew Johnson, whose family came originally from the Scottish Borders, took over. Lincoln's Democrat opponent in the election of 1864 had been General George McClellan. McClellan failed in his bid for the presidency, but in 1869 Ulysses S Grant would become the sixth president of the United States with Scottish origins.

Presidents Johnson and Grant presided over the period of post-war reconstruction. The Civil War was deeply traumatic for a young nation which had not yet defined itself geographically or culturally. Although there were plenty people in the north – among them a young man from Scotland called Andrew Carnegie – who benefited economically, the economy of the south was in tatters, and so was the social structure; a way of life had been destroyed. The labour force on which so much depended had either vanished or had to be paid wages. The task of Andrew Johnson, born into a North Carolina community, was to bring the southern states back into the union and start the process of integration and revival.

Legislation aimed at ensuring equal rights for freed slaves was put in place, but the old order resisted this and Johnson made it easy for them. Some southern states enacted Black Codes, which enabled them to treat freed slaves as virtual serfs and made it very difficult for blacks to own or lease land. Johnson's successor, Grant, continued the reconstruction process, but whatever gains were made were effectively reversed by President Rutherford Hayes, elected in 1877, who allowed the return of white rule in the southern states. Hayes was the son of an Ulster Scots minister. James Buchanan, who had preceded Lincoln as president, was also from an Ulster Scots family, with origins in Stirlingshire. Thus, four of the five presidents who had to deal directly with issues of slavery and their legacy were of Scottish descent. Not one of them was an unambivalent abolitionist.

A significant factor in the old south's resistance to change was the birth in December 1865 of an organisation that would become synonymous with the fight for white Protestant supremacy. In Pulaski, Tennessee a group of former Confederate soldiers of Scottish descent got together to form a secret society called the Ku Klux Klan. Their purpose was to undermine the rights of blacks and their weapon was terror. Dressed in white robes and hoods, they carried out beatings, rapes and lynchings against blacks and any who supported them. Their rituals were designed to create fear and dismay. Between 1867 and 1871 there were in Kentucky alone 116 acts of violence attributed to the Klan.

The Ku Klux Klan deliberately invoked largely spurious images of Highland clanship and heritage, crudely expressed in a book by Scottish American Thomas Dixon of North Carolina, called *The Clansman* (1904). He explicitly presents an old heroic Scotland reborn in a new valiant south. He makes his intentions clear in his introduction:

How the young South, led by the reincarnated souls of the Clansmen of Old Scotland, went forth under this cover and against overwhelming odds, daring exile, imprisonment, and a felon's death, and saved the life of a people, forms one of the most dramatic chapters in the history of the Aryan race.

His characters have Highland names and are inspired by 'the heritage of centuries of heroic blood from the martyrs of old Scotland'. This goes hand-in-hand with spine-chilling racism. Dixon's book was drawn on by DW Griffith for his reverberating film *The Birth of a Nation*, released in 1915.

The Klan's activities declined in the 1870s, after Federal efforts to control it, but it did not disappear. In the 1920s and '30s it resurfaced, when its targets included non-Protestants, Jews and foreigners as well as blacks. In 1924 it had 4.5 million members. Now it has around 15,000. The Ku Klux Klan's uncomfortable evocation of clanship inevitably colours other aspects of Scottish heritage in the southern states. The works of Sir Walter Scott, which encouraged a romantic version of Highland history, were embraced with enthusiasm. The Confederate flag incorporates the saltire. Later, the fiction of the kailyard, evoking a homely, non-industrial, containable past which chimed with what many exiles wanted to remember, was enormously popular in the United States. The defeated south derived comfort from such links with a nation which had heroically resisted its more powerful neighbour. To be Scottish was a source of pride and could fuel defiance. The association with white supremacism still lingers but the legacy of Scots in the southern states expresses itself most overtly in less threatening and more celebratory ways. The biggest Highland Games in North America takes place every year at North Carolina's Grandfather Mountain, which allows the thousands assembled to express an often invented but generally harmless Scottish heritage.

With the Civil War over there was a huge movement westward. Migration had continued during the war, in spite of the fact that some tribes took advantage of troops being engaged elsewhere to harass settlers. One of the most destructive episodes, for all concerned, was the 1862 rising of the Minnesota Sioux, provoked by encroachment on what remained of territory allocated to them. Among settlers, the death toll may have been 700. Among the Sioux it is impossible to say, although 38 of 306 Sioux captured were hanged. Scots had been settling in Minnesota since the 1830s. More would follow, especially when the railway arrived after the Civil War. In a famous photograph of refugee families fleeing the uprising, a young girl stares out at the camera wrapped in a tartan plaid.

The lure of the west was not just the landscape and sparkling air that impressed John Clay, but commercial potential and the promise of fortunes to be made, directly and indirectly, from land, cattle, gold and silver. After 1864, more than ever, the frontier was attracting not only settlers and prospectors, but a chaotic mix of people displaced by war: ex-soldiers who could not settle to a peacetime existence, guerrillas who had fought in the border states, diverse opportunists, freed slaves. It is probable that there were Scots in every category, even the latter, as some may well have been the product of the union of black slaves and Scots.

Until the 1850s the 'far west' was the territory across the Mississippi: Illinois, Iowa, Wisconsin and Minnesota, Missouri and Arkansas. To the west of Missouri was Kansas, which saw some of the bloodiest guerrilla fighting in the Civil War, and to the west of Arkansas was Indian Territory, now home to the displaced Cherokees, Creeks, Choctaws and Seminoles. Further south was Texas, keen to attract settlers, competing with California and Oregon. After the Civil War the potential of the vast Great Plains area was beginning to attract attention. The fact that there were people there already was not a deterrent.

In 1865 it was estimated that there were around 225,000 Native Americans in the territory between the Missouri River and the Sierras, and around 400,000 white settlers. With the conflict between the states at an end, the US Army turned its attention to the 'Indian problem'. Many veterans of the Civil War became Indian fighters. Colonel Ranald Mackenzie, born in New York of Highland parents, was a ruthless scourge of the Kiowa and Comanche, although he had respect for some Indian nations. 'I regard the Cheyenne tribe of Indians,' he said, '...as the finest body of that race which I have ever met.' Involved in persuading the Cheyennes to accept reservation life, he was indignant at their treatment: 'I am expected to see that Indians behave properly whom the government is starving – and not only that, but starving in flagrant violation of agreement.'

But there was a powerful current of opinion that was distinctly less sympathetic. 'Either the Indians must give way, or we must abandon all west of the Missouri River,' announced General Sherman, who played a key role in the last round of Indian wars. Horace Greeley, one of the most influential journalists of the time, was ruthless in his opinion of the aboriginals: 'Squalid and conceited, proud and worthless, lazy and lousy, they will strut out or drink out their miserable existence, and at length afford the world a sensible relief by dying out of it.' The pressures of expansion and the sometimes aggressive response of the tribes made it convenient to go along with such views, but there were Scots who regarded the native tribes with sympathy and sometimes admiration, and a number who recognised a degree of kinship. Sometimes the kinship was actual, in cases of those like half-Cherokee John Ross or Samuel Muir from Ayrshire, who married a Sac-Fox woman. But there were others on the frontier who, though not necessarily directly linked with Indian tribes, understood that a willingness to learn Native skills was a key to survival. The early explorers and mountain men would have had little success without this recognition, and some of those who fought the Indians, such as Thomas McGregor from Paisley, had a respect for their courage and dignity, which was mutual.

Angus MacDonald, fur trader and frontiersman who married a Nez Perce woman and spoke several tribal languages, described participating in a Montana celebration in 1850:

> I stripped with the leading men, painted with vermillion the groves and dimples of my upper body, mounted my black buffalo charger with my full eagle feather cap and cantered round and round with them, keeping time to the song. This new sight of a white man to them and to myself they never forgot to speak of.

His son Duncan did his best to assist the Nez Perce in their final stand against the US army in 1877. As well as speaking Nez Perce, English and French, he spoke Gaelic. Descendants of Angus and Duncan MacDonald still live in Montana. The MacDonalds are striking examples of Highland empathy with Indians, but there are other sources that indicate support. An article in an 1840 issue of the Gaelic periodical *Cuairtear nan Gleann* commented sympathetically on the predicament of the Indian:

> There is no people on the face of the earth who, in matters of war or hunting, can surpass the Indians who inhabit the region of America which is not inhabited by white people.

They are now, alas! few in number compared to what they were at one time; for, as the white people become more numerous and more powerful, the Indians are scourged backwards before them, from place to place; and are injured by every sort of the most merciless brutality and violence.

When Charles Augustus Murray and his companions set off in 1834 from Fort Leavenworth on the Missouri on an expedition westwards, he relied on Pawnee guides and adopted their style of travelling. They departed each day at 4am, on empty stomachs, and continued for nine hours before they stopped for food. They were received hospitably by the main tribe, were invited to feasts, took part in buffalo hunts and survived a Cheyenne attack. Although Murray, in his *Travels in North America* (1854), refers to 'savages', he describes the Pawnee way of life with sympathetic interest. He also wrote a novel based on his experiences, *The Prairie-Bird* (1845). But as increasing numbers of settlers penetrated the shrinking territory allowed to the hard-pressed tribes, attitudes were less understanding. The view remained widespread that Indians were barbaric and that the West would not be safe until they were contained and re-educated, if not obliterated.

One of their most outspoken defenders was RB Cunninghame Graham who was in New Orleans and Texas in 1879. Native Americans, he believed, had been 'tricked by all, outwitted, plundered by the Christian speculator'. He insisted that those responsible for destroying the beaver and the buffalo and replacing them with whisky and smallpox owed 'some reparation beyond a small-bore bullet'. He argued, he said, not as a sentimentalist but 'as one who has passed many a night staring into the darkness watching his horses when Indians were about', and he went on:

I am one of those who think that the colour of the skin makes little difference to right and wrong in the abstract, and who fail to see so much difference between an Indian sitting over a fire gnawing a piece of venison, and a tailor in the East-end of London working in a gas-lit den sixteen hours a day for a few shillings a week.

The last phase of Indian resistance had already been played out when Cunninghame Graham wrote this in 1890. One of the key figures was General George Crook, born in Ohio of partly Scottish descent. After the Civil War he was posted west, first to Idaho, then taking charge of the Department of Arizona with the task of subduing the Apaches, who resisted containment in reservations. Crook gained a reputation for fairness – 'He was a good man,' said Wooden Leg of the Cheyennes, 'always kind to the Indians.' At the same time he was unshakeably determined. He fought the Sioux in Wyoming and Montana, then was called back to Arizona in 1882, where increasingly resentful bands of Apaches were breaking out of the reservations and attacking ranchers and soldiers (episodes that have provided material for countless Westerns). It was the final chapter. Crook, now not only a seasoned Indian fighter but also sympathetic to the Apache predicament, in an unusual move arranged meetings to hear their grievances. It became clear to him that 'they had lost confidence in everybody, and did not know whom or what to believe'. Unscrupulous agents and middlemen had cheated the reservation Apaches of their supplies and land-grabbers squatted on their territory. Crook argued that the Apaches needed to be convinced that they would receive fair treatment: 'we are too culpable, as a nation, for the existing condition of affairs. It follows that we must satisfy them that hereafter they shall be treated with justice, and protected from inroads of white men.'

In 1886 Geronimo, last of the great Apache chiefs, surrendered to Crook, who promised that although the Apaches would initially be sent to a reservation in Florida, after two years they would be allowed to return to their own country. The War Department was furious that he had taken it upon himself to make such a promise, Geronimo took off, and General Crook was reprimanded. He resigned. Eventually Geronimo and his people were dispatched to the Florida swamps, where many of them died of tuberculosis.

Crook's favourite scout was Archie McIntosh, part Scots, part Chippewa, whose father had been employed by the Hudson's Bay Company. Born in Michigan, he was sent to Edinburgh at the age of twelve for two years' schooling. By 1855 he was a US army scout, working first with Donald McKay, another Indian Scot, before joining Crook's Geronimo campaign. He married a woman from the San Carlos reservation in Arizona, and settled there.

In the north, Colonel James Forsyth had taken command of the 7th Cavalry, General George Armstrong Custer's former regiment. (The 'Armstrong' signals Custer's connection with the Scottish Borders.) Custer, ambitious and eager to further his military career in the west, had in 1868 led a raid on a Cheyenne camp on the banks of the Washita River in Kansas. Large numbers of men, women and children were killed. The memory of this massacre fuelled the Sioux and Cheyenne attack eight years later at the Little Bighorn in which Custer lost his life. By the 1880s, the now defeated Sioux tribes were settled on reservations in Dakota. Chief Sitting Bull, after several years of exile in Canada and then as a performer in Buffalo Bill's Wild West Show, joined them.

Pressure on their land continued. The agent at Pine Ridge was Dr Valentine McGillycuddy, a Scottish ex-army surgeon described by Edgar Bronson in his *Reminiscences of a Ranchman* (1908) as 'a man in a million... [who] saw that his Indians got the last pound of provisions and supplies and the last yard of goods the Indian Bureau allowed'. In Bronson's view if there had been more agents like McGillycuddy, 'half our Indian wars had never happened'. It was Dr McGillycuddy who recommended that the authorities should not interfere when the Ghost Dance cult swept through the reservations promising the Sioux that the old ways would come again and the white soldiers would 'sink into the earth'. The authorities did not listen. Alarmed, they sent in the Indian police to apprehend Sitting Bull, but he was not arrested, he was murdered. Colonel Forsyth arrived with the 7th Cavalry to quell the uproar that ensued.

Colonel Forsyth's men rounded up a band of Minneconjou Sioux, 120 men and 230 women and children, and camped at Wounded Knee Creek. The next morning, while the Minneconjou were handing over their weapons to the soldiers one of their guns went off. The soldiers began firing. Hotchkiss guns mounted round the camp raked the Indian tepees with shrapnel. As many as 300 Sioux may have been killed; 25 soldiers were dead and 39 wounded. The Sioux had believed that their ghost shirts would protect them from the soldiers' bullets. It was a few days after Christmas, 1890, and by the end of the day snow was falling. Cunninghame Graham's comment, in a letter to the *Daily Graphic* in January 1891, was: 'One's very soul revolts in disgust from the account of the cruel butchery, the shooting down of fleeing savages with Gatling guns, the useless and cruel slaughter of the women and children.'

A year after the carnage at Wounded Knee, Buffalo Bill Cody's Wild West show was in Glasgow playing to enthusiastic audiences. With Cody was a man called George C Crager who had spent time among the Sioux and now offered to sell a collection of North American Indian material to Glasgow's Kelvingrove Museum. Included was a ghost shirt. In 1995 and 1998, representatives of the Lakota (Sioux) visited Glasgow to request its return. In August 1999, Glasgow's ghost shirt was restored to Lakota people, including 28 descendants of the victims, gathered at the site of the massacre. At the ceremony the bagpipes were played. The day before, at Eagle Butte on the Cheyenne River reservation, a pibroch composed in 1995 by Farquhar MacDonald of Skye was played. It was called '*An Lèine Thaibhse* – The Ghost Shirt'. Another Skye pibroch was also played, 'Lament for the Children' by the famed MacCrimmon. The piper was a Scottish-American from Ohio.

For those heading for Oregon and California in the 1840s, the dry and monotonous plains they had to cross were empty of all but vast herds of buffalo and a handful of tribes. There was no temptation to linger, especially with a destination in view that promised fertile land or gold. Throughout the Civil War, the movement continued: wagon trains and mule trains, then the stagecoach and the pony express, finally the railroad. It was the railroad and ranching that spearheaded the last phase of settlement. In 1862 the Homestead Act allowed each American adult to purchase 160 acres in the public domain for $1.25 an acre. For those squatters who had cultivated the same claim for five years, the land was free; it seemed impossible that it could run out. By the late 1880s cattle ranching had transformed the plains from Texas to Wyoming, and the railroad crossed the continent, with lines also running north and south and dozens of branches linking the growing towns. By 1889 there was a perception that land was getting scarce and public pressure persuaded the government to open Indian Territory to settlement, once regarded as fit only for displaced tribes. Competing claimants raced to get their hands on what they believed to be the last available land.

In that quarter of a century, Scots played a conspicuous role in transforming the last frontier. They put money, engineering expertise and labour into America's railroads. They financed and pioneered cattle and sheep ranching. They were among the thousands of ordinary people who settled and built communities in often unpromising circumstances. They were prominent on the Pacific coast, in Portland, Seattle and San Francisco. There were attempts to found new Scottish colonies. George Grant, a crofter's son from Banffshire, established a community in Kansas in 1872 which was intended to attract people of some substance. It didn't last, but one of those who joined the colony was Scotty Philip, a sixteen-year-old from Dallas, Morayshire. He went off to prospect for gold in Dakota's Black Hills, married a Sioux, thus becoming brother-in-law to Crazy Horse, and settled down to ranch in South Dakota. It was a Scot, John Muir from Dunbar, who recognised that the wilderness which had once seemed so formidable a barrier was under threat, and acted to protect it. Some of those involved in this new wave of settlement had been in the US for generations, others were newly arrived, sometimes in response to recruitment drives. Scots continued to filter south from Canada, tempted by the possibility of cheaper land or better pay. In 1882 James Bruce and John Sinclair made their way to North Dakota. John McIntosh arrived with his ox-wagon from Manitoba. The South Dakota community of Botineau had a distinctly Scottish character.

The first trans-Mississippi railroads were being constructed in the 1850s, but it was 1869 when the Central Pacific and Union Pacific Railroads met at Promontory Point in Utah and it became possible to cross the continent by rail. Scots continued their early involvement with railroad and locomotive building, and travelled the new lines along with thousands of other immigrants. The best-known account of such a journey is Robert Louis Stevenson's *Across the Plains*, which describes travelling from New York to California ten years after the link was completed. The experience was not a happy one.

He boarded the train in Jersey City, in a desperate crush of distressed immigrant families who were wet, hungry and exhausted. 'I have never seen fellow creatures so stricken down,' Stevenson wrote, 'nor suffered, in my own person, such complete paralysis of mind. The whole business was a nightmare while it lasted, and is still a nightmare to remember.' He changed trains at Pittsburgh, where he managed to get his first meal since leaving New York, and woke the next morning to find the train travelling through Ohio, and then on through Indiana, Illinois and Iowa to Council

Bluffs on the Missouri. He provides a vivid description. The country was 'rich and various, and breathed an elegance peculiar to itself. The tall corn pleased the eye; the trees were graceful in themselves, and framed the plain into long aerial vistas; and the clean, bright, gardened townships spoke of country fare and pleasant summer evenings on the stoop.' But it was also cold and damp:

> Day came in with a shudder. White mists lay thinly over the surface of the plain, as we see them more often on a lake; and though the sun had soon dispersed and drunk them up, leaving an atmosphere of fever heat and crystal pureness from horizon to horizon, the mists had still been there, and we knew that this paradise was haunted by killing damps and foul marasmus... At the point of day, and while we were all in the grasp of that first chill, a native of the state, who had got in at some way station, pronounced it, with a doctoral air, 'a real fever and ague morning'.

At Council Bluffs he and his fellow travellers were herded onto a Union Pacific train, 'branded', and 'sorted and boxed'. Families travelled in one carriage, single men in another and Chinese in a third. The carriages were overcrowded and airless with primitive sleeping arrangements. Meals were only available at stations. Stevenson quickly discovered that emigrant trains were a lower form of traffic and that the emigrants themselves were despised. He dryly commented: 'Equality, though conceived very largely in America, does not extend so low down as to an emigrant.' He was particularly outraged at the treatment of the Chinese.

The train crossed the Nebraska plains: 'an empty sky, an empty earth; front and back, the line of the railway stretched from horizon to horizon, like a cue across a billiard board'. Occasionally tiny dots would appear which would turn out to be wooden cabins, which then 'dwindled and dwindled in our wake until they melted into their surroundings'. Stevenson reflected on what it must have been like for the earlier generation of emigrants, 'painfully urging their teams, with no landmark but that unattainable evening sun for which they steered'.

> They had nothing, it would seem, to overtake; nothing by which to reckon their advance; no sight for repose or for encouragement; but stage after stage, only the dead green waste under foot, and the mocking, fugitive horizon... It is the settlers, after all, at whom we have a right to marvel. Our consciousness, by which we live, is itself but the creature of variety. Upon what food does it subsist in such a land? What livelihood can repay a human creature for a life spent in this huge sameness? He is cut off from books, from news, from company, from all that relieve existence but the prosecution of his affairs. A sky full of stars is the most varied spectacle that he can hope.

After the monotony of the plains came the mountains, but they too were dreary, 'mile upon mile, and not a tree, a bird or a river'. Nevertheless, in Stevenson's eyes the railway had a meaning beyond the journey itself. In a few lines he evokes an emblematic American experience, and suggests an icon for the nineteenth century generally:

> when I think how the railroad has been pushed through this unwatered wilderness and haunt of savage tribes, and now will bear an Emigrant for some twelve pounds from the Atlantic to the Golden Gates; how at each stage of the construction, roaring, impromptu cities, full of gold and lust and death, sprang up, and then died away again, and are now but wayside stations in the desert; how in these uncouth places, pig-tailed Chinese pirates worked side by side

with border ruffians and broken men from Europe, talking together in a mixed dialect, mostly oaths, gambling, drinking, quarrelling and murdering like wolves; how the plumed, hereditary lord of all America, heard, in this last fastness, the scream of the 'bad medicine waggon', charioting his foes; and then when I go on to remember that all this epical turmoil was conducted by gentlemen in frock coats and with a view to nothing more extraordinary than a fortune and subsequent visit to Paris, it seems to me, I own, as if this railway were the one typical achievement of the age in which we live.

That emigrant or ruffian or gentleman in a frock coat was often a compatriot of Stevenson's.

Six years before Stevenson's transcontinental journey, a woman from Edinburgh boarded a train in Truckee, California to travel east through the Humboldt mountain range to Cheyenne, Wyoming. Her experience was rather different from Stevenson's. She had a 'luxurious bed' with linen sheets and 'costly California blankets' in a thickly carpeted carriage hung with green and crimson curtains. If the food was not up to much – 'coarse, greasy meals' – the scenery and sunset were beautiful. They descended into Utah with the wheel marks of the wagon road running parallel to the track, scattered with the bleached bones of oxen. Cheyenne proved to be 'detestable', although no longer taken over by 'the sum of advancing civilisation' responsible for 'murders, stabbings, shootings, and pistol affrays'. Isabella Bird was an extraordinarily adventurous traveller and explored the Rocky Mountains on horseback, often alone for days at a time. She was a skilled horsewoman and handy with a gun as well as being an acute observer and vivid writer. She described her experiences in *A Lady's Life in the Rocky Mountains* (1879).

By the time Bird was adventuring in the Rockies the transformation of the Great Plains was under way, brought about partly by the railroad itself, which left a string of towns and settlements in its wake, and partly by the extraordinary expansion of cattle ranching. The railroad companies were about more than building track and running trains. They owned the land on either side of the lines, which they sold on, encouraging the plantation of communities to provide passengers and freight. Railways abhorred a vacuum. There were casualties, however. In 1881 the City of Glasgow Bank collapsed, having overstretched its American railroad involvement. The judge who presided over the court case commented: 'a Scotch Bank buying and working a railroad in America is about as startling a thing as one can conceive'.

William J Menzies, an Edinburgh lawyer, visited the US three times after the Civil War, and was convinced that it offered unrivalled opportunities for investment. In 1872 he reported on 'the wonderful fertility' of America's virgin soil, 'the multitude and variety of its productions and manufactures, the rapid development of its railroad system'. These, along with the high level of immigration, were the ingredients of 'almost illimitable resources and the creation of material wealth'. A group of Edinburgh men, including the publisher Thomas Nelson, got together to form the Scottish-American Investment Company. Many more such companies would follow. In 1877 the American Mortgage Company of Scotland was set up, and a year later came the Edinburgh American Land Mortgage Company. With the help of agents on the ground these companies loaned money for developments in Illinois, Iowa, Minnesota, Missouri and Dakota, as well as Oregon and Washington and states in the south.

Dundee-based companies were also keen to invest in the US. Dundee had a well-established relationship with America, which was a destination for Dundee linen and jute. Dundee cloth provided sails for ships, the material for the covered wagons that crossed the plains, and for tents. During the Civil War jute was in demand for sandbags. Dundee merchants and businessmen did not hesitate to buy into companies that promised high interest rates. One of these was the Scottish American Investment Trust, set up in 1873. Another was the Oregon and Washington Investment Trust, chaired by the Earl of Airlie. The Dundee Land Investment Company sent out William Smith of Montrose to investigate possible land deals. The plan was to encourage Scots to emigrate and buy land on an instalment plan. Indiana, Wisconsin, Texas, Missouri and Minnesota were considered. Two townsites were purchased in Minnesota and named Airlie and Dundee. Land was also acquired in California and Kansas City. The Scots spread their net wide.

Mining, especially after 1880 in Utah, California, Colorado, Arizona and New Mexico, also attracted investment, although the returns were not so encouraging. Many of the smaller ventures proved unsuccessful, though two large-scale enterprises, the Scottish Pacific Coast Mining Company in California and the Arizona Copper Company did well. The latter got off to a shaky start but after reorganisation in 1884 grew into a huge and profitable business. Many Scots, particularly in Edinburgh, benefited, and others were more directly involved in a practical way. When smelting works were built to process the copper the furnaces were the work of two firms whose Scottish names indicate their origins: Fraser and Chalmers of Chicago, and Rankin, Brayton and Company of San Francisco.

Americans looking for capital soon identified Scotland as a likely source. As the newspaper *The Statist* put it in January 1885: 'in the summer of 1882 hardly a train came into Edinburgh from the West or the South which did not bring a Yankee with a cattle ranche in one pocket, a "timber limit" in another, and perhaps an embryo Erie Railway up his sleeve'. The said Yankee acted as a magnet to dozens of individuals and syndicates with cash to spare, cash that was itself the consequence of Scottish industrial success. In the 1870s it was the cattle ranches in particular that were attracting attention.

In the 1860s an Indian trader called Jesse Chisholm, part Scot, part Cherokee, carved out a trail north from Texas to Indian Territory (now Oklahoma). His grandfather John Chisholm had arrived from Scotland in 1777 and was involved in land deals and trade with several tribes. His son Ignatius, Jesse's father, married the daughter of a Cherokee chief. The Chisholm Trail became the main route for cattlemen who needed to get their beasts to market. In 1867 the Kansas Pacific Railroad was making its way west and small towns sprang up along the track. Abilene in Kansas became the destination for cattle heading for slaughter in Kansas City and Chicago. In 1871, 700,000 longhorn cows were driven to the Abilene stockyards. As the railroad moved west the destinations changed: Ellsworth, Hays City, Dodge City, Wichita are names that resonate with all aficionados of the Western. With the problem of access to markets solved, cattle ranching on an unprecedented scale followed.

Scotland had a centuries-old tradition of cattle-raising and cattle-droving, and Scottish names crop up often in the story of American ranching. Scots were hard-bitten cowboys, they were ranch managers, and from the late 1870s they put a huge amount of money into cows. The demand for beef was not confined to America. Large quantities of live cattle, and with the coming of refrigeration in the 1870s of carcasses, were exported; the biggest market was Britain. In 1877 James Macdonald was sent by *The Scotsman* newspaper to investigate the American cattle industry, and the following year published a book called *Food from the Far West* (1878). A Royal Commission was appointed to do the same. The Earl of Airlie, chairman of the Scottish-American Mortgage Company, also visited the West. All brought back a story of vast acreages of cheap grassland sustaining a booming business, though Lord Airlie warned against emigration without sufficient capital. Between 1880 and 1882 several companies were set up to enter the ranching business. The Prairie Cattle Company was born in Edinburgh, and acquired land in Colorado, New Mexico and the

Texas Panhandle; the Texas Land and Cattle Company sprung from Dundee. The Swan Land and Cattle Company was another Scottish venture, run by four formidable brothers with an extensive ranch in Wyoming. Baron Tweedmouth, who had turned his Strathglass estate into a deer forest in the 1850s, in 1883 became the main investor in the Panhandle's Rocking Chair Ranch, and sent out his youngest son Archibald to become co-manager.

One of the most famous of these ventures was Dundee's Matador Land and Cattle Company, registered at the end of 1882. The first chairman of the board was William Robertson, an engineer. The company purchased the Matador Ranch: 100,000 acres of Texas land and 40,000 head of cattle. One of the vendors was Henry Campbell, who was kept on as ranch superintendent. Born in North Carolina of Scottish descent, he had been in Texas since before the Civil War. The Matador was originally stocked with cattle acquired from John Chisum (possibly related to Jesse Chisholm) in Lincoln County, New Mexico, which was Billy the Kid's stamping ground. Chisum presided over a vast cattle empire; he was reincarnated by John Wayne in the Andrew McLaglen movie *Chisum* (1970).

The Matador Ranch was later managed by Murdo Mackenzie from near Tain in Easter Ross, the son of a tenant farmer. He had started his working life as a bank clerk. He began his American career as manager of the Prairie Cattle Company and took over the Matador in 1891. By this time it had expanded considerably, and was running cattle in Wyoming and South Dakota as well as Texas. Mackenzie went on to become president of the American National Livestock Corporation and was appointed by Theodore Roosevelt to the National Conservation Commission. Later he went to Brazil to manage the Brazilian Land and Cattle Company, but returned to take over the Matador again in 1922. Somewhat improbably, Mackenzie banned drinking and gambling on the range. After his death in 1937 he was succeeded by his son John. According to John Clay, Mackenzie's 'name is a household word both in North and South America'. The town of Murdo, South Dakota, is named for him. The Matador Ranch survived until 1951, when the land was sold for oil drilling.

John Clay, himself a participant, described the excitement in Edinburgh drawing rooms which 'buzzed with the stories of this last of the bonanzas, staid old gentlemen who scarcely knew the difference betwixt a steer and a heifer discussed it over their port'. Clay was asked to investigate possibilities in Wyoming, and reported favourably: the result was the Wyoming Cattle Ranche Company. At around the same time, 1882, the Edinburgh-based Western American Cattle Company was also set up and acquired Wyoming land. Clay acted for them too. In that year a total of ten substantial British-American cattle companies were initiated, all of which, whether based in England or Scotland, had Scottish involvement.

Two years later James Tait returned to Scotland from the American West and published a pamphlet entitled *The Cattle Fields of the Far West*. It summed up the attraction of investing in cattle:

> The cattle fields of Western America extend with slight interruption from Montana to Southern Texas, north and south, and from the Mississippi Valley to the Pacific, east and west. On the vast plains or prairies embraced in this area, cattle roam all the year round, foraging entirely for themselves, and with the expenditure of a minimum of care and outlay on the part of the owners.

The future of cattle raising was, in Tait's view, 'luminous with promise'. But in fact the bonanza was over, and although Tait himself was involved in several ranching and colonising ventures none of them succeeded. Two especially severe winters demonstrated that cattle could not, in fact, survive without food and shelter, and cattle ranges proved not to be limitless after all. Settlers continued to pour in, challenging the ranchers' unlawful fencing of land. In 1886 ten large cattle companies in Laramie County, Wyoming, among them the Swan Land and Cattle Company, were listed as having fenced land they did not own.

One of the best known battles over range resources was the Johnson County War, fought out in Wyoming in 1892 and involving John Clay, who was managing the Swan ranch at the time, and other Scots with local ranching interests. Increasing numbers of homesteaders were settling on land where ranchers had run their cattle. The ranchers, represented by the Wyoming Stock Growers Association, were also concerned about cattle rustling, a growing problem which they laid at the door of the homesteaders. To sort things out the Stock Growers brought in a band of 50 gunmen, who disposed of two alleged rustlers before being confronted by a posse led by Sheriff Angus of Buffalo (also a Scot). Although several ranchers were implicated, including Clay and close associates, none were brought to trial. Clay's own account emphasises the depredations of the rustlers and, almost, defends vigilantism. 'In this world of complex conditions it is hard to define where law ends and individuality begins,' he remarks, adding: 'Great reforms are brought about by revolutionary methods.' Clay's attitude towards homesteaders, many of whom were from Central Europe, was ambivalent. He saw them as an unstoppable enemy to open-range ranching, but also as the mainstay of frontier life.

Clay's book, *My Life on the Range*, highlights the close relationship between Scotland and the American West. There are many Scots in its pages, on both sides of the Atlantic. AD Adamson, 'a big, burly, openhearted Scotchman', managed the Ferguson Land and Cattle Company in Wyoming. Among those who tried to hunt down rustlers were Jimmy Craig and George Henderson. John Stewart, a wholesale grocer from Council Bluffs who also had a ranch on the Sweetwater River, was, according to Clay, 'full of enterprise and aggressive push'. Charles Campbell was president of the Cheyenne Club, 'a splendid type of the Scotch-Canadian, solid, conservative, popular, loyal, with a fine practical knowledge of the cow business'. Clay lists the membership of the Wyoming Stock Growers. Many names are or could be Scottish: Anderson, Baxter, Blair, Gilchrist, Guthrie, McFarlane, Rankin, Robertson are just some of them. The fact that in 1927 Cheyenne erected a statue of Robert Burns indicates the strength of the connection.

Towards the end of the nineteenth century, another threat to the cattleman emerged: sheep. With their long tradition of shepherding, Scots were leading developers of sheep farming in the US. James Baird from Dumfriesshire emigrated in 1883 and worked on the construction of the Northern Pacific Railroad before settling in Minnesota to raise sheep. Alex McKay from Perth was a sheep farmer in California before moving on to mining in Arizona, where he founded the town of Oracle. Robert Burnett, who would later inherit the title to Crathes Castle in Aberdeenshire, was in the 1880s running a large herd of sheep in Southern California. Robert Taylor from Hawick in the Borders arrived in Wyoming by way of Pennsylvania and California and by 1913 was running 65,000 sheep, as well as cattle and horses, on 75,000 acres of land. He was a pioneer in Wyoming sheep farming. WA McKay started his working life as a sheep farmer in Dunbartonshire and transplanted his skills to Wyoming, with an intervening period repairing locomotives for the Union Pacific Railroad.

William Dunbar from Inverness started sheep ranching in New Mexico in the 1890s and by the time he died in 1937 had 12,000 acres. McIntosh in New Mexico takes its name from brothers William, Donald and John, who ran a sheep farm and employed several other Scots. Perhaps the best-known Scot in the sheep business was Andrew Little from Moffat, who turned up in Caldwell, Idaho with his two collies and became an enormously successful farmer, running 165,000 sheep in the Boise Valley. Historian Ferencz Szasz comments: 'What Andrew Carnegie was to steel, Andrew Little was to western sheep ranching – the ultimate success story.' Seven of his eight brothers joined him. The sheep dogs who emigrated with their owners became part of the story, fast, clever, agile and much prized.

By the 1890s the heyday of the range cattle industry was over, with the farmers taking over. Even in Montana the cattle ranges were shrinking, a process hastened by the completion of the Great Northern Railroad. At Great Falls, Montana in 1902 the great railroad builder James J Hill, born in Canada of Scottish parents, predicted that 'churches and schools will be erected where now bands of cattle and sheep roam'. But beef was still needed to feed America, cattle were still raised, and cowboys were still needed. In 1900 Murdo MacLean from Wester Ross arrived in Billings, Montana, where with other Scots he worked as a cowboy. They stayed at a Billings hotel run by Gaelic speakers.

One of the first to recognise the implications of the closing frontier and a shrinking wilderness was John Muir, born in Dunbar, East Lothian in 1838. Eleven years later his family emigrated, intending to go to Canada but persuaded by accounts of Wisconsin and Michigan to change destinations. They made their way slowly and painfully west. They had brought far too much luggage, including tools and equipment, 'as if all America were still a wilderness in which little or nothing could be bought,' wrote Muir in his autobiography. In Buffalo, New York his father purchased a cast-iron stove and a set of pots and pans, and 'provisions enough for a long siege', all of which were shifted to their destination in Wisconsin. Daniel Muir found land by a lake, and with the help of neighbours built a shanty, later replaced by a frame house. John and his brother David instantly responded to the 'pure wildness' that they found – the woods, the grasses and flowers, the lake, the birds, 'the frogs and snakes and turtles in the creeks and springs'. 'Coming direct from school in Scotland,' Muir wrote, 'while we were still hopefully ignorant and far from tame – notwithstanding the unnatural profusion of teaching and thrashing lavished upon us – getting acquainted with the animals about us was a never-failing source of wonder and delight.'

It was a hard upbringing, but his passion for the natural world far outweighed the rigours of settlement life and the tyranny of his father. He paid his own way through Wisconsin University, before embarking on what he described late in life as 'a glorious botanical and geological excursion, which has lasted nearly fifty years and is not yet completed, always happy and free, poor and rich, without thought of a diploma or making a name, urged on and on through endless, inspiring, Godful beauty'.

He walked a thousand miles to the Gulf of Florida, and explored the West extensively on foot, in particular the Sierra Nevadas. He was the first to articulate the need for wilderness conservation and he campaigned passionately and with eventual success for legislation to create national parks. The first was Yosemite National Park, founded in 1890. He was joined in his work by William Keith from Aberdeenshire, who had arrived in New York at the age of twelve and served an apprenticeship as an engraver. In 1858 he went west, and based in San Francisco worked as a landscape painter. 'There's naebody like a Scotchman to see beauty,' was Muir's comment.

Like John Clay, John Muir responded to the lure of the West, and for some of the same reasons. But whereas Clay saw the wilderness as offering potential for exploitation and making money, Muir quickly identified cause for concern at the human onslaught on wilderness resources. For many, he was the enemy, inhibiting development, standing in the way of mines and dams and reservoirs that were seen as essential for growing communities and economic prosperity. The two men had grown up in Dunbar and Kelso respectively, towns not so many miles distant from each other, and were both imbued with an appreciation of freedom as well as determination, which had led them both west.

CHAPTER EIGHT

Muscle and Brain

[The Scots] bring us muscle and brain and the tried skill
and trustworthiness in many of our great industries of
which they are managers of the most successful ones.
NEAL DOW, 1880

IN 1881 THE Fife town of Dunfermline witnessed an extraordinary event. A middle-aged man was making a visit to his birthplace, which he had left 33 years earlier. He was a twelve-year-old then, the son of a handloom weaver who gave up the struggle to make a living in a declining trade, and like thousands of others at that time departed with his family for the USA. The son returned to Scotland a very rich man. He had donated $25,000 to enable Dunfermline to build its first public swimming baths, and the same amount for a public library. His name was Andrew Carnegie.

His entry into the town was, according to one account, like a royal progress:

> the American stars and stripes waving everywhere, even over the noble old abbey where Scottish kings lie in their stone coffins. Bells were ringing, drums beating, people shouting. The Chief, taken by surprise, his sunburnt cheeks pale, and, as he confessed, a big lump in his throat, could only bow right and left, while the crowd swarmed about the coach windows and a hundred hands were outstretched to grasp his mother's.

It wasn't just the town's gratitude that caused this enthusiastic reception. It was also an acknowledgement of spectacular success, a celebration of a son of Dunfermline who made the American dream a reality, on a scale that in the 1840s no one in Scotland, least of all the Carnegie family, could have imagined.

Dunfermline had for decades been primarily a weaving and coal-mining town. Andrew's father, William Carnegie, and grandfather had produced fine linen damask, for which the town was famous. A key export destination was the US. But the 1840s brought economic depression and unemployment; handloom weaving was being superseded by factory production. William and his wife Margaret Morrison had both inherited a tradition of radicalism and the family were committed supporters of Chartism, which called for parliamentary reform and an extension of the vote. Margaret's brother Tam Morrison was jailed for his involvement in Chartist riots.

Hard times had already pushed many people out of Scotland. Both Margaret's sisters and their husbands, Ann and Andrew Aitken and Kitty and Thomas Hogan, went to Pennsylvania. A letter from Ann, dated May 1844, urged William and Margaret to follow. 'This country's far better for the working man than the old one,' she wrote, '& there is room enough & to spare, notwithstanding the thousands that flock into her borders.' Four years later, the Carnegies, with their two young sons Andrew and Thomas, followed Ann's advice.

The journey took them across the Forth from Limekilns to Bo'ness, and through the Forth and Clyde Canal to Glasgow. They sailed from the Clyde's Broomielaw on the *Wiscasset*, an American-built former whaling ship, which took them to New York. From New York they proceeded up the Hudson by steamer to Albany, then on a crowded packet boat on the Erie Canal to Buffalo; from Buffalo by steamer to Cleveland, Ohio, another packet boat on another canal, the Ohio and Erie, to Akron and then Beaver, Pennsylvania. The final stage of their journey took them down the

Ohio River to Pittsburgh. They had travelled a vast arc of waterways to arrive at a point due west of New York. There was not yet a railway.

Pittsburgh had been given its name by General John Forbes, who had once owned the Pittencrief estate in Dunfermline. In colonial times it had been an outlying fur-trading post, but by the early nineteenth century it was an expanding mass of industrial activity, ironworks fed by local coal, cotton mills, slaughterhouses and tanneries, casting up a pall of smoke that every visitor commented on. Everything, inside and out, was coated in a layer of soot. Charles Augustus Murray, visiting in the 1830s, called it 'an emporium of smoke and dirt'.

The Carnegies joined the Aitkens in Allegheny City, by that time a part of Pittsburgh. With his father unable to find work – there was not much call for handloom weavers – Andrew, the elder boy, had to find a job. He was taken on as a bobbin boy at a mill owned by a Scot. His second employer was another Scot at another mill. But before long his working life took a different direction, when through his uncle, Thomas Hogan, he got a job with the Atlantic and Ohio Telegraph Company. In a letter of 1852 to a cousin back in Scotland Andrew expressed his confidence that he had done the right thing in coming to the US:

> I am sure it is far better for me that I came here. If I had been in Dunfermline working at the Loom, it's very likely I would have been a poor weaver all my days, but here, I can surely do something better than that if I don't it will be my own fault, for anyone can get along in this country, I intend going to night school this fall to learn something more and after that to teach my self some other branches.

He was not yet seventeen. The following year he joined the Pennsylvania Railroad as a telegraph operator, recommended for the job by another Scot, James Reid. Andrew Carnegie was ambitious and determined, but it is possible that without the help of family and an existing Scottish network, and without the opportunity offered by the Civil War, his career would have been unremarkable.

Communications were vital to the conduct of the war. Carnegie soon found himself with a key role in repairing track and moving troops. At the same time, he was investing in other areas that were stimulated by wartime needs. When he returned to Dunfermline for the first time in 1862 he was already a successful man, and he found his home town somewhat small and mean. In 1865 he resigned his railroad job and never looked back. When he made his 1881 visit to Scotland he was a steel magnate and extremely rich.

Although Carnegie had his finger in many pies and made many shrewd investments it was the Pittsburgh steel mills that were the core of his success. He was single-minded, at times ruthless, and demanded a great deal from those who worked with and for him. He wanted to make money and he wanted the kind of life a large amount of money could buy. But he always intended to use any surplus for 'benevolent purposes', as he put it in his famous Christmas letter of 1868, and he emphasised in particular promoting education and improving prospects for the poorer classes. He believed that those with money had a moral obligation to ensure that they provided some benefit for society as a whole. 'I cannot shut my eyes,' he wrote, 'to the fact that the production of wealth is not the work of any one man and the acquisition of great fortunes is not possible without the cooperation of multitudes of men.' His philanthropy was paternalistic – he believed he knew what was best for working people and right for society – but over the years he provided many millions in Britain and the US for libraries, parks, educational institutions, swimming baths, concert halls, museums, art galleries and latterly church organs.

Carnegie's benevolence did not mean that he was generous to his own labour force. If the market dictated, wages were cut and jobs were lost. Many of his workers lived in squalid conditions, working twelve hours a day. Among them were fellow-countrymen. One of them, Thomas Crawford, remarked that, although he had always hoped to educate himself, he had little time for studying: 'After working twelve hours, how can a man go to a library?' If Carnegie acknowledged that his success depended on his workers, he was unshakeably convinced that his workers' well-being depended on his leadership and astuteness as a businessman. 'The interests of capital and labour are one,' he stated in a speech in 1889 when he opened a library at Braddock, Pennsylvania, the location of his first steel enterprise. But capital and labour inevitably clashed.

Carnegie was in Scotland when, in the summer of 1892, trouble broke out at the Homestead Steel Works on the banks of the Monongahela River, six miles from Pittsburgh. When negotiations on wages and conditions broke down, a strike and lock-out followed. Members of the Amalgamated Association, a steel and iron workers' union, determined to take over the plant. In response, the management turned to the Pinkerton organisation which supplied 300 armed men to break the strike. Violent clashes between the strikers and the Pinkerton men resulted in several deaths and many wounded, with the Pinkertons getting the worst of it. Some were beaten to death by a furious mob.

Public opinion was divided. There was outrage at the brutality of the strikers, but also sympathy, and criticism of Carnegie, who was anxious to distance himself from the whole affair. The *London Financial Observer* was unambivalent:

Here we have this Scotch-Yankee plutocrat meandering through Scotland in a four-in-hand [Carnegie's private coach], opening public libraries and receiving the freedom of cities, while the wretched workmen who sweat themselves in order to supply him with the ways and means for this self-glorification are starving in Pittsburgh.

Like many self-made men, Carnegie believed that the way to the top was open to anyone who was sufficiently dedicated and hard-working, especially if they had access to one of the institutions he financed. In his *Autobiography* he described the Homestead strike as the 'one serious quarrel with our workmen in our whole history'. It was the only quarrel that erupted on a major scale, but there were legitimate grievances: steel production was a dirty and dangerous business, and those closest to the dirt and danger were ill-rewarded.

Carnegie's money was made in the US but he spent a great deal of it in Scotland, not only for philanthropic purposes but on a splendid home for himself and his wife and daughter. For ten years he leased Cluny Castle in Perthshire, where the family spent their summers. 'The exile may be excused if his fondness for his native land knows no bounds,' he stated in a speech in Inverness, and went on: 'Return to Scotland was ever to me the prize of life.' In 1898 he purchased Skibo Castle in Sutherland, where he played golf, stalked deer, and entertained large numbers of guests. In 1901 he sold out his Pittsburgh steel concerns for $400 million, and continued to give away large sums of money. Carnegie libraries were opening in four continents. To his great satisfaction he was able to buy Dunfermline's Pittencrief estate and hand over to the city as a public park the grounds in which as a boy he had been forbidden to play. He set up the Carnegie Peace Fund, the Carnegie Hero Fund, a Trust for the Universities of Scotland, and several other trust funds. But not everyone was impressed. 'Push and screw; buy cheap and sell dear... Presently the American ideal of life will be our own,' was the disapproving comment in *Blackwood's Magazine*. He died in August 1919, bitterly disappointed by the failure to avoid world war.

The Pinkerton men who were brought in to quell the Homestead strike were only briefly part of Carnegie's story, but they have a place also in the bigger picture of Scots in nineteenth-century America. Allan Pinkerton grew up in Glasgow's Gorbals, like Carnegie the son of a handloom weaver. His mother worked in a cotton mill. He was apprenticed as a boy in a pattern-making shop, and in 1837, at the age of eighteen, became a journeyman cooper. Over the next few years Allan Pinkerton, again like the Carnegies and the Morrisons, became involved in Chartism. He was soon a leading activist, taking part in strikes and demonstrations, and before long was wanted by the police. He had to go into hiding. In March 1842 he and Joan Carfrae, a bookbinder from Paisley, were secretly married. Less than a month later they were smuggled on board a ship on the Clyde, and sailed for Montreal. When work ran out in Montreal Allan and Joan Pinkerton made their way south to Chicago where they made contact with a fellow Glaswegian with whom they worked for a while.

Scots had played a part in the founding of Chicago which by the time the Pinkertons arrived was a vigorous, rapidly growing but still raw frontier town. They stayed only for a few months, before deciding to join a community of Scots on the Fox River fifty miles northeast of Chicago. The place where they made their new home and Allan set up a cooperage business was called Dundee. He and Joan were soon involved in the abolitionist movement, keen activists in the underground railroad that helped escaped slaves cross the border into Canada. But he had other talents. He became deputy sheriff of Kane County, then of Cook County, which meant returning to Chicago.

By the early 1850s Chicago was 'feverishly booming', in the words of historian JC Furnas, and attracting criminals and opportunists in large numbers. The crime rate soared. Pinkerton was appointed Chicago's first detective. Then in 1850 he and a lawyer called Edward Rucker set up their own agency 'for the purpose of transacting a general Detective Police Business in Illinois, Wisconsin, Michigan and Indiana' which would investigate 'frauds and criminal offences'. Their aim was 'the detection of offenders, procuring arrests and convictions, apprehension or return of fugitives from justice, or bail; recovering lost or stolen property, obtaining information etc'. It was the start of, not the world's first, but certainly the world's best-known detective agency.

Within a few years Pinkerton's Agency had gained contracts to protect several railroads, which were particularly vulnerable to robberies, as countless tales of frontier rail heists record. And all the time he was pursuing criminals he was himself actively engaged in challenging the law, through his involvement in the anti-slavery movement. Slavery, he said, was 'a curse to the American nation'. Among those who were always welcome at the Pinkerton home was the fanatical abolitionist John Brown, and when he arrived on the doorstep in the early hours of a March 1859 morning with twelve rescued slaves Pinkerton helped to house and care for them, and raised money to send them on the next stage of their journey.

Pinkerton's Agency was doing well, but the Civil War brought new opportunities, just as it had for Carnegie. They began with guarding President Lincoln, and continued with the setting up of a spy network which operated behind Confederate lines. Pinkerton was a fervent admirer and close associate of General McClellan, and it was McClellan who initiated the spy project. In his book about this period of his life, *Spy of the Rebellion* (1883), Pinkerton described what was involved:

> I was to have as much strength of force as I required. It was arranged I was to go whenever the army moved. I was to go forward with the General, so that I might always be in communication with him. My corps was to be continually occupied in procuring from all possible sources, information regarding the strength, position and movements of the enemy.

All spies, counter brands, deserters, refugees and prisoners of war coming into our lines from the front were to be carefully examined by me, and their statements taken in writing.

The efforts of Pinkerton and his men had mixed results, but Lincoln thought highly of him. When Lincoln was assassinated, Pinkerton expressed his belief that if he himself had been on duty at the theatre that night a better job would have been done in protecting the president. Throughout the war, Pinkerton's agency continued its civilian detection work, and in the difficult years immediately following its close there was more call than ever for his men and the occasional woman. The post-war slump in the economy, the return of one-and-a-half million men to the labour market, and a high level of immigration meant that crime flourished. Pinkerton opened offices in New York and Philadelphia. The expansion of the railroad network and the growth of telegraphic communication made it easier to run things at a distance, though they also increased targets for criminals. Pinkerton thrived. His men had a hand in quelling the activities of many of the frontier's most notorious outlaws, among them the Reno gang in Indiana, and the James and Younger brothers in Missouri. Perhaps most spectacular was the Pinkerton agents' pursuit in the 1890s of members of the Wild Bunch, including Butch Cassidy and Harry Longbaugh, the 'Sundance Kid', which took them almost the length and breadth of the US and down into South America.

In 1870 Pinkerton built a house and developed an estate on land he had bought six years earlier. He called the estate 'The Larches', although there were no larches. When he found they were unobtainable in the US, he sent to Scotland for 85,000 larch trees which were planted alongside the estate's driveways. His sons Robert and William joined the business. Increasingly, the agency was involved in countering industrial unrest and in strike breaking. Their role was bitterly resented. In the Pennsylvania coalfields there was growing violence as mine workers, particularly a band of Irishmen known as the 'Molly Maguires', reacted against appalling conditions and exploitative mine owners. Pinkerton agents infiltrated the 'Mollies' and ringleaders were identified and arrested. There were nineteen executions. Other strike-breaking activities followed, and Pinkerton agents were soon identified by the labouring classes as instruments of corporate oppression. It was against this background that they entered the stage of the Homestead strike in 1892, and met the unleashed fury of the workforce. By this time Allan Pinkerton was dead and his sons had taken over.

Carnegie and Pinkerton had much more in common than similar backgrounds, a similar experience of their homeland, and parallel if not similar ambitions. They were both highly contradictory individuals. Carnegie's drive for wealth and ruthless business practice warred with his Chartist inheritance and his belief that he had a responsibility to the less fortunate. Pinkerton took huge risks as a political radical in Scotland and an abolitionist in the US, yet helped crush the attempts of labour to win fairer treatment. Both men demanded a great deal of themselves and of those who worked for them; they were both realists with a broad streak of sentiment. However remarkable their careers, Carnegie's especially, they were characteristic of many of the Scots who arrived in the US in the middle of the nineteenth century, ambitious, hard working, committed to their families, committed to Scotland although they adapted so readily to the raw new world in which they found themselves.

Carnegie and Pinkerton were both helped in their early weeks and months in the US by fellow Scots. The Scottish connection continued to be accepted and respected, although such clannishness could be unpopular, as it had been a century earlier. Scottish achievement after the Civil War was not just a story of a few remarkable individuals. There were thousands who made decent lives for themselves and their families, and hundreds who did strikingly well. By the late 1860s the US was recovering from post-war economic depression and the opportunities that benefited Carnegie dramatically re-established the nation's magnetism as the land of promise.

Scots, and Scottish money, responded. Robert Fleming, son of a Dundee tradesman, began his career as bookkeeper in the textile firm of Baxters, which in 1870 sent him to the US as their agent. Impressed by American potential, Fleming returned convinced that Scottish money would do well on the other side of the Atlantic. Dundee linen and jute manufacture was thriving and reserve funds were healthy. Fleming and his associates set up the Scottish American Investment Trust, and others followed. Although investment specifically in land and the cattle trade was prominent, the portfolio was mixed. Many who profited from these ventures never set foot in America, but these close financial links strengthened the Scottish-American connection and fostered interest in American events. They helped to ensure that the United States bulked large in the consciousness of those considering departure from Scotland.

Between 1870 and 1900 the US was the destination of over half of all those who emigrated. They did not all remain. Some were not inspired by what they encountered, and returned to Scotland disappointed and disillusioned. But others did well enough to sustain the dream, which attracted Scotland's expanding middle class as well as struggling labourers. John Stevenson, for example, was from a prominent Glasgow family and had a degree from Glasgow University. He went to Pittsburgh in 1872 where he was employed at the Carnegie Steel Works. He became a partner in the firm of Mackintosh, Hemphill and Co, then in an iron production firm based in Newcastle, Pennsylvania. His firm was taken over by US Steel, which bought out Carnegie. In 1905 he set up a plant manufacturing ordinance. He became a noted Republican. His brother, Sir Daniel Macaulay Stevenson, stayed in Glasgow and also had a successful career, becoming Glasgow's Lord Provost and chancellor of Glasgow University, and a prominent benefactor particularly to education. These parallel careers highlight correspondences between American and Scottish attitudes. American visitors often identified Glasgow as a city similar in many respects to commercially vibrant and socially open cities in the US.

George Bain from Stirling arrived in St Louis in 1865, by way of Montreal, Portland and Chicago. He became a merchant and flour miller, establishing St Louis as the US centre of milling. David Nicholson's success story was also located in St Louis. He was from Perthshire, and he, too, had made his way to St Louis via Canada and Chicago. He started a dry goods business in 1843. By 1870 he was running one of the largest stores in the country. Dugald Crawford was another successful Scot in the St Louis retail business, while Robert Borthwick did well in Buffalo. Another store-owning success was William Donaldson from Milnathort, Kinross. Beginning in 1877 as the employee of a Scottish dry goods firm in Providence, Rhode Island, he went on to St Paul where he set up his own business, which grew into a five-storey department store employing 900 people. He became a leading figure in the area, and chairman of the Businessmen's Union of Minneapolis.

Scotland's transatlantic financial adventures were not confined to investment. Many Scots became directly involved in American accountancy, insurance and banking. Particularly striking is the connection between Aberdeenshire and Wisconsin and Illinois, states that were attracting large numbers in the mid-nineteenth century. In 1836 Patrick Strachan from Aberdeen became manager of the Illinois Company and then director of several other banking and insurance companies. William Scott, accountant with the Illinois Investment Company, was himself an astute investor, and around 1858 was able to return to a well-heeled retirement in his native Aberdeen.

George Smith, born in Old Deer, Aberdeenshire, went to the US first in 1833 where he did well in Chicago and Wisconsin land speculations. He returned to Scotland and with his cousin Alexander Anderson, lawyer and banker, set up the Scottish Illinois Land Investment Company. Back in the US in 1839 he launched the Wisconsin Marine and Fire Insurance Company, and went on to make a great deal of money through banking, the railways and land investment, contributing significantly to frontier development. He spent his latter years in London, and died worth $52 million. Aberdonian John Johnston went to Milwaukee in 1856 where he became an accountant with Smith's Wisconsin Marine and Fire Insurance Company. Company directorship and the vice-presidency of a bank followed. His success enabled him to donate land for Milwaukee's city hospital, which was named after him. Another Aberdeenshire lad, Alexander Mitchell, joined the same company and eventually became its president. He moved into railroads, initiated major expansion of the Milwaukee and St Paul Railroad, and became a Republican member of Congress.

The railways continued to attract Scottish involvement and money. John Kennedy from Blantyre in Lanarkshire made his first visit to the US in 1850, representing an iron and coal firm. He returned in 1857 and became a prominent banker and a director of several railroad lines, as well as an active philanthropist. A close friend was James J Hill, Canadian born of Scottish parents, whose railroad building career began in the US. Both men were members of the syndicate that created the Canadian Pacific Railway Company. John Lundie from Arbroath worked on several American railroad projects and was a key figure in the electrification of the Illinois Central's suburban lines. Alexander Winton, among many other things, built railroad cars. Born in Grangemouth, he was an apprentice engineer on the Clyde before emigrating to New York in 1878. After a period as a ship's engineer he began a cycle business in Cleveland, where in 1897 he built one of the first motorcycles.

With his founding of the Winton Motor Carriage Company he graduated to four wheels. In 1911 he started a marine engine business.

David Laing came from Dunbar but by 1848, aged eighteen, he was in Pennsylvania. With his American-born wife and family he moved on to Indiana, where he worked first as a day labourer and later in a railway maintenance shop in Logansport, becoming foreman in 1876. Many of his fellow workers were Scots or English. Life wasn't easy. The workshop maintained 86 locomotives and 400 miles of track. In a letter to his sister of February 1874 he wrote of hard times: 'There are thousands here that are out of employment this winter and those that have work are working at reduced wages'. Of his five children only two survived.

Charles Macalester's origins were in Argyll. His father, from Campbeltown, had emigrated to Philadelphia in 1786, and did well as a trader and banker, founding a Presbyterian Church in Philadelphia. The son's success as a banker enabled him to provide land for Macalester College in Minneapolis. The habit of good works long pre-dated Andrew Carnegie. All of these men were agile in responding to opportunities to profit from the growing nation's need for infrastructure and communications, and Scotland's own well-recognised track record in insurance and banking gave them authority as well as experience.

The transcontinental railroad link was completed in 1869. California, where gold had already attracted huge numbers of both those who hoped to find gold and those who hoped to help the lucky ones spend their money, became more accessible. But Alexander Henry from Leith had arrived by sea in 1867. He was thirty years old and had served as a marine in the Crimean War before joining the merchant navy. He jumped ship in San Francisco, and settled in the German wine-growing area of Anaheim. On a ranch which he called 'Caledonia Grove' he started his own winery but when blight struck his vines he turned to growing oranges and walnuts. Another Anaheim settler was Richard Melrose, who made his home there in 1870. As a lawyer, politician and newspaper editor he involved himself in local issues, including support for Japanese immigrants who were banned from owning property and from white schools.

The Scottish imprint on San Francisco was lasting. Robert Dollar from Falkirk was prominent in California shipping, operating a fleet of cargo vessels that plied up and down the coast. By the 1920s he had a shipping empire that extended to the Far East and was playing an important role in opening up Chinese trade. He initiated the first round-the-world passenger service.

Most visitors to San Francisco take a ride on the cable car. Its mechanism was the work of Andrew Hallidie from a Dunfermline family. Visitors will probably also walk in the Golden Gate Park. It was the work of John McLaren, who grew up on a farm near Stirling. He was employed at Edinburgh's Royal Botanic Garden before emigrating. In California he worked as a landscape gardener and gained expertise in reclaiming areas of coastal sand dunes. In 1887 he became San Francisco's superintendent of parks. He transformed 1,000 acres of dunes and scrub to create the Golden Gate Park, planted with a million trees. He also created El Camino Real Park.

Scotland's own industrial base was feeding the transformation of the United States into a major industrial nation. It was not only money, enterprise and energy that came from Scotland, but labour, which was particularly evident in mining, quarrying and iron and steel. When after the Civil War Alexander McDonald, British miners' union leader, travelled in the US he found thousands of Scots in the major coalfields, although many hundreds of them worked there for the summer season only, returning to Scotland in October. McDonald, whose own two brothers were working in mines in Ohio and Illinois, encouraged Scottish miners to emigrate and take advantage of the higher wages and better conditions (although longer hours) to be found on the other side of the Atlantic. Scots were at the coal face and the blast furnace but they were also managers and engineers. William Goold left Glasgow for Pennsylvania in 1852 and his prospecting for coal led to the opening of several new mines. In Alabama he was responsible for producing the state's first coke.

The 1870 Census reveals that 46% of immigrant Scots were working in industrial jobs. Scots were to be found in the lead mines of the upper Mississippi and in the Michigan copper mines. George Hardie, a farmer's son, emigrated in 1852 and did well in the copper mines and was able to settle into a comfortable retirement in Illinois. Scots were plentiful in the expanding iron and steel works, and in building the railway locomotives for which demand surged after the Civil War. 'There is not a railway machine shop in America, or iron shipbuilding establishment, where Scotch mechanics may not be found,' wrote Peter Ross in 1896. James Sherriffs from Banff became a foundry superintendent at Menomonee, Wisconsin and later set up his own manufacturing company. Henry Elliott, who had worked for English locomotive builder George Stephenson, set up a locomotive works in Illinois. Peter Arthur, born in Paisley in 1831, was eleven when he went to the US, and was working on the railways from the age of eighteen. He was 32 when he became head of the Loco Engineers Union, which he remained until his death in 1903. In his hands the union was a powerful force. At the same time he took advantage of US opportunities by speculating successfully in real estate.

Industry required coal and the building of cities required stone. Scots were prominent in America's quarries and were particularly numerous in New England. Many of them were skilled stone masons from Aberdeenshire, often making an annual trip to the US and working for a few months at much higher wages than at home. The close relationship between Aberdeen and centres of the granite industry such as Quincy, Massachusetts and Barre, Vermont lasted well into the twentieth century. At Quincy, John Westland from Aberdeen and Gordon McKenzie and George Patterson from Huntly introduced the mechanical polishing of granite using machinery modelled on that already in use in Aberdeen.

As the nineteenth century came to an end, returning sojourners continued to spread the news of employment possibilities and encourage others to go. Those who set up their own businesses back in Scotland attracted American orders through their contacts, while in the US the experience and technical skills of Scottish quarrymen and masons were widely recognised. Peter Ross claimed that:

> Scotch masons long held the lead in this country; wherever a stone building was being erected, Scotsmen in greater or lesser numbers were sure to be found. Every building of any size in that country, it may be safe to say, owes something to Scottish ingenuity.

Among the buildings listed by Ross as having a Scottish input are the Capitol in Albany, Boston's State House, the Metropolitan Museum in New York and Chicago's City Hall. Gilbert Cameron from Greenock helped to build the Smithsonian. He returned to Greenock to live in a house he called 'Washington Cottage'. John Campbell, a stone mason from Blair Atholl, went to Illinois in 1851 and after doing well as a mason took up farming. Mormon John Sharp from Clackmannanshire became superintendent of the granite quarry in Utah where Scots were among those cutting the stone for the Mormon Temple in Salt Lake City. In 1902 the *Granite Cutters' Journal* was proclaiming, 'From the Atlantic to the Pacific comes the cry for more men.'

Robert Gillespie Reid was a stone mason from Couper Angus who went first to Australia before heading for North America. In Australia he was building railway viaducts. In New York State he helped to construct Buffalo's International Bridge before building more bridges in Canada. The expansion of railways meant that he was in great demand, and back in the US he built bridges for the Southern Pacific, and across the Delaware Water Gap. The 1890s saw him in Newfoundland. He initiated the Alphabet Fleet, ships built in Scotland for plying the Newfoundland coastal waters, and all with Scottish names – *Argyle, Bruce, Clyde, Dundee.*

In the latter part of the nineteenth century huge numbers of emigrants from all over Europe flooded into the United States, and except in specialised areas the demand for labour slackened. In spite of the need for particular skills, the prospects for emigrants were less attractive and many had to accept working for minimal wages. Scots had to take their chance with thousands of others. Ships crammed with emigrants queued up on arrival at New York to decant their passengers. They all had to be processed, at Manhattan's Castle Garden until 1892, and then at Ellis Island, which could handle 8,000 emigrants a day. Most of the Scots could at least speak English, although even for them the experience of being harassed by sometimes unscrupulous agents and herded onto a train bound for a destination that meant little to them was traumatic. Many headed for existing Scottish communities, in Pittsburgh or Chicago perhaps, or in Seattle where by this time there were large numbers of Scots.

The US was finding it increasingly difficult to absorb the flood of unskilled labour that was pouring into the country. But without it fortunes like Carnegie's and the more modest successes of hundreds of others would have been rather harder to achieve. Labour was plentiful, and if there were problems there was always another wave of new arrivals to take the place of those who protested at conditions or wages. Plenty of Scots joined the army of migrants on the search for work. John McIntosh of Rochester, New York, published a poem in 1876 which gives a flavour of the experience. It takes the form of a dialogue between a tramp and a farmer:

TRAMP
Poor and ragged, I think you said,
Right; and we come for a little bread,
To help us along our weary way,
Asking for labor from day to day,
That is the reason we're here, you see,
Forced from the city by poverty...
We canvassed the city through and through,
Nothing to work at. Nothing to do;
The wheels of the engines go no more,
Bolted and barred is the old shop door...

FARMER
What! Rob us? Hear the old villain, Jim,
We'll be murdered, too, by the likes of him.
And yet they will ask for food and drink,
Guess you ain't quite so bad off's you think.
I say to you as I allus say:
No man need starve in Ameriky.

According to Stephen Graham, a journalist who joined tramps in
Pennsylvania in 1913, there were more tramps in the USA than in
any other country except Russia. The archetypal 'wanderin' workin'
man' is expressed in his life and in his songs by Woody Guthrie,
the descendant of Scots, who took to the road at the age of thirteen.
He in turn inspired and nourished the folk revival of the 1960s.

When Robert Louis Stevenson arrived in New York in 1879 he
brought with him a clutch of romantic preconceptions, which he
described in his book *The Amateur Emigrant*:

A few wild story-books which delighted his childhood form
the imaginative basis of his picture of America. In course of

time, there is added to this a great crowd of stimulating details – vast cities that grow up as by enchantment; the birds, that have gone south in autumn, returning with the spring to find thousands camped upon their marshes, and the lamps burning far and near along populous streets; forests that disappear like snow; countries larger than Britain that are cleared and settled, one man running forth with his household gods before another, while the bear and the Indian are yet scarce aware of their approach; oil that gushes from the earth; gold that is washed or quarried in the brooks or glens of the Sierras; and all that bustle, courage, action and constant kaleidoscopic change that Walt Whitman has seized and set forth in his vigorous, cheerful, and loquacious verses.

His notion of the US as a nation of promise and profusion did not last long. In his first hours in New York he met 'two Scots lads, recent immigrants' who for six weeks had been looking for work without success. Another had been searching for work for three months. Stevenson's experience of the US, east coast, west coast, and travelling across the continent, was full of contradictions. Although he had a vision of 'a land of promise' he soon discovered that the dispossessed who arrived in their thousands were generally despised and often struggled to make something of their new lives. Yet that image of promise survived and in the twentieth century the USA's magnetism did not diminish. The 1920s saw 300,000 Scots leaving, most of them for North America with more than ever before going to the US.

In September 1937 a young couple from Edinburgh sailed on the Anchor Line's *Tuscania* from Glasgow to New York, 'a joint adventure into a new world'. Thirty-four years later, in the second of two autobiographical volumes, David Daiches wrote about their arrival. 'We were both very Old World in family traditions and habits of thought,' he said, and added, 'I was conscious of the whole history of Europe and the Mediterranean lying behind me.' Like generations of Atlantic travellers who left Europe, David and Isobel Daiches had expectations and images gleaned from books and word-of-mouth and meetings with Americans, and like most of their compatriots were familiar with the USA on celluloid. Although there was a powerful sense of entering the unknown – 'To sail to America was in a way to voyage beyond history' – there was also a sense of familiarity. As the ship made its way up New York's North River, the city they had imagined became real. They were on their way to Chicago, but first stayed on the twentieth floor of the Beekman Tower Hotel from where they looked down onto First Avenue and 49th Street. 'All the varied life of the great city seemed to rise up to me as I looked down, and I was deeply moved.'

The fact that in the 1920s and '30s, America, like Europe, experienced an economic slump and severe unemployment did not tarnish the image. Many Scottish Canadians were tempted across the border by the prospect of jobs and better wages: industrial centres such as Detroit and Boston were key destinations. 'Boston! One could easily have yelled "Gold!" and received the same effect in eastern Nova Scotia during the decades between 1880 and 1920,' wrote George Sandfield MacDonald of Montreal, and Boston continued to attract struggling Nova Scotians. Scottish Canadians felled trees in the Michigan forests and helped to build American railways. So many Ontario Scots crossed the border that there was said to be 'a new Glengarry' in Dakota.

In Scotland, American movies, American music and American books fuelled an interest. The idea of America was encapsulated in dozens of powerful icons which influenced the aspirations of Europeans – cowboys, Cadillacs, blues and blue jeans, wide open spaces and upward mobility. In the second half of the twentieth century, although Scots still transplanted themselves permanently to the US, it became increasingly possible – and desirable – to visit, as a student, on holiday, or working temporarily. The notion of the US attracting the most challenging and most enterprising minds took hold, and the phrase 'brain drain' was coined. Compared with what Scotland – and Britain as a whole – offered, the American academic world seemed less constrained and better rewarded. The frontiers of scientific research were expanding; the approach to business was more open and adventurous; the professional climate was more invigorating. There still seemed plenty of scope for 'muscle and brain'.

CHAPTER NINE

Fire on the Mountain

*When the fire's on the mountain we'll be
coming home again.*
THEME SONG, GRANDFATHER MOUNTAIN GAMES

IN 1829 THE St Andrews Society of Charleston was 100 years old.
It celebrated with a procession to the city's First Presbyterian Church
where those assembled were addressed by a Scot, the Reverend
Mitchell King, who lauded Scots as 'benefactors of mankind'. 'Their
praises are on every tongue,' he said. 'Their works are on every
hand.' And he went on:

> They form the text books of our schools and colleges. They
> are found in the shop of the mechanic, in the counting house
> of the merchant, on the table of the physician and lawyer, in
> the study of the philosopher, in the cabinet of the statesman,
> and in the desk of the divine. There is no language or people
> where their voice is not heard – where they do not improve
> the heart, and instruct and influence the mind.

Nearly a century later, Woodrow Wilson, whose grandfather had
been born in Scotland and whose father was Moderator of the
General Assembly of the American Presbyterian Church, expressed
the same sentiment more concisely: 'every line of strength in our
history is a line coloured by Scottish blood'.

In 1997 the governor of North Carolina announced the
instatement of Tartan Day, with the claim that 'North Carolina

has the largest number of people of Scottish heritage of any other state or country in the world'. The following year, borrowing from Canada, 6 April, the day on which the Declaration of Arbroath was signed, became National Tartan Day in the US. On this day massed pipe bands march down New York's Fifth Avenue. Balls and dinners and award ceremonies take place. Tartan is exuberantly worn by many who embrace a Scottish ancestry, whether Highland or Lowland.

The celebration of Scottish identity never vanished in the United States, but as the twentieth century drew to a close it experienced a revival that had been building for several decades. In the 1970s, clan and heritage societies had proliferated. The Council for Scottish Clans and Associations was founded in 1974, with the stated aim of 'the preservation and promotion of the customs, traditions and heritage of the Scottish people through support of Scottish-oriented organizations'. Clan societies with their emphasis on clan tradition, much of which had little historical reality, and events such as Highland games, became a focus of the self-conscious reinvention of Scottishness. The much older St Andrews Societies had been founded for a different purpose. Their tradition of providing help for Scots in difficulty had grown out of the need for a support system in the early years of emigration. The first such organisation was Boston's Old Scots Charitable Society founded in 1657. In 1729, when the first St Andrews Society was born in Charleston, most large cities and identifiable Scottish communities founded something similar. They were usually open only to Scots and the sons of Scots (they were generally men only and many remain so); by default part of their rationale was the preservation of Scottish identity and connections.

The rules of the Scots Thistle Society, founded in Philadelphia in 1799, give a flavour of the intentions of this kind of philanthropy:

The Society reflecting upon the situation of many of their

friends and countrymen that emigrate from home, who, although endued with Virtue and talents, arrive on an unknown shore, destitute of friends, without the means of support and frequently in circumstances of real distress. That if it is in their power as a Society whose views are directed to relieve distress... to render to their distressed brothers emigrating from the same Country, so far as in their power, the necessary assistance which they may require.

Scots had a reputation for looking after their own, and at times this 'clannishness' was criticised, seen as running contrary to the 'melting pot' ethos which insisted on a new identity for the thousands who arrived. Interestingly, the process of building that identity borrowed from Scottish examples. The Scottish democratic tradition influenced education in America and also, directly and indirectly, the Constitution. The ideas of the Scottish Enlightenment crossed the Atlantic in many different forms. Scottish voices were highly significant in the process of American discovery of ways of describing themselves.

Scottish emigrants carried with them the poetry of Robert Burns and through Burns Clubs and annual Burns Suppers kept the poetry, the language and their Scottish connections alive. It seems clear that it was not only Scots who responded to Burns. The first American edition of Burns was published in the US only two years after the original Kilmarnock edition of his poems appeared in Scotland in 1786, and it was followed by dozens more. In 1811 an article in the *American Review* claimed that the poetry of Burns was better understood in the US than in England. The Scottish dialect, it suggested, was more familiar to American than to English readers. Scots words entered the language of Appalachia. Historian David Fischer lists several examples, including 'cracker', slang for poor white, from the Scots word meaning 'boaster' or 'gossip'. Americans were primed to respond sympathetically to ideas and publications emanating from Scotland: 'We look with more reverence upon the literary and scientific character of Scotland, and are always prepared to receive with admiration, the intellectual off-spring of her capital which we consider as the metropolis of genius and learning.'

In 1820 a group of Scots in New York celebrated Burns's birthday, 25 January, and 27 years later the first US Burns Club was born, also in New York. When Charles Murray was travelling in the US in 1834 he found figures of Tam O'Shanter and Souter Johnnie displayed in a Baltimore museum. Statues of Robert Burns can be found all over the US, often in unexpected places. Cheyenne, Wyoming, for example, put up a statue of Burns in 1927, funded by a woman called Mary Gilchrist.

Another Scottish writer who was received 'with admiration', if not with adulation, in the United States, as indeed he was throughout most of Europe, was Walter Scott. Scott was hugely popular and an inspiration in many ways. He provided a historical narrative for a country that had been shocked into a whole new climate of existence, first by the Union of the Parliaments in 1707 and then by the Jacobite Risings that ended in 1746. Out of a violent and divided history he created the possibility of a progressive future without losing the heroic and rugged romance of the past. He produced fiction that was distinctively Scottish, in language, landscape and character. The United States of America was born in violence, and division haunted its first hundred years, and still does. Like Scotland it had a wild and beautiful terrain, an environment of bold action and idealistic endeavour. Americans enthusiastically embraced Scott's heroic version of Scotland's past. Plantations in the southern states took their names from Scott's novels and there was a craze for putting on medieval-style tournaments modelled on the one described in *Ivanhoe*.

Perhaps part of Scott's appeal lay in the recognition that, as in Scotland, there was a need for ways of presenting the young nation that did not borrow from England. James Fennimore Cooper, whose novels of the American frontier began appearing in the 1820s, was welcomed as a genuinely American writer who could do for the US what Scott had done for Scotland. Scott set the standard for how Americans could project themselves and their history. There was even a parallel between Native Americans and the Gaels, who had themselves been compared with America's 'savages'.

Burns and Scott were pre-eminent in the transatlantic literary landscape, but there were others. Allan Ramsay's poems and his play *The Gentle Shepherd*, published in America in 1750, were very popular. James Macpherson's *Ossian* was published in the US in 1790, and several editions followed. The debate about its authenticity engaged Americans as much as those on the other side of the Atlantic. The same year saw the American publication of Home's play *Douglas*. A very popular work was Jane Porter's novel *The Scottish Chiefs*, published in 1810, which retold in highly-coloured style the story of Wallace and Bruce. James Hogg and John Galt were also read enthusiastically. American journals and magazines kept the reading public abreast of Scottish writing. Some of these were aimed specifically at a Scottish audience. The *New York Literary Gazette*, for example, was initiated in the 1820s and specialised in Scottish material. The *Scottish-American Journal*, which ran from 1857 to 1919, had around 15,000 subscribers. Other Scottish interest papers of the nineteenth and early twentieth century included the *Caledonian Advertiser*, begun in 1869 and merged with *The Scotsman* in 1874, the *Boston Scotsman*, and the monthly *Caledonian*.

Scottish books helped to nourish, in some cases to create, an interest in Scotland itself, and American tourists crossed the Atlantic to inspect the country that had been made vivid to them by Scott above all. Benjamin Silliman, professor of chemistry and natural history at Yale, came to Scotland in 1805, the year in which Scott's *The Lay of the Last Minstrel* was published. He spent six months in Edinburgh, relishing the opportunity to mix with 'a constellation of scientific and literary men'. He found Scots generally sympathetic to America and Americans. His writes of a dinner at which his host 'remarked that it was a very delightful thing to see people born and educated some 3000 miles from each other sitting down in friendship at the same table, and finding a common language, mutual feelings, and identical manners'. Scottish visitors to America may have disagreed on the subject of manners. Thomas Hamilton and others were appalled at American eating habits, which Hamilton described as unknown 'beyond the limits of the Zoological Gardens'. 'Each individual,' he wrote, 'seemed to *pitchfork* his food down his gullet, without the smallest attention to the wants of his neighbour.'

Washington Irving's visit to Scotland was a return to his homeland. His father William had left Shapinsay in Orkney for New York in 1763. He established himself as a merchant and remained after the war. His admiration for the American Revolution is indicated by the name he chose for one of his three sons, all born in New York. Washington Irving spent many years in Europe, including a spell assisting in the family hardware business in Liverpool and a stay in Scotland, which he chronicled in his *Tour in Scotland 1817*. While he was there he met Scott and other literary figures. His tour included the Highlands which, for him as much as for Americans with no Scottish connections, represented picturesque romance at its most dramatic. Although Irving had already published his first work, it was after this visit that his literary career took off and he created his best known character, Rip Van Winkle. Europe in general and Scotland in particular clearly stimulated his writing, and influenced his creation of work that was popular on both sides of the Atlantic.

Transatlantic tourism was not an option for most Americans, whatever their origins. The Scots who settled in the US rarely returned to the old country for a visit, although some gave up their

American adventure and returned for good. The well-heeled Americans who did make tours of Scotland, as well as those who maintained the tradition of seeking a Scottish education, did much to keep the United States aware of the small nation which had played so significant a part in its colonial history. And it was history as well as landscape that visiting Americans sought. In 1832 Calvin Colton, foreign correspondent of the *New York Observer*, was in the Highlands. He wrote:

A people born and bred among such hills and vales, familiar with such mountains and lakes, challenging the stronger emotions of the soul, and the bolder flights of fancy, ought to be extraordinary. I never looked out upon the face of that country, but my mind was quickened – equally by what strikes the eye, and by historical associations.

Americans were hungry for history, and hungry, too, to create their own environment of learning and literature. Scots had contributed to that before the revolution, and a Scottish ambience, as well as Scottish individuals, continued the tradition. Colton struggled to reconcile the grandeur of the landscape with the meanness of the circumstances in which many Highlanders lived, but managed to make the necessary leap of imagination: 'It is not difficult to believe that they have done such exploits, as are ascribed to them in the historical legends of that classic ground.' In North America the legacy of the Gaelic past survived, but only patchily in the United States.

Living in Edinburgh from 1810 was a woman who had spent ten of her childhood years in colonial America. After 22 years as wife of the minister in the Highland parish of Laggan, who died in 1801, Anne Grant renewed her interest in America, publishing her *Memoirs of an American Lady* in 1808. Americans were frequent visitors to her Edinburgh home. She was a literary figure of some reputation on both sides of the Atlantic, producing essays and poems as well as two volumes of memoirs. For many Americans she provided a gateway to the Edinburgh literary scene and she, in turn, clearly enjoyed their company. 'The American character has been much raised among our literary people here,' she wrote in 1819 to a friend in the US, 'by a constellation of persons of brilliant talents, and polished manners, by whom we were dazzled and delighted last winter.' According to cultural historian Andrew Hook, 'no other individual did so much to encourage and develop personal ties between Americans and Scots'.

Blackwood's Magazine commented approvingly on American visitors to Scotland:

> Not a few are with us every year in Scotland; and were we to form our opinion of their countrymen in general from the young Americans with whom we have made acquaintance-ship and friendship, we should think almost as highly of our brethren across the western wave as of ourselves.

Francis Jeffrey, editor of the *Edinburgh Review* from its foundation in 1802 to 1829, was pro-American and keen to reach an American readership. The *Review* was an influential outlet for those sympathetic to the US. Jeffrey visited the US himself in 1814. He was greeted with enthusiastic respect, met both President Madison and Secretary of State James Monroe, and acquired an American wife. Not surprisingly, his positive attitude towards the US continued, and he welcomed many American visitors to his home.

Books from Scotland kept the home country vivid in the hearts and minds of exiles and helped to create an image of a valiant little nation, which bred a distinctive race of rugged and enterprising people who held their own against tremendous odds. Their landscape was romantically beautiful and their defeats were romantically courageous. They were egalitarian and determined, ideal material for pioneering of all kinds.

Scottish writers entered the mainstream of the infant republic's imagination, and in some respects remained there. Mark Twain famously blamed Walter Scott for the Civil War, believing that the South had taken from his books an inappropriate code of chivalry and aristocracy which fuelled a dangerous sense of difference from the north. In *Huckleberry Finn* the wrecked paddle steamer is called the *Walter Scott*. A later generation responded enthusiastically to Robert Louis Stevenson, particularly to his *Strange Case of Dr Jekyll and Mr Hyde* (1886). American readers may not have been aware of its essentially Scottish character (the story is set in London) but there was a continuing appetite for his work. Newspapers competed for his journalism. Samuel McClure, an Ulster Scot from Antrim via Glasgow, signed up Stevenson for regular contributions. McClure, who had emigrated initially to Indiana and was educated at Knox College in Illinois, had begun his magazine career by starting a cycling magazine called *The Wheelman*. He later ran a newspaper syndicate, through which Stevenson was published, and *McClure's Magazine*, which serialised some of Stevenson's later fiction.

The American appetite for Scottish fiction continued with the next generation of Scottish writers, especially those of the Kailyard school whose picture of a cosy rural domesticity attracted American readers. It may not have been just nostalgia for the old country. George Blake saw a parallel between rural Scotland's kailyard and rural America's cabbage-patch. They were both, he said, 'primitive communities', and pointed out that 'a kailyard is a cabbage-patch', suggesting in both cases 'the rural cottage and its modest kitchen garden, a sort of inner shrine of decent living in pious poverty'. The three key Kailyard writers were JM Barrie, Samuel Crockett and Ian Maclaren. The latter in particular was hugely popular in the America; his *Beside the Bonnie Brier Bush* was in 1895 the bestselling work of fiction in the US. Clearly, it was not only those of Scottish heritage who found in it a message relating to American values. MacLaren himself (the Reverend John Watson) died in Iowa while on his third literary tour of the States.

More recently, American enthusiasm for RL Stevenson has contributed significantly to a widespread revival of interest in a writer who, like Burns and Scott, produced work that is distinctively Scottish yet crosses borders with ease. There was a public monument to Stevenson in San Francisco before there was one in Edinburgh. The Stevenson House at Monterey and museum at Silverado are maintained with dedication and hard work. American Mormons financed the refurbishment of Vailima, the house in Samoa in which Stevenson spent his final years. The American scholarly contribution to Stevenson studies rivals that in Scotland, and several American writers, among them Donna Tartt, acknowledge the influence of Stevenson on their work.

Two American writers who impressed Stevenson were Walt Whitman, who acknowledged the influence of Scott, and Herman Melville, who was descended from a Fife family. Stevenson saw them as distinctively American but they have qualities of vigour and conviction which suggest a Scottish influence. A Scottish inheritance flavours the fiction of the American West, in which many Scottish names appear: the Lone Ranger, who made his first appearance on radio in 1933, was the alias of John Reid, a clearly Scottish Texas Ranger created by George W Trendle. Scots populate the novels of William Faulkner, who was himself of Scottish origin. In *Intruder in the Dust* (1948), for example, most of the protagonists are of Scottish descent and there is a deliberate evocation of a Highland heritage. The sixteen-year-old hero has been brought up to be aware of 'the mountains in Scotland where his ancestors had come from but he hadn't seen yet' – implying that one day he will see them. His uncle talks of:

> people named Gowrie and McCallum and Fraser and Ingrum that used to be Ingraham and Workitt that used to be

Urquhart only the one that brought it to America and then Mississippi couldn't spell it either, who loved brawling and fear God and believe in Hell...

The murdered Vinson Gowrie is buried in the graveyard of the Caledonia Church.

Norman Maclean in *A River Runs Through It* (1976) and Ivan Doig in his novels also specifically acknowledge their Scottish origins. They both grew up in Montana. Ivan Doig's memoir *This House of Sky: Landscapes of the Western Mind* (1987) describes how in the 1890s his grandfather's family arrived at Helena from a village near Dundee, and then moved on with 'a double handful of Scottish families' to the Big Belt range of hills, where they settled. 'Two deep Caledonian notions seem to have pulled them so far into the hills: to raise sheep, and to graze them on mountain grass which cost nothing.' At the end of a country track 'worn bald by iron wagon-wheels and later by the hard tires of Model T's' the families made their homes and survived savage winters beset by blizzards and howling wolves and coyotes.

The impact of Scotland on some of the most distinctively American music genres is widely acknowledged. From the Borders the ballad tradition travelled to Ulster and on across the Atlantic where it re-emerged in the Bluegrass music rooted in the Appalachians. The well-known ballad 'Barbara Ellen', for example, has an Appalachian version extraordinarily close to the original, but there are many others which are current on both sides of the Atlantic. Songs of the Western frontier were also descended from the Border ballads – not surprisingly as the ballads' original environment was frontier territory, with all the instability and need for self-reliance that that implies. Ballads narrating the exploits of Jesse James or Sam Bass echo the Border ballads 'Kinmont Willie' or 'Hughie the Graeme'. The reiver who may have inspired the latter was probably among Grahams transported to Ulster. Some of their descendants undoubtedly went on to America.

The legacy of Scottish and Irish fiddle music is easily detectable in Appalachian and Cajun styles of both fiddle and banjo playing and in the American square dance. The Scottish originals of some Appalachian fiddle tunes can be precisely identitifed. Historian Richard Blaustein lists 'Hop High Ladies' ('Miss McLeod's Reel'), 'Leather Britches' ('Lord MacDonald's Lament') and 'Too Young to Marry' ('My Love is but a Lassie Yet') as examples. In almost any recorded compilation of Bluegrass music the Scottish origins sing out. In the 1980s the Shetland fiddler Aly Bain explored the connections between Scottish and North American music in an illuminating journey that took him from Nova Scotia to New Orleans and produced a series of recordings of 'transatlantic sessions'.

Plenty of Scottish names appear in the story of American folk and country music: Woody Guthrie, so hugely influential; Bill Monroe, Bluegrass pioneer; Glen Campbell, one of the best-known names in country music; and many others. Some Scottish tunes resurface in American versions almost intact. The tune of 'Red River Valley' is said to have been borrowed from a Gaelic song, a reminder that the Gaels were as strong an influence as the Lowland Borderers. Professor Willie Ruff of Yale University, a jazz musician as well as an academic, has suggested that the style of unaccompanied Gaelic psalm singing directly influenced the early gospel choirs. He was reported in *The Independent* newspaper as claiming that 'it was in the Highlands that I found the cultural roots of Black America'. We know that in North Carolina there were black Gaelic-speaking congregations and the correspondence in style and texture between Gaelic lining-out, the congregation following the lead of the precentor, and gospel singing is very striking.

Traditional Gaelic song and eighteenth-century dance tunes travelled to America, in published form as well as with musicians, suggesting that they were enjoyed in drawing rooms as well as barns and taverns. And in Scotland there was music that reflected the new Atlantic horizons. James Boswell famously described 'a dance called America' in his *Journal of a Tour to the Hebrides*, which historian and musician Hugh Cheape believes may have been a tune called 'The American Reel' published by Niel Gow in his fifth book of fiddle music. Now, American country music is widely popular in Scotland, although enthusiasts may not be aware that Scottish music has a place in its origins.

Scottish music was absorbed into newly emerging American musical idioms. Other signifiers of the Scottish homeland were more conspicuous. Tartan also travelled across the Atlantic, initially as part of regimental uniform and of the ordinary dress of emigrant Highlanders. Later, it travelled as a deliberate symbol of the old country. The museum at Ellis Island has in its collections a tartan outfit worn by a small boy on his arrival in the US early in the twentieth century. His family were expecting to become citizens of the United States; if anything, this increased the need to make a statement about their origins.

As early as 1765 a Scottish cloth merchant in Philadelphia was advertising 'best Scotch Plaids' for making up into Highland dress. The presence of Highland regiments in the colonies may have encouraged the adoption of the kilt by Scots who would not normally have associated themselves with traditions of the Gael. James Macpherson's Ossian versions were delighting readers with epic tales evoking a romantic Highland past with which many were eager to be linked. Tartan was a shortcut to the Highlands. In the next century, tartan spread in popularity on both sides of the Atlantic, boosted by Queen Victoria's passion for the Gaeltachd and the adoption of tartan into mainstream fashion. It became required dress for any Scottish function, whether Burns Supper or Highland Games.

Tartan soon became formalised, although the dress code did not necessarily bear much relation to the way tartan was originally worn. The codification of clan tartans was a nineteenth-century phenomenon. The programme for the 63rd Scottish Games of the Caledonian Club of Philadelphia, held in 1922, features a photograph of 'Chief William Morton' in kilt, plaid, sporran, tartan stockings, bonnet with majestic eagle feathers, huge plaid pin, claymore and several daggers. The black-and-white picture does not allow identification of the tartan. A few decades later the kilt was sometimes obligatory at such events. In 1965 the Grandfather Mountain games instituted a Parade of Tartans. There are now more than 300 officially registered tartans, including those for the US Navy, Air Force and Marine Corps, the Military Academy at West Point, the Citadel Military Academy at Charleston, and the State of Georgia. There is a Confederate Memorial tartan. New traditions such as 'the kirkin of the tartan' have evolved. There is a Scottish Tartans Museum and Heritage Centre at Franklin, South Carolina.

In Compton Mackenzie's novel *The Monarch of the Glen* (1941) Chester Royde Jr is an American millionaire visiting the Highlands. He and his wife Carrie, a Canadian of Scottish descent in search of her roots, fall in love with tartan. His sister falls in love with a kilt-wearing Glaswegian Scottish nationalist. Chester acquires two dazzling kilts, one in orange, one in purple – he is advised to avoid tartan. Mackenzie's good-natured mockery of American infatuation with the Highlands has a more serious undertone, as he reminds us that much of what seems so attractive is either a distortion of history or the result of just that displacement of people that sent thousands across the Atlantic. There is some irony in the fact that the televised version of *The Monarch of the Glen* has proved very popular in North America.

In the twentieth century burgeoning clan societies and expanding Highland games nurtured the wearing of tartan and the reinvention of tradition. In 1836 the Highland Society of New York organised what was probably the first 'modern' Highland games, although the origins reputedly go back to the eleventh century, when Malcolm III ('Canmore') organised competitive sports on the Braes of Mar. The Braemar Highland Society had been founded in 1817 and within a few years was promoting sporting activities in addition to preserving other aspects of Highland culture. Queen Victoria's acquisition in 1852 of nearby Balmoral helped the Braemar Gathering to become a key sporting event and influential on many others, including the Highland games at Grandfather Mountain, North Carolina, founded in 1956. By this time there was a well-established tradition of Highland games in North America; to them has been attributed the origins of track and field events in mainstream sporting meetings. But Grandfather Mountain soon became the biggest, with thousands of Scottish American families assembling, many of them camping for the duration of the games and meeting together for all kinds of informal events as well as the programmed activities.

The first Grandfather Mountain Games was opened on 19 August, the date on which Prince Charles Edward Stewart raised his standard in Glenfinnan. The link with Jacobitism was thus explicit, and the Scottish American empathy with the defeated clans, particularly in the southern states, is an influential factor in the way the Highland heritage is commemorated in the US. Although a minority of the clans supported the Jacobites, and the early Scottish emigrants to America were as likely to have been Covenanters as clansmen, it is the emblem of heroic defeat that has most resonance. The tone is caught expressively in North Carolina's Loch Norman Games, which have been going for only a decade. The programme of the opening games in 1994 proclaimed:

> Far out of that dark nowhere, in the time before we were born, men who were flesh of our flesh and bone of our bone went through fire and storm to break a path to the future.

> We are part of the future they died for... What they did, the
> lives they lived, the sacrifices they made, the stories they told,
> the songs they sang and, finally, the deaths they died make
> up a part of our own experience. We will remember and set
> an example for those who will follow.

Loch Norman is an area settled by Ulster Scots, most of whom
originated in southern Scotland, yet this does not inhibit the forging
of a direct and intimate connection with Highland experience. It is
not just that Scotland's past is romanticised, but that participants
in these events feel it is crucial to claim a slice of that particular
'dark nowhere' for their own.

Parallels with the more recent past in the American South are
sometimes explicitly evoked. At Aberdeen in the Cape Fear Valley
there is an annual festival which combines music and crafts and a
replicated Confederate encampment. The venue is Shaw House
and the Malcolm Blue Farm, the latter the farm settled by Malcolm
Blue who arrived from Argyll in 1825. The celebration of Scotland
as a warrior society flows into the urge to keep alive a Southern
heritage that emphasises romantic Confederate heroism. In both
cases there is a sense of loss and a need to commemorate. One of
the aims of the Clan Fraser Society is 'to mark with plaques and
statuary, historic battle sites in Scotland and North America where
members of the clan have gained undying fame'.

Around 300 Highland games take place in North America every
year. Although about half are located in the southern states, they
are also found in the north and west. The annual games at Loon
Mountain, New Hampshire, are described on the website of the
New Hampshire Gathering of the Scottish Clans Inc as 'a Scottish
cultural celebration of music, dance, athletics, Scottish imports and
food' and have an array of corporate sponsors. But these events
are just the most conspicuous expression of a Scottish legacy. For
over 250 years clan societies, Celtic, Gaelic and Highland Societies,

Caledonian Clubs, St Andrews Societies, Burns Clubs and societies representing Scottish places of origin have nurtured the old country connection. In the early decades of the nineteenth century Minnesota had a St Andrews Society, a Caledonian Club and a Lewis Society. The *Denver Republican* reported the Colorado Caledonian Club St Andrew's Day ball of 1882 in tones approaching envy: 'If any people know how to enjoy themselves it's the Scotch. Of course, they are somewhat clannish but a people coming from a country so rich in historical reminiscences have a right to be.'

In 1912 the Oakland California Caledonian Club brought together some 5,000 people for their 4th Annual Gathering. An Oakland magazine called *The Maple Leaf* indicates that many of the Scottish community had arrived there by way of Canada. In the 1920s Clan Stewart of Duluth gathered at Fond du Lac on Lake Superior. Many of Minnesota's Scots had also come from Canada. A decade or so later the Duluth Lewis Society's annual picnic was reported in the *Stornoway Gazette*. About 100 people got together for bowling, races and shinty, the latter of a somewhat wild nature:

> the whistle blew, the battle was on; and believe you me, mate, it was no child's play: some of those fellows were using golf clubs, walking sticks, barrel staves, and what not, and one was lucky to miss their wild swings, and not get his head knocked off. The ladies served 'a lovely supper' and on the bus back to town Gaelic songs were sung all the way home, and a hilarious time was had by all.

Some of them may have sailed to Canada from Lewis on the *Metagama* in 1923 or the *Marloch* the following year. Many of this group of emigrants had a difficult time in Canada's prairie provinces and some drifted south hoping for better things in the

US. They were welcomed by existing Lewis communities.

Some societies were particularly concerned with assisting Scots in Scotland: in 1885 the Scottish Land League of America was set up in Chicago to support the Highland crofters in their battle for a fairer land policy. In 1925 the American Iona Society based in New York City had among its members several prominent citizens, including the editors of the *Wall Street Journal* and the *New York Times*. It came up with a proposal to found a 'seat of learning' in the Highlands, 'a rallying centre for economic as well as academic pursuits'. The society's aim was 'to persuade all worthy fellow-citizens to give tangible recognition to the fact that many of the finer elements in our civilisation are a heritage from the Scots pioneers, who lived and fought for American liberty and progress'. The proposed institution was seen as an acknowledgement of this debt (although most of those who fought for American liberty were not Highlanders). However, the idea did not go down well in Scotland and the plan was dropped. There is now a University of the Highlands and Islands and a Gaelic College, Sabhal Mor Ostaig, on Skye. Americans are among those who attend the courses run by the latter.

Well into the nineteenth century there were significant numbers of native Gaelic speakers in the US. James Stuart was in South Carolina in 1828, where he encountered Argyll-born Gaelic-speaking Duncan Macmillan: 'his pleasure in seeing me was increased when he found that I could ask him how he was in Gaelic'. But the Reverend John Sinclair, who when he first went to North Carolina in 1858 reported that Gaelic was widely spoken, fourteen years later had to admit that 'the customs and manners of the old Gaels' were disappearing, and Gaelic itself 'nearly dead'. William Fraser from Inverness-shire emigrated to Elgin, Illinois in 1846. Nearly 40 years later he made a trip to the west coast where in Oregon he encountered Scottish communities. He put his comments in verse:

Some of the Scots in this country
Have completely rejected every fine custom
That followed their ancestors throughout the generations
They have no interest in sustaining them
But like the Gentiles around them
Grow cold-hearted with their wealth
And refuse to speak Gaelic, disparaging it instead
Even though they were sustained by it in their youth.

Some enclaves of Gaelic speakers survived at least until the end of the nineteenth century. It was estimated that in 1884 there were 4–5,000 Gaelic speakers in Chicago. The Scottish Gaelic newspaper *An Gaidheal*, founded in 1871, had subscribers in North Carolina and the mid-west, and *MacTalla*, published in Sydney, Nova Scotia from 1892 to 1904, had quite a wide US circulation, reflecting the flow of Gaels across the border. Seattle was attracting Highlanders from Quebec and Prince Edward Island. Many second generation Scottish Canadians drifted south. Four of the children of Finley McRitchie from Lewis, who had settled in Quebec in 1843 aged two, made their lives in the US. A 1934 editorial in *An Gaidheal*, concerned at the diminishing numbers of Gaelic speakers in Scotland, called for a strengthening of links with those in America. From time to time there were efforts to revitalise Gaelic in North America, more successful in Canada than in the US.

One of the most important twentieth-century collectors of Gaelic songs and folklore was the late Margaret Fay Shaw, born in Pennsylvania to a family whose ancestors had emigrated from Scotland to Philadelphia in 1782. She first visited the Hebrides in 1924 and was at once intrigued by the Gaelic tradition. She later lived for six years in South Uist, until her marriage to John Lorne Campbell in 1935. From their base on the island of Canna, they recorded and documented what grew into a uniquely valuable archive of Gaelic material, and explored the Gaeltachd's cultural migrations across the Atlantic.

Language, literature, music, tartan: all of these crossed the Atlantic and survived the passage, even if they did not all transplant equally well. But there were other enthusiasms that travelled with emigrant Scots. There can be few Americans who do not immediately associate pipe bands and tartan with Scotland, but there are probably many who are unaware that ice hockey is the child of shinty, the fast and furious game played at the Duluth Lewis Society picnic. The New York Highlanders Shinty Club was founded in 1903. The aim of the club was, as reported in the *Kingussie Record*, 'to keep alive in the land of [the members'] adoption the game which in their youth, afforded them such delight, and which in some measure at least gave them that grit and pluck which are essential in fighting the stern battle of life'.

Football – soccer – also travelled with Scots, not an exclusively Scottish sport but one that has been played in Scotland for centuries and has dominated Scottish sporting life for more than a hundred years. It's not surprising to find that there were Scottish football teams in the US. Chicago, Pittsburgh, St Louis, Denver, San Francisco, Seattle, Tacoma, New York and Philadelphia all had Scottish teams. The Detroit soccer team was founded by a Scot. The influence of Highland games on modern athletics has already been mentioned.

But of course the Scottish game that Americans have taken to their hearts, and which brings many Americans to Scotland, is golf. Golf, according to historian John Burnett, is, with whisky and people, 'Scotland's greatest export'. Scotland's links, grassy stretches of sandy coastline, were ideal for the development of golf and by the second half of the nineteenth century the game was widely played by Scots and by visitors to Scotland. It was inevitable that it would cross the Atlantic. The first US golf clubs emerged in the

1870s and '80s. One of the earliest grew out of the golfing activities
of John Reid from Fife and his fellow enthusiasts. The resulting St
Andrews Golf Club in Westchester County, New York, had many
members with Scottish connections, including Andrew Carnegie.
Golf soon became popular throughout the US, and in the early
twentieth century professional players were being recruited from
Scotland to tutor Americans. In 1950 it was estimated that the
amount of US land given to golf was equal to a strip of land over
four miles wide extending the length of Scotland.

When Charles Augustus Murray travelled in the US in the 1830s
he was able to state confidently:

> In no other part of the world has my national pride been
> more gratified than in this country; which, abounding as it
> does in settlers from almost every nation in Europe, affords
> a fairer opportunity than can be found at home of compar-
> ing their respective characters under similar circumstances.
> I think I can confirm with equal truth and pleasure, that the
> Scotchmen who have settled in the United States, have earned
> for themselves a higher average character for honesty, perse-
> verance, and enterprise, than their rival settlers from any
> other part of the world.

A similar confidence has influenced the emergence of a Scottish
identity in the US today, with a higher profile than it has had since
the success of the Scottish tobacco traders in Virginia and Maryland
250 years ago. A US Information Agency pamphlet of 1950 argued
that it was impossible 'to determine the exact extent of Scottish
influence – except to say that it is large, and has become part of the
bone and sinew and the character of America'. Similarly, America
has become a part of Scotland. The USA has entered the lives of
Scots in ways that are now so commonplace they are scarcely
noticed: American films, accents, music, language. Some of this is

the return of the Scottish American: there are in the Edinburgh area alone eleven branches of McDonalds. If at times it seems as if the coca-cola culture is obliterating Scottish distinctiveness, there is also a recognition that American influences can be positive and productive. In an interview of 1962 documentary film-maker John Grierson said, 'it was from America that we in Glasgow, Scotland, got our first sight of most things new in the arts'. Grierson himself was hugely influential on both sides of the Atlantic. Glasgow's annual Celtic Connections festival regularly features US artists. American authors at the Edinburgh International Book Festival attract large audiences.

Through the twentieth century the United States retained a magnetic attraction for Scots. It remained the land of opportunity, especially between the wars when Scotland was struggling with economic depression and unemployment. The fact that hard times in the UK were linked with hard times in the US was not necessarily a deterrent. The American dream, sustaining a belief that moving on would bring something better, inspired Scots as it inspired Americans themselves. The sense of space and freedom, so powerfully expressed by Walt Whitman – 'The east and west are mine; and the north and south are mine' – permeated notions of what the USA could offer. Today the belief that the US is a place of energy and possibility, a 'can-do' society, is widespread. There is also a surviving acknowledgement of connection with the Scottish pioneers of the eighteenth and nineteenth centuries. It is captured in Margaret Elphinstone's novel *Voyageurs*, and in Tom Hubbard's sequence of poems, *From Soda Fountain to Moonshine Mountain* (2004). Both explore a kinship between Scot and Indian, celebrated particularly in Hubbard's 'Charles Kerr's Praise-Poem to the Appalachians':

Wadna my ain forefolk, sons o thon same Gret Speerit,
As brithers o aa races hauden-doun and movit-on,

Wadna they bless the embrace o thir twa launds,
My Scotland, my America; oor Alba, oor Appalachia...

The two world wars brought Americans to Scotland in significant numbers, and until recently there was a tangible legacy in American airforce and naval bases. After World War II many Scottish women departed for the US as GI brides, young girls 'jitterbugging up the gangplank' as Lydia Robb's poem 'GI Bride' puts it:

The band playing *California Here I Come*
Then *Auld Lang Syne*

Descendants of these departures, and of the thousands that went before, now return to Scotland curious about the people and places that are part of their heritage. North Sea oil has also brought numbers of Americans working for US companies, who make their home in Scotland, at least temporarily. Meanwhile in the US, a Scotland survives that Scots may not recognise, but which has a powerful reality for those who subscribe to its blend of heightened images. When Scots visit the United States, as they do in increasing numbers, they too respond to icons which may have little relevance to the lives of millions of Americans – Disneyland, Times Square, the Grand Canyon, the Golden Gate.

In the mid-1990s the Scottish writer Duncan McLean travelled to Texas. He was in search of 'western swing', 'square dances, reels, and schottisches, stomps, rags and waltzes... strings, brass and lap steel guitars, jive-talking, yodelling and scatting', an amalgam that could only be American yet, as his description suggests, owes more than a little to music from Scotland. He had stumbled on a western swing recording in an Edinburgh junkshop. His search starts in Nashville, Tennessee, where in a café he finds himself listening to 'Billy Ray Pinkerton, all the way from Elgin,

Alabama'. He doesn't comment on the Scottish connections. His journey ends in McLean, Texas. He drives there from across the border in Oklahoma, where he eats pinto beans and cornbread in a town called Duncan. McLean is on Route 66, the highway from Chicago to Los Angeles, sometimes described as Main Street, America. It is a dusty prairie town, population 849. McLean the writer doesn't tell us who McLean the town is named for, but plenty of Scots made their way to Texas, some probably following Route 66 west.

McLean is a dying town. Its mainstay, a brassiere factory, closed sometime before and there is now little work. The young people leave. 'I walk up the Main Street of McLean, then turn on to the eastbound carriageway of The Main Street of America,' Duncan McLean writes in his account of his trip, *Lone Star Swing* (1997). He ponders the legendary significance of Route 66, and why it is that all journeys seem to head west. 'Travelling west does seem to be associated here with progress, with moving forwards; going east is essentially retrograde, nostalgic.'

In James Kelman's *You Have to Be Careful in the Land of the Free* (2004), the central character, Jeremiah Brown, is about to return to Glasgow after living for twelve years in the United States, contemplating an eastward rather than westward journey. After years of struggling to make a living he feels dispossessed and alien, deeply ambivalent about the realities of American life which force so many into the margins of existence. He is also ambivalent about the images of Scotland current in the US, the tartan, the bagpipes, 'Highland chieftains in the style of auld William Wallace'. In conversation with an American who aspires to visit Scotland he sums up the dream, the Scottish as opposed to the American dream:

> Ye all want to go to the motherland in the off chance ye bump into one of yer ancestors' descendants, a long-lost cousin. What ye hope to discover is if ye are related to a clan

chieftain, if ye are descended from royal blood and maybe own a mountain or something, if ye have any cheap servants at yer disposal, with luck they'll be wearing a kilt and sing praise songs for yer wife and family; bodies like me, we'll call ye sir, hump yer suitcases and dedicate pibroch airs and fiddle tunes to this race of which you are a leading member if not the central progenitor.

This is pretty much what Compton Mackenzie describes in *The Monarch of the Glen*. The Scotland Jeremiah Brown (a name that could as well be American as Scottish) hopes to return to is less romantic but perhaps equally illusory. His picture of home is a Glasgow that would be embraced by his half-American daughter whom he no longer sees, a place of parks and green grass and swings, of mutual support. 'My wee yin would love Glasgow, and people would love her, my faimly.' Although he despises sentiment, and reproves himself for nursing what is probably a fantasy, he dreams of returning to a Scotland of warmth and solid values. 'I read someplace the emigrants werenay the best people, the best people steyed at hame '

Jeremiah has no belief that the Scottish 'home' can be recreated in America, in the way implied by the Grandfather Mountain Games theme song. Scots don't go to America to look for Scotland. They go – and in the twenty-first century they still go – in search of a new life, a different experience, images nurtured over the last hundred years by song and screen rather than by emigration agents and letters from the New World. They may go, as Jeremiah did, to escape from Scotland. They may go because west is the hopeful direction.

Duncan McLean heads west on a journey that started in Orkney. When he checks in at the Cactus Inn, McLean, Texas, the desk clerk is puzzled: 'Your name, he says, It's the same as this town.'

'I know,' is the reply.

MAP 1: Scotland

Shetland Islands

Lerwick

0 10 20 30 40 50 60 70 80 kilometres

North

Orkney Islands
Stromness
Pentland Firth
Thurso

Lewis Stornoway
Caithness
Sutherland
Kildonan

Loch Broom

North Uist Harris
Wester Ross
Easter Ross
Dornoch
Cromarty Moray Firth
Forres Craigellachie Peterhead
Benbecula
Strathglass Inverness Dufftown
Banff
South Uist
Kintail
River Spey
Barra
Knoydart Aberdeen
Glengarry
Morar
Fort William
Angus Montrose
Coll
Tobermory Morven Glencoe River Tay Aberfeldy
Tiree
Mull Glen Dochart Killin Dundee Firth of Tay
Iona Perth
Argyll
Colonsay Jura Stirling Fife
Alloa
River Forth Kirkcaldy Firth of Forth
Greenock Dumbarton Falkirk Leith
Islay Bute Paisley Glasgow Edinburgh
River Clyde
Lanark Kelso
Arran Kilmarnock Selkirk
Campbeltown Ayr Hawick
Kintyre
Firth of Clyde
Galloway Dumfries

Solway Firth

216

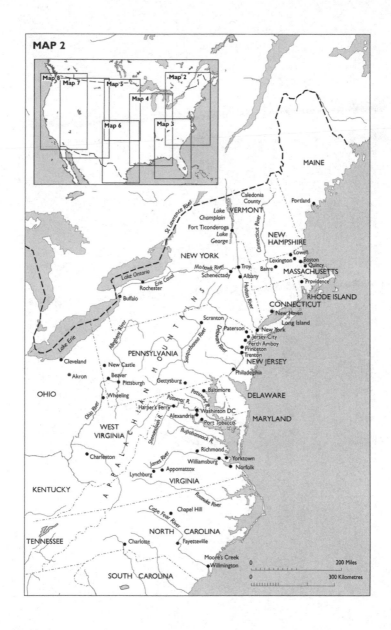

MAP 2

Map 8 Map 7 Map 5 Map 2
        Map 4
        Map 6 Map 3

MAINE

Caledonia
County
Portland

Lake
Champlain
VERMONT
Fort Ticonderoga
Lake
George
NEW
HAMPSHIRE

Lowell
Lexington Boston
Barre Quincy
MASSACHUSETTS
Providence
RHODE ISLAND

St Lawrence River

Connecticut River

NEW YORK

Mohawk River Troy
Schenectady Albany

Lake Ontario
Erie Canal
Rochester

Hudson River

Buffalo

CONNECTICUT
New Haven
Long Island

Lake Erie

Scranton
Paterson
Jersey City
Perth Amboy
Princeton
Trenton
NEW JERSEY

New York

Allegheny River

Susquehanna River

Delaware River

Cleveland
New Castle
PENNSYLVANIA

Akron
Beaver
Pittsburgh
Gettysburg
Philadelphia

OHIO

Wheeling

Baltimore
DELAWARE

Ohio River

Harper's Ferry
Potomac R.
Washinton DC
Alexandria
Port Tobacco
MARYLAND

Patapsco R.

WEST
VIRGINIA

Shenandoah R.

Rupahannock R.

Charleston

James River

Richmond

Williamsburg Yorktown
Norfolk

KENTUCKY

Lynchburg Appomattox
VIRGINIA

Roanoke River

Cape Fear River Chapel Hill

NORTH CAROLINA

TENNESSEE

Charlotte Fayetteville

Moore's Creek
Wilmington

SOUTH CAROLINA

0   200 Miles

0   300 Kilometres

APPALACHIAN MOUNTAINS

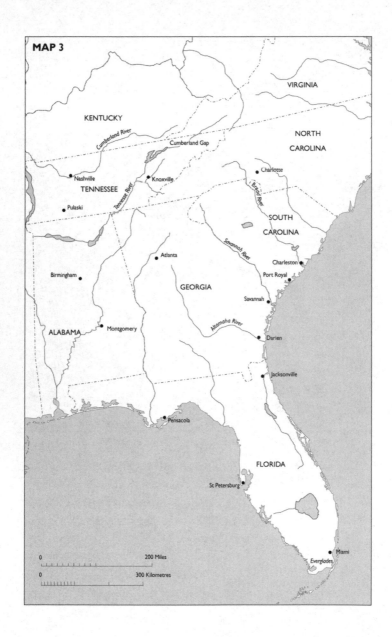

MAP 3

VIRGINIA

KENTUCKY

Cumberland River

Cumberland Gap

NORTH
CAROLINA

Charlotte

Nashville

Knoxville

TENNESSEE

Tennessee River

Broad River

Pulaski

SOUTH
CAROLINA

Atlanta

Savannah River

Charleston

Birmingham

Port Royal

GEORGIA

Savannah

ALABAMA

Montgomery

Altamaha River

Darien

Jacksonville

Pensacola

FLORIDA

St Petersburg

Miami

Everglades

| 0 | | 200 Miles |
| 0 | | 300 Kilometres |

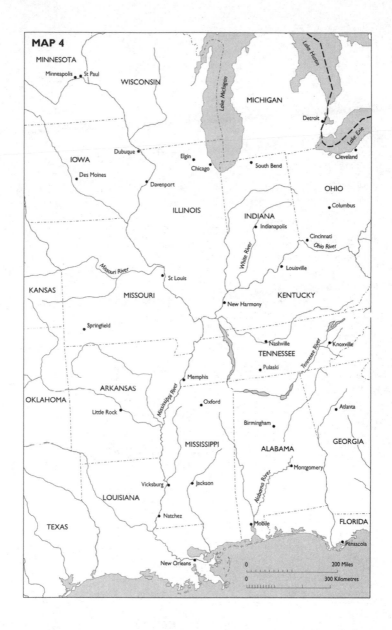

MAP 4

MINNESOTA
Minneapolis • • St Paul
WISCONSIN
MICHIGAN
Lake Michigan
Lake Huron
Detroit •
Lake Erie
IOWA
Dubuque •
Elgin •
Chicago •
• South Bend
Cleveland •
Des Moines •
Davenport •
OHIO
Columbus •
ILLINOIS
INDIANA
• Indianapolis
White River
Cincinnati •
Ohio River
Missouri River
St Louis •
Louisville •
KANSAS
MISSOURI
KENTUCKY
• New Harmony
Springfield •
Nashville •
TENNESSEE
Tennessee River
Knoxville •
• Pulaski
ARKANSAS
Mississippi River
Memphis •
OKLAHOMA
• Oxford
Atlanta •
Little Rock •
Birmingham •
MISSISSIPPI
ALABAMA
GEORGIA
Alabama River
• Montgomery
Vicksburg •
• Jackson
LOUISIANA
TEXAS
• Natchez
Mobile •
FLORIDA
Pensacola •
New Orleans •

0   200 Miles
0   300 Kilometres

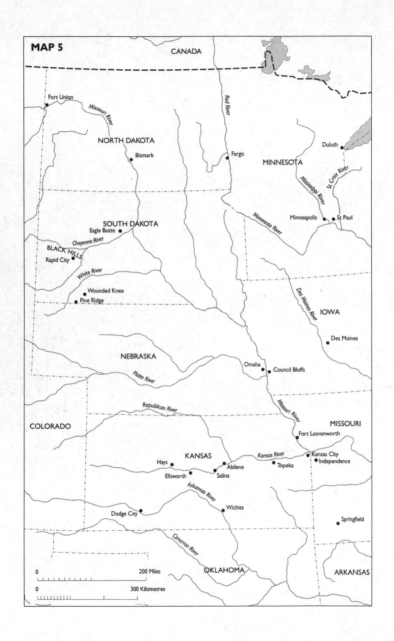

MAP 5

CANADA

Fort Union

Missouri River

NORTH DAKOTA

Bismark

Red River

Fargo

MINNESOTA

Duluth

St Croix River

Mississippi River

Minneapolis ● ● St Paul

Minnesota River

SOUTH DAKOTA

Eagle Butte

Cheyenne River

BLACK HILLS

Rapid City

White River

Wounded Knee

Pine Ridge

Des Moines River

IOWA

Des Moines

NEBRASKA

Platte River

Omaha ● Council Bluffs

Republican River

Missouri River

COLORADO

MISSOURI

Fort Leavenworth

KANSAS

Kansas River

Kansas City

Independence

Hays

Abilene

Topeka

Ellsworth

Salina

Arkansas River

Dodge City

Wichita

Springfield

Cimarron River

OKLAHOMA

ARKANSAS

0   200 Miles

0   300 Kilometres

220

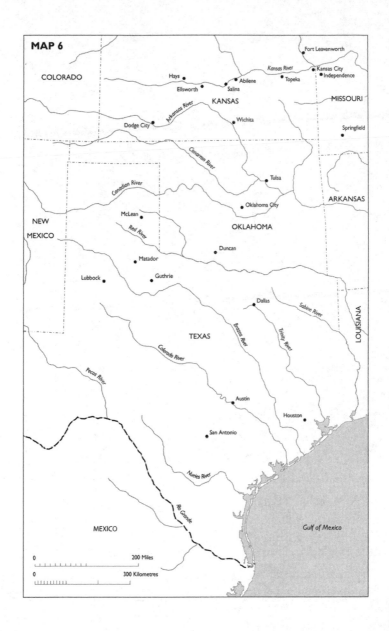

MAP 6

COLORADO

Fort Leavenworth

Kansas River

Kansas City
Independence

Hays

Ellsworth

Abilene
Salina

Topeka

MISSOURI

KANSAS

Arkansas River

Wichita

Dodge City

Springfield

Cimarron River

Tulsa

Canadian River

NEW
MEXICO

McLean

Red River

Oklahoma City

ARKANSAS

OKLAHOMA

Duncan

Matador

Lubbock

Guthrie

Dallas

Sabine River

LOUISIANA

TEXAS

Brazos River

Trinity River

Colorado River

Pecos River

Austin

Houston

San Antonio

Nueces River

Rio Grande

MEXICO

Gulf of Mexico

0   200 Miles

0   300 Kilometres

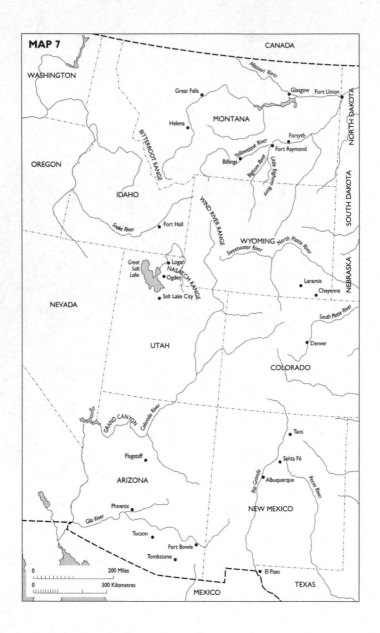

MAP 7

CANADA

WASHINGTON

Missouri River

Great Falls

Glasgow   Fort Union

MONTANA

Helena

BITTERROOT RANGE

OREGON

Forsyth

Yellowstone River   Fort Raymond

Billings

Bighorn River

Little Bighorn River

IDAHO

WIND RIVER RANGE

Snake River   Fort Hall

WYOMING   North Platte River

Sweetwater River

NEBRASKA

SOUTH DAKOTA

NORTH DAKOTA

Great
Salt
Lake   Logan

WASATCH RANGE

Ogden

Laramie

Cheyenne

NEVADA   Salt Lake City

UTAH

South Platte River

Denver

COLORADO

GRAND CANYON

Colorado River

Taos

Flagstaff

Santa Fé

ARIZONA

Albuquerque

Rio Grande

Pecos River

NEW MEXICO

Phoenix

Gila River

Tucson

Fort Bowie

Tombstone

El Paso

0   200 Miles

0   300 Kilometres

MEXICO   TEXAS

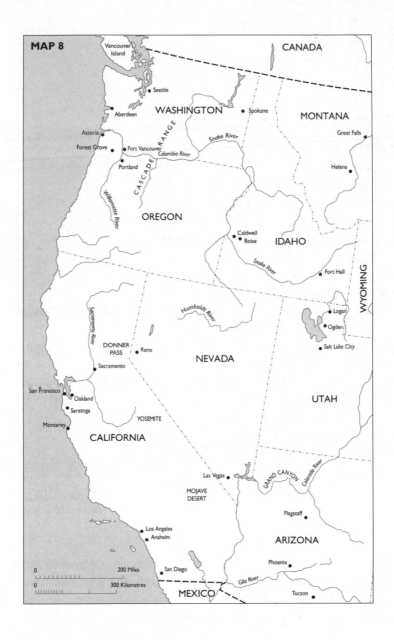

MAP 8

CANADA

Vancouver
Island

Seattle

WASHINGTON

Spokane

MONTANA

Aberdeen

Astoria

Forest Grove

Fort Vancouver

Great Falls

Snake River

Columbia River

Portland

Helena

CASCADE RANGE

Willamette River

OREGON

Caldwell
Boise

IDAHO

Snake River

Fort Hall

WYOMING

Sacramento River

Humboldt River

Logan

Ogden

Salt Lake City

DONNER
PASS

Reno

NEVADA

Sacramento

San Fransisco

Oakland

Saratoga

UTAH

Monterey

YOSEMITE

CALIFORNIA

Las Vegas

MOJAVE
DESERT

GRAND CANYON

Colorado River

Flagstaff

ARIZONA

Los Angeles
Anaheim

Phoenix

0   200 Miles

0   300 Kilometres

San Diego

Gila River

Tucson

MEXICO

223

Chronology

1611 Scots begin to settle in Ulster
1620 Pilgrim Fathers arrive in New England
1624 Virginia becomes first British crown colony
1626 Dutch found New Amsterdam
1630 British colonists begin to settle in New England in significant numbers
1650 Battle of Dunbar; Covenanter prisoners transported to New England
1651 Battle of Worcester; more Covenanter prisoners transported
1657 Charitable Association of Boston founded, first Scottish association in the colonies
1663 Navigation Act barring Scottish involvement in colonial trade
1664 British gain Dutch colony of New Amsterdam, becomes New York
1668 Port Glasgow built for American trade
1670 Hudson's Bay Company set up
1683 First Scottish colony, East New Jersey
1684 Scottish settlement at Stuart's Town, South Carolina
1689 James VII and II deposed, William III becomes king
1693 Foundation of College of William and Mary by James Blair
1695 Company of Scotland founded
1698 Scottish colony founded at Darien, on isthmus of Panama
1704 John Campbell starts America's first newspaper, the *Boston News-letter*
1707 Union of Scottish and English parliaments

1715   Jacobite Rising; Jacobite prisoners transported to colonies
1718   Substantial immigration of Ulster Scots begins
1729   First St Andrews Society founded in Charleston, South Carolina
1736   Recruitment of Highlanders to settle Georgia
1738   Settlement of Argyll families at Lake George, New York
1739   Organised settlement of Highlanders along Cape Fear River, North Carolina
1746   Defeat of Jacobites at Culloden; College of New Jersey (Princeton University) founded
1747   Philadelphia St Andrews Society founded
1748   British defeat of Spain
1755   Outbreak of French and Indian War
1758   Glasgow dominates colonial tobacco trade
1763   Treaty of Paris
1765   Stamp Act; James Wilson sails for Philadelphia
1768   John Witherspoon sails for Philadelphia
1772   Scots American Company of Farmers formed
1773   Boston tea party
1774   First Continental Congress meets in Philadelphia
1776   Declaration of Independence signed; Battle of Moore's Creek
1783   Treaty of Paris
1787   Constitution of USA agreed
1788   Burns published in USA
1789   University of North Carolina at Chapel Hill chartered
1803   Louisiana Purchase; first of several UK Passenger Acts
1804   Lewis and Clark expedition sets off from St Louis
1807   UK abolition of slave trade
1808   Importation of slaves into US banned
1812   War between Britain and US
1814   Battle of Horseshoe Bend

1823 David Douglas's first collecting trip to US
1825 Community of New Harmony set up in Indiana by
       Robert Owen
1836 Texas declaration of independence; the Alamo, San
       Antonio, falls to Mexican forces
1838 Cherokees and other tribes forced west on the 'Trail of
       Tears'
1842 Allan Pinkerton leaves Glasgow for Chicago
1845 Texas joins the US; US invades Mexico
1846 Potato blight in Scotland; Smithsonian Institution
       founded in Washington, DC
1848 Treaty of Guadalupe Hidalgo gives New Mexico and
       California to the US; Carnegie family leaves Dunfermline
       for Pittsburgh; discovery of gold in California
1849 Muir family leaves Dunbar for Wisconsin
1852 *Uncle Tom's Cabin* by Harriet Beecher Stowe published
1859 John Brown attacks US arsenal at Harper's Ferry
1861 Outbreak of American Civil War
1862 Homestead Act
1863 President Lincoln gives Gettysburg Address
1865 General Lee surrenders at Appomattox courthouse; Ku
       Klux Klan founded
1867 Chisholm Trail opened from Texas to Abilene, Kansas
1869 Transcontinental railroad completed
1870 Scottish American Investment Trust set up
1873 Beginning of major Scottish investment in American West
1876 Battle of the Little Bighorn
1882 Matador Land and Cattle Company set up
1886 Crofters Act; Apache chief Geronimo surrenders to
       General Crook
1890 Massacre at Wounded Knee Creek; John Muir founds
       Yosemite National Park
1892 Strike at Homestead Steelworks, Pennsylvania

1901 Carnegie sells his steel holdings for $400 million
1945 With end of World War II 'GI brides' depart for US
1956 Grandfather Mountain Highland Games founded in
        North Carolina
1974 Foundation of Council of Scottish Clans and
        Associations
1998 National Tartan Day established as US annual event
1999 Re-established Scottish Parliament opens

Places to Visit

Scotland

EVIDENCE OF THE place of emigration in Scotland's history can be found in small museums all over the country. The **Museum of Scotland** in Edinburgh has a gallery on emigration and Scots abroad called 'Scotland and the World' which includes American material. The **National War Museum** in Edinburgh Castle has displays relating to Scottish regiments involved in North American wars.

The **People's Palace** museum in Glasgow and the **McLean Museum** in Greenock have material related to the Clyde's connections with North America. The **Andrew Carnegie Birthplace Museum** in Dunfermline displays material related to Carnegie's life and work. Material on Burns, Scott and Stevenson, whose work had a huge impact on the US, can be found at Edinburgh's **Writers' Museum**.

Many museums display material connected with departures from Scotland and the circumstances behind them. Some of these are: the **Highland Folk Museum**, Kingussie; **Timespan**, Helmsdale; **Cromarty Courthouse Museum** in Easter Ross; **Laing Museum**, Newburgh; **Forres Museum**, Moray.

For archive and genealogical material visit the **Scottish National Archive** and the **National Library of Scotland**, both in Edinburgh. The **SEALLAM! Visitor Centre**, Northton, Harris, focuses on material relating to emigration from the Western Isles and has a wealth of genealogical information.

USA

MANY HISTORY MUSEUMS and historic sites in the US contain material that relates to Scottish experience even if Scots are not specifically identified. What follows is a highly selective list. More information can be obtained from www.MuseumsUSA.org.

Ellis Island Immigration Museum, New York, contains displays and information relating to immigration from 1892. The **National Museum of American History,** part of Washington's **Smithsonian Institution,** includes material on settlement, the American Revolution, and many other aspects of US history in which Scots were involved. Most states and cities have historical societies, some of which maintain their own museums. Three museums relating specifically to the expanding frontier are the **Museum of the Fur Trade,** Chalron, Nebraska; the **Museum of Westward Expansion,** St Louis, Missouri, and the **Emigrant Trail Museum,** Truckee, California. **The Alamo,** San Antonio, Texas, commemorates the famous defeat.

In southern states places and events of interest include **The Scottish Heritage Center** at St Andrews Presbyterian College, Laurinburg, North Carolina; **Moore's Creek** battlefield site, North Carolina, US National Parks; Scottish Heritage Days, a festival of Scottish-American links held at Darien, Georgia under the auspices of **Fort King George,** Historic Site; **North Carolina Scottish Heritage Society;** the **Malcolm Blue Farm,** Aberdeen, North Carolina.

Museums and sites related to Scots in California include the **Stevenson House** at Monterey, the **Silverado Museum** at St Helena, the **San Francisco Cable Car Museum,** the **John Muir National Historic Site, Golden Gate Park,** and the **Balclutha,** a Clyde-built sailing ship at the **San Francisco Maritime National Historic Park.**

Bibliography

Included in this list are all the books referred to in the text, and other relevant sources.

Adams, Ian and Somerville, Meredith: *Cargoes of Despair and Hope*, Edinburgh, 1993

Allsop, Kenneth: *Hard Travellin'*, London, 1967

Andrews, EW with Andrews, Charles McLean (eds): *Journal of a Lady of Quality*, New Haven, 1934–43

Aspinwall, Bernard: *Portable Utopia: Glasgow and the United States 1820–1920*, Aberdeen, 1984

Bailyn, Bernard and Barbara DeWolfe: *Voyagers to the West: Emigration from Britain to America on the Eve of Revolution*, New York, 1986

Baines, RT Dudley: *Emigration from Europe 1815–1930*, Basingstoke, 1991

Bird, Isabella: *A Lady's Life in the Rocky Mountains*, London, 1982

Black, George F: *Scotland's Mark on America*, New York, 1921

Blake, George: *Down to the Sea*, London, 1937

Blaustein, Richard: *The Thistle and the River: Historical Links and Cultural Parallels Between Scotland and Appalachia. Contributions to Southern Appalachian Studies*, 7, Jefferson, 2003

Boswell, James: *Journal of a Tour to the Hebrides*, London, 1785

Brock, William: *Scotus Americanus: A Survey of the Sources for Links Between Scotland and America in the 18th Century*, Edinburgh, 1982

Bronson, Edgar: *Reminiscences of a Ranchman*, Lincoln, 1962

Cage, RA (ed): *The Scots Abroad 1750–1914: Labour, Capital, Experience*, London, 1985

Calder, Jenni: *There Must Be a Lone Ranger: The Myth and Reality of the American West*, London, 1974

— (ed) *Present Poets 2: Scotland to the World to Scotland*, Edinburgh, 1999
— *Scots in Canada*, Edinburgh, 2003

Carnegie, Andrew: *Autobiography*, Boston, 1986

Carrothers, WS: *Emigration from the British Isles*, London, 1965

Chambers, W: *The Emigrant's Manual: British America and the USA*, Edinburgh, 1851
— *Things as They Are in America*, Edinburgh, 1857
— *The Emigrants' Guide to the United States and the Dominion of Canada*, 1872

Cohen, Michael: *The Pathless Way: John Muir and American Wilderness*, Madison, 1984

Coleman, Terry: *Passage to America*, London, 1972

Court, Franklin: *The Scottish Connection: The Rise of English Literary Study in Early America*, Syracuse, 2001

Cunningham, Tom: *The Diamond's Ace: Scotland and the Native Americans*, Edinburgh, 2001

Dakin, Susan Bryant: *A Scotch Paisano in Los Angeles*, 1978

Defoe, Daniel: *Tour Thro' the Whole Island of Great Britain*, ed GDH Cole, London, 1927

Devine, TM: *The Tobacco Lords*, Edinburgh, 1970
— *A Scottish Firm in Virginia, 1767–1777: W Cunninghame and Company*, Edinburgh, 1984
— (ed) *Scottish Emigration and Scottish Society*, Edinburgh, 1992
— *Scotland's Empire 1600–1815*, London, 2003

Dobson, David: *Scottish Emigration to Colonial America, 1607–1785*, Athens, Georgia, 1994

Doig, Ivan: *This House of Sky: Landscapes of the Western Mind*, 1987

Donaldson, Emily Ann: *The Scottish Highland Games in America*, Gretna, 1986

Dixon, Thomas: *The Clansman: An Historical Romance of the Ku Klux Klan*, New York, 1905

Dudgeon, Thomas: *A Nine Years Residence and a Nine Months Tour on Foot in the States of New York and Pennsylvania*, Edinburgh, 1841

Eckhardt, Celia Morris: *Fanny Wright, Rebel in America*, Cambridge, Massachusetts, 1984

Edwards, OD and George Shepperson (eds): *Scotland, Europe and the American Revolution*, Edinburgh, 1976

Elphinstone, Margaret: *Voyageurs*, Edinburgh, 2004

Erickson, Charlotte: *Invisible Immigrants: The Adaption of English and Scottish Immigrants in 19th century America*, Ithaca, 1972

Faulkner, William: *Intruder in the Dust*, London, 1949

Ferguson, Fergus: *From Glasgow to Missouri*, Glasgow, 1878

Fischer, David Hackett: *Albion's Seed: Four British Folkways in America*, New York, 1989

Fitzgerald, Patrick and Ikringill, Steve(eds): *Atlantic Crossroads. Historical Connections Between Scotland, Ulster and North America*, Newtownards, 2001

Fitzpatrick, Rory: *God's Frontersmen: The Scots-Irish Epic*, London, 1989

Flint, James: *Letters from America*, Edinburgh, 1822

Fry, Michael: *The Scottish Empire*, Edinburgh, 2002
— *Bold, Independent, Unconquer'd and Free: How the Scots Made America Safe for Liberty, Democracy and Capitalism*, Ayr, 2003

Furnas, JC: *The Americans: A Social History of the United States 1587–1914*, New York, 1969

Galt, John: *Lawrie Todd or Settlers in the Woods*, London, 1832

Gibson, Rob: *Plaids and Bandanas: from Highland Drover to Wild West Cowboy*, Edinburgh, 2003

Gilchrist, MM: *Patrick Ferguson 'A Man of Some Genius'*, Edinburgh, 2003

Graham, Ian Charles Cargill: *Colonists from Scotland: Emigration to North America, 1707–1783*, Ithaca, 1956

Graham, RB Cunninghame: *The North American Sketches*, ed John Walker, Edinburgh, 1986

Grahame, Fred B (ed): *The Diary of William Richard Grahame in the United States and Canada, 1831–1833*, Dundas, Ontario,

Grant, Anne: *Journal of an American Lady*, New York, 1901

Griffin, Patrick: *The People with No Name: Ireland's Ulster Scots, America's Scots Irish, and the Creation of a British Atlantic World 1689–1764*, Princeton, 2001

Hamilton, Thomas: *Men and Manners in America*, Edinburgh, 1833

Harper, Marjory: *Adventurers and Exiles: The Great Scottish Exodus*, London, 2003

Haws, Charles H: *Scots in the Old Dominion 1685–1800*, Edinburgh, 1980

Herman, Arthur: *The Scottish Enlightenment: How the Scots Invented the Modern World*, London, 2002

Hewitson, Jim: *Tam Blake & Co: The Story of the Scots in America*, Edinburgh, 1993

Hook, Andrew: *Scotland and America 1750–1835*, Glasgow, 1975
— *From Goosecreek to Gandercleuch: Studies in Scottish-American Literary and Cultural History*, East Linton, 1999

Horan, James D: *The Pinkertons: The Detective Dynasty that Made History*, New York, 1967

Hubbard, Tom: *From Soda Fountain to Moonshine Mountain*, Kirkcaldy, 2004

Hunter, James: *A Dance Called America*, Edinburgh, 1994
— *Glencoe and the Indians*, Edinburgh, 1996

Irving, Washington: *Tour in Scotland, 1817*, ed Stanley T Williams, Newhaven, 1927

Jackson, W Turrentine: *The Enterprising Scot: Investors in the American West after 1873*, Edinburgh,1968

Karras, Alan A: *Sojourners in the Sun: Scottish Migrants in Jamaica and the Chesapeake 1740–1800*, Ithaca, 1992

Kelly, Douglas, with Kelly, Caroline Switzer: *Carolina Scots: An Historical and Genealogical Study of over 100 Years of Emigration*, Dillon, 1998

Kelman, James: *You Have to be Careful in the Land of the Free*, London, 2004

Krass, Peter: *Carnegie*, Hoboken, 2002

Landsman, N: *Scotland and Its First American Colony, 1683–1765*, Princeton, 1985

Lavender, David: *The Penguin Book of the American West*, Harmondsworth, 1969

Lehmann, WC: *Scottish and Scotch-Irish Contributions to Early American Life and Culture*, New York, 1978

MacDonnel, Margaret: *The Emigrant Experience: Songs of the Highland Emigrants in North America*, University of Toronto Press, Toronto, 1982

Macinnes, Allan I, Harper, Marjory-Ann D and Fryer, Linda G (eds): *Scotland and the Americas, c.1650–c.1939*, Edinburgh, 2002

Mackay, Alexander: *The Western World and Travels in the US 1846 and 1847, 1849*

Mackenzie, Compton: *The Monarch of the Glen*, London, 1941

Mackenzie, Eneas: *An Historical, Topographical, and Descriptive View of the United States of America*, Newcastle, 1819

McLean, Norman: *A River Runs Through It*, Chicago, 1976

MacRae, David: *The Americans at Home: Pen and Ink Sketches of American Men, Manners, and Institutions*, New York, 1868
— *American Presidents and Men I Have Met*, Glasgow, 1908

Meyer, Duane: *The Highland Scots of North Carolina, 1732–1776*, Chapel Hill, 1961

Miller, Sally M: *John Muir: Life and Work*, University of Mexico Press, Albuquerque, 1993

Mitchell, Ann Lindsay: *David Douglas: Explorer and Botanist*, London, 1999

Muir, John: *The Story of My Boyhood and Youth*, ed Frank Tindall, Edinburgh, 1987

Murray, Charles Augustus: *Travels in North America*, London, 1854

Newton, Michael: *We're Indians Sure Enough: The Legacy of the Scottish Highlanders in the United States*, Saorsa Media, 2001

'Old Scene Painter': *The Emigrant's Guide, or A Picture of America*, London, 1816

Parker, Anthony: *Scottish Highlanders in Colonial Georgia: The Recruitment, Emigration and Settlement at Darien, 1735–1748*, Athens, 1997

Pennant, Thomas, *Tour of Scotland and a Voyage to the Hebrides*, London, 1773

Pinkerton, Allan, *Spy of the Rebellion*, New York, 1883

Preston, Richard Arthur (ed): *For Friends at Home: A Scottish Emigrant's Letters from Canada, California and the Cariboo 1844–1864*, Montreal, 1974

Ray, Celeste: *Highland Heritage: Scottish Americans in the American South*, Chapel Hill, 2001

Redmond, Gerald: *The Caledonian Games in Nineteenth-Century America*, Cranbury, Nova Scotia, 1971

Regan, John: *The Western Wilds of America*, Edinburgh, 1859

Richards, Eric: *The Highland Clearances*, Edinburgh, 2000

Ross, Peter: *The Scot in America*, New York, 1896

Ruddock, Ted (ed): *Travels in the Colonies in 1773–1775, Described in the Letters of William Mylne*, Athens, Georgia, 1993

Rush, Benjamin: *The Autobiography of Benjamin Rush*, ed George W Corner, Princeton, 1948

Scotus Americanus: *Information Concerning the Province of North Carolina*, Glasgow, 1773

Scott, Walter: *Rob Roy*, Edinburgh, 1817

Sher, RB and Smitten, JR (eds): *Scotland and America in the Age of Enlightenment*, Edinburgh, 1990

Stevenson, Robert Louis: *From the Clyde to California*, ed Andrew Noble, Aberdeen, 1985 [includes *The Amateur Emigrant* and *Across the Plains*]

Stuart, James: *Three Years in North America*, New York, 1833

Szasz, Ferenc: *Scots in the North American West 1790–1917*, Norman, 2000

Van Vugt, William: *Britain to America: Mid-Nineteenth-Century Immigrants to the United States*, Chicago, 1999

Ward, Jean M and Maveety, Elaine A (eds): *Pacific Northwest Women 1815–1925*, Corvallis, 1995

Wills, Gary, *Inventing America: Jefferson's Declaration of Independence*, New York, 1978

Wright, Frances: *Views of Society and Manners in America*, Cambridge, Mass, 1963

Zinn, Howard: *A People's History of the United States 1492–Present*, New York, 2001

Abercrombie, Lord James, 9
Aberdeen, 4, 30, 45, 46, 69, 75, 135,180,
    184, 185
Aberdeen Journal, 12
Aberdeen, North Carolina, 206
Aberdeenshire, 29, 35, 76, 165, 167, 180,
    181, 184
Abilene, 161
Academy of Natural Sciences, 127
Across the Plains, 155
Act of Union, 3, 5, 27, 54, 194
Adams, John, 67, 68
Adamson, AD, 164
Affleck, Thomas, 129
Agar, Herbert, 144
Ainslie, Hew, 114
Airlie, 160
Airlie, Earl of, 160, 161
Aitken, Andrew and Ann, 170, 171
Akron, 170
Alabama, 90, 93 136, 141, 142, 184, 213
Alamo, The, 132-33
Alamo, The (film), 132
Albany, 48, 49, 50, 52, 170, 185
Albany Gazette, 129
Alasdair, Alasdair MacMhaighstir, 142
Alexander Walker & Co, 57
Alexandria, 55, 56
Alison, Francis, 70
Allason, William, 57
Allegheny City, 171
Allegheny Mountains, 36, 43, 45, 88, 91, 97,
    116, 144
Allen, David, 11, 17
Allison, Ebenezer, 143
Allison, Margaret, 143
Alloa, 130
Altamaha River, 33
Altowan, 109
Amalgamated Association, 173
Amateur Emigrant, The, 23, 187–88
American Farmer, The, 127
American Fur Company, 106, 107
American Iona Society, 208
American Iron Works, 76
American Mortgage Company of Scotland, 159
American National Livestock Corporation, 162
American Ornithology, 127
American Review, 193
American Volunteers, 81
Americans at Home, The, 143
Anaheim, 182, 183
Anchor Line, 22, 95, 188

Ancrum, 73
Anderson, Alexander, 181
Anderson, Rev James, 60
Angus, William 'Red', 164
Annan, 56
Annandale, 37
Annapolis, 66
Antietam, 144
Antrim, 199
Apache people, 151
Appalachian Mountains, 28, 34, 62, 91, 99,
    103, 141, 201, 202
Appin, 89
Appomattox Court House, 144
Arbroath, 122, 181, 192
Argyle, 130
Argyll, 7, 38, 41, 42, 48, 51, 73, 82, 182,
    206, 208
Argyll, Earl of. See Campbell, Archibald,
    Earl of Argyll
Argyll Patent, 51
Arizona, 151, 152, 160, 165
Arizona Copper Company, 160
Arkansas, 141, 147, 148
Arnprior Society for Emigrants, 12
Arran, 49
Arthur, Peter, 184
Ashleigh River, 32
Astor, John Jacob, 105, 106
Astoria, 106, 107
Atlantic Ocean, 1, 2, 5, 7, 10, 11, 14, 21, 22,
    27, 33, 41, 45, 49, 55, 57, 73, 84, 95, 101,
    120, 125, 164, 179, 184, 185, 193, 195,
    198, 201, 203, 210
Atlantic and Ohio Telegraph, 171
Atlantic Steam Ferry Company, 122
Augusta, 43, 64
Australia, 185
Autobiography (Carnegie), 174
Autobiography (Fletcher), 86
Autobiography (Jefferson), 70
Ayr, 113, 127
Ayrshire, 32, 55, 69, 83, 114, 118, 121, 122,
    126, 127, 149
Azores, 56

Bahamas, 62
Bailyn, Bernard, 44
Bain, Aly, 202
Bain, George, 180
Baird, James, 165
Ballindalloch, 35
Balmoral, 11, 205

Baltimore, 55, 88, 98, 109
Banff, 184
Banffshire, 129, 154
Bank of the United States, 56
Barclay, Robert, of Urie, 29, 30
Barre, 185
Barrie, JM, 199
Bass, Sam, 201
Basse, Jeremiah, 31
Bath, 90
Battle of Bloody Marsh, 33
Battle of Bull Run, 142, 143, 144
Battle of Culloden, 7, 9, 76, 77
Battle of Dunbar, 4, 54
Battle of Horseshoe Bend, 93, 94, 132
Battle of Princeton, 76
Battle of San Jacinto, 133, 134
Battle of Worcester, 4
Baxters (Dundee), 179
Beaver, 170
Belfast, 8, 31, 93
Bell, Ninian, 54
Bennett, James Gordon, 129
Bermuda, 51, 62
Berwickshire, 122
Beside the Bonnie Brier Bush, 199
Bethune, Joanna, 125
Big Raft Swamp, 82
Biggar, 120
Bighorn River, 105
Billings, 166
Billy the Kid. See Bonney, William
Bird, Isabella, 158
Birth of a Nation, The, 146
Black Hills, 154
Black Sea, 80
Black Watch, 9
Blackfeet people, 105
Blackwood's Magazine, 101, 174, 198
Bladen County, 38
Bladensburg, 55
Bladnoch, 121
Blair Atholl, 185
Blair, James, 59
Blairdrummond, 68
Blake, George, 2, 199
Blantyre, 181
Blaustein, Richard, 202
Blue, Duncan, 82
Blue, Malcolm, 206
Bogle Corbet, 18
Boise Valley, 165
Bonney, William, 'Billy the Kid', 162

Boone, Daniel, 44
Boonesborough, 44
Borders (Scotland), 4, 8, 17, 30, 73, 139,
    144, 165, 201
Borlum, 33
Borthwick, JD, 113, 136
Borthwick, James, 20
Borthwick, Robert, 180
Boston, 4, 66, 67, 90, 95, 122, 129, 185,
    189, 192
Boston Scotsman, 195
Boswell, James, 203
Botany Bay, 86
Botineau, 155
Bowie, James, 132
Boyd, John, 60
Brackenridge, William Dunlop, 127
Braddock, 173
Braemar Gathering, 205
Braemar Highland Society, 205
Brandywine, 76, 80
Brazil, 162
Brazilian Land and Cattle Company, 162
Bridgewater, 59
Bristol, 54
British Chronicle, 130
British Columbia, 108
British North America. See Canada
Broad River, 36
Brock, William R, 61
Bronson, Edgar, 152
Brooklyn, 122, 123
Broomielaw, 22, 170
Brown, Rev Clark, 110
Brown, George, 130
Brown, John, 141, 176
Brown, Jonas, 36
Brown, Peter, 130
Brown, Tabitha Moffat, 110
Brownlee, James, 120
Bruce, James, 155
Bruce, Robert, King of Scots, 195
Buchan, Earl of, see Erskine, David, Earl of
    Buchan
Buchanan, President James, 145
Buchanan Street, Glasgow, 55
Buchanan, Thomas, 51
Buchanan, Walter, 51
Buffalo Bill, see Cody, William
Buffalo, New York, 166, 170, 180
Buffalo, Wyoming, 164
Burden, Henry, 122
Burgoyne, General John, 81

Burnett, John, 210
Burnett, Robert, 165
Burns Clubs, 193, 194
Burns, George, 95
Burns, James, 95
Burns, Robert, 101, 193, 194, 195, 200
Burntisland, 20
Burr, Aaron, 83
Businessmen's Union of Minneapolis, 180
Bute, Lord. See Stewart, John, Earl of Bute
Butler, Major John, 79
Butler's Rangers, 79

Caithness, 38, 50
Caldwell, 165
Caledonia County, 12
Caledonia Grove, 182
Caledonian, The, 130, 195
Caledonian Advertiser, The, 130, 195
Caledonian Clubs, 204, 207
Caledonian Mercury, 13, 14, 58
Caledonian Volunteers, 79
California, 24, 37, 109, 122, 128, 133,
   134–36, 141, 154, 155, 158, 160, 165,
   182–83, 207
Cameron, 90
Cameron, Dougald, 90
Cameron, Gilbert, 185
Cameron, Colonel James, 142
Cameron Guards, 142
Cameron Rifles, 142
Cameron's Highlanders, 142
Campbell, Alexander (merchant), 26, 89
Campbell, Alexander (stonemason), 143
Campbell, Archibald, Earl of Argyll, 31
Campbell, Charles, 164
Campbell, Duncan, 122
Campbell, Sir George, 32
Campbell, Glen, 202
Campbell, Henry, 162
Campbell, Hugh, 38
Campbell, James, 143
Campbell, John (Maryland), 55
Campbell, John (stonemason), 185
Campbell, John A, 143
Campbell, John Lorne, 209
Campbell, Captain Lachlan, 7, 48
Campbell, Lord Neil, 31–2
Campbell, Robert, 107
Campbell, Samuel, 43
Campbell, Thomas, 1, 26
Campbell, Colonel William, 81
Campbelltown, 38

Campbeltown, 38, 91, 182
Canada, 3, 9, 17, 18, 25, 47, 85, 88, 99,
   120, 126, 152, 155, 166, 175, 180, 192,
   207, 209
Canada Company, 101
Canadian Pacific Railway, 181
Canna, 209
Cape Fear River, 27, 37, 38, 41, 42, 43, 77,
   79, 89, 206
Cape Horn, 106, 128, 135, 136
Cardross, 134, 135
Cardross, Lord. See Erskine, Henry, Lord
   Cardross
Carfrae, Joan, 95, 175
Caribbean. See West Indies
Carlyle, Alexander, 2
Carlyle, John, 56
Carnegie, Andrew, 145, 165, 169–74, 175,
   176, 178, 179, 182, 186
Carnegie, Margaret. See Morrison, Margaret
Carnegie, Thomas, 170, 171
Carnegie, William, 95, 124, 170, 175
Carolina Company, 32
Carson, Kit, 133
Cassidy, Butch, 177
Cattle Fields of the Far West, The, 163
Cattle ranching, 160-65
Cavalry, 7th, 152, 153
Celtic Connections, 212
Central Pacific Railroad, 155
Cessnock, 32
Chambers Journal, 18
Chancellorsville, 143
Chapel Hill, 44
Charles II, 3, 4
Charleston, 53, 67, 74, 81, 94, 125, 141,
   143, 192, 204
Chartism, 170, 175, 178
Cheape, Hugh, 203
Cherokee people, 9, 44, 46, 93, 13–32, 148,
   149, 161
Cherokee Regiment, 129
Chesapeake Bay, 5, 7, 54, 55, 58, 82
Cheyenne, 158, 194
Cheyenne Club, 164
Cheyenne people, 148, 150, 151, 152
Cheyenne River, 153
Chicago, 95, 130, 142, 160, 161, 175, 180,
   185, 186, 189, 208, 209, 210
Chickasaw people, 116, 131
Chippewa people, 152
Chisholm, Ignatius, 161
Chisholm, Jesse, 160–61, 162

Chisholm, John, 161
Chisholm Trail, 161
Chisum, John, 162
Chisum (film), 162
Choctaw people, 131, 148
Church of Jesus Christ of Latter-day Saints.
  See Mormons
Cincinnatti, 91, 96, 97, 98, 121, 129, 135
City of Glasgow Bank, 159
Civil War, 122, 123, 124, 129, 134, 137,
  139, 141-45, 147, 148, 151, 154, 159,
  162, 172, 176, 178, 183, 184, 199
Clackmannanshire, 185
Clan Fraser Society, 206
Clansman, The, 146
Clark, William, 104, 105
Clark & Co, 124
Clay, John, 139, 147, 162, 163, 167
Cleveland, 170, 181
Cluny Castle, 174
Coats, J & P, 124
Cochrane, Sir John, 32
Cody, William, 'Buffalo Bill', 152, 153
Coldingham, 118
College of New Jersey. See Princeton
  University
College of Pennsylvania. See University of
  Pennsylvania
College of Philadelphia, 71
College of William and Mary, 59, 68, 70
Colonsay, 15, 38
Colorado, 160, 161
Colter, John, 104–05
Colton, Calvin, 197
Columbia Fur Company, 107
Columbia River, 104, 105, 106, 107, 110, 128
Comanche people, 148
Congressional Globe, 133
Connecticut, 76
Connecticut River, 12, 49, 123
Constitutional Convention, 83
Continental Congress, 67
Cook County, 175
Cooper, James Fenimore, 195
Cooper, Peter, 123
Cornwallis, General Charles, 81, 82, 83
Council Bluffs, 155–56, 164
Council for Scottish Clans and
  Associations, 192
Couper Angus, 185
Courier and Enquirer, 129
Covenanters, 4, 7, 32, 205
Crager, George C, 153

Craig, Alexander, 121
Craig, Hector, 113
Craig, James, 45
Craig, Jimmy, 164
Craig, John, 36
Craigsville, 113
Craignish, 51
Cranston, 59
Crathes Castle, 165
Crawford, Dugald, 180
Crawford, Thomas, 173
Crazy Horse, 154
Creek people, 93, 94, 131, 148
Crimean War, 142, 182
Crockett, Davy, 132
Crockett, Samuel, 199
Crofting Act, 19
Cromarty, 16, 106
Cromwell, Oliver, 4
Crook, General George, 143, 151–2
Crooks, Ramsay, 106
Cross Creek, 37, 38, 40, 44, 76
Cuairtear nan Gleann, 149
Culross, 128
Cumberland County, 43
Cumberland, William Augustus, Duke of, 48
Cumberland Gap, 44, 91
Cumming, John, 50
Cunard, Samuel, 95
Cunard Shipping Company, 95
Cunninghame, William, 55
Currie, James, 6
Custer, General George Armstrong, 152

Daiches, David and Isobel, 188–89
Daily Graphic, 153
Dale, David, 114
Dalkeith, 101
Dallas, 155
Darien, Georgia, 33, 93
Darien, Panama, 31, 32
Davenport, 136
Davenport and St Paul Railroad, 136
Davis, Jefferson, 141
Declaration of Arbroath, 192
Declaration of Independence, 67, 70, 73,
  74–5, 84, 85
Defoe, Daniel, 5, 6
Delaware, 45, 60, 141
Delaware and Hudson Canal Company, 122
Delaware River, 36, 45, 98
Dempster, George, 87, 111
Denmark, 129

Denver, 210
Denver Republican, 207
Derry, 8
Detroit, 189, 210
De Voto, Bernard, 109
Dickie, George, 122
Dickson, Thomas, 122
Dickson Manufacturing Company, 122
Dinwiddie, Robert, 62
Dixon, Joseph, 104
Dixon, Thomas, 146
Dodge City, 161
Doig, Ivan, 201
Dollar, Robert, 183
Donahoe, 136
Donahoe, James, 135–36
Donahoe, Michael, 135–36
Donahoe, Peter, 135–36
Donaldson, William, 180
Donegal, 36
Donner family, 134
Dornoch, 20, 107
Dougalston, 55
Douglas, 195
Douglas, David, 128
Douglas, James, 108
Douglas, Thomas, Earl of Selkirk, 109
Douglas, William, 68
Dow, Neal, 169
Drummond, James, Earl of Perth, 29, 30
Drummond, William, 37
Dudgeon, Thomas, 95
Duff, William, 142
Duluth, 207, 210
Dumfries, 55, 129
Dumfriesshire, 45, 56, 165
Dunbar, 4, 155, 166, 167, 182
Dunbar, Captain George, 33
Dunbar, William (Indian trader), 35
Dunbar, William (sheep rancher), 165
Dunbartonshire, 55, 134, 165
Dunblane, 122
Dundee, 113, 114, 159, 162, 179, 201
Dundee, Illinois, 95, 130, 175
Dundee Land Investment Company, 160
Dundee, Minnesota, 160
Dunfermline, 76, 169, 170, 171, 172, 174, 183
Dunlop, James, 75
Dunlop Street, Glasgow, 55
Dunmore, Lord. See John Murray, Lord Dunmore
Dunn, Mary, 25
Eagle Butte, 153

East Florida Society, 35
East Lothian, 40, 43, 71, 166
Easter Ross, 20, 95, 107, 122
Eckford, Henry, 122
Economy, 116
Edinburgh, 6, 7, 8, 19, 30, 46, 53, 60, 63,
    64, 73, 74, 85, 86, 90, 117, 122, 125, 126,
    129, 130, 142, 152, 159, 160, 161, 163,
    183, 188, 196, 197, 198, 213
Edinburgh Advertiser, 11, 21, 67
Edinburgh American Land Mortgage
    Company, 159
Edinburgh International Book Festival, 212
Edinburgh Review, 101, 198
Edinburgh University, 51, 61, 62, 68, 107,
    126, 130
education, 28, 59, 61, 68-9, 70–1, 73, 83,
    122, 125–28, 193
Edward Warren, 109
Eigg, 142
Elgin, 142
Elgin, Alabama, 213
Elgin, Illinois, 130, 208
Elliot, Henry, 184
Elliott, Milford, 134
Ellis Island, 24–5, 186, 203
Ellsworth, 161
Elphinstone, Margaret, 106, 212
Emigrant's Guide, 99, 118
Encyclopaedia Britannica, 86
Erie Canal, 123, 170
Erie Railroad, 123, 160
Erskine, David, Earl of Buchan, 85
Erskine, Rev John, 85
Erskine, Henry, Lord Cardross, 32
Erskine, Robert, 76

Falkirk, 183
Falmouth, 55, 57, 89
Faulkner, William, 200–01
Fayetteville, 38
Ferguson, Rev AN, 90
Ferguson, James, 123
Ferguson Land and Cattle Company, 164
Ferguson, Patrick, 81, 84
Fife, 20, 117, 128, 200, 211
First National Gold Bank, 136
First Ohio Volunteers, 135
Firth of Forth, 130, 170
Fischer, David, 193
Flamborough Head, 80
Fleming, Robert, 179
Fletcher, Mrs Archibald, 86

Floral College for Women, 126
Florida, 35, 93, 141, 151, 152, 167
Food from the Far West, 161
Fond du Lac, 207
Forbes, General John, 171
Forbes, William, 38
Forest Grove, 110
Forsyth, Colonel James, 143, 152, 153
Fort Dunmore, 62
Fort Hall, 108, 110
Fort Laramie, 107
Fort Leavenworth, 150
Fort Raymond, 105
Fort Riley, 143
Fort Ticonderoga, 9, 51
Fort Union, 107
Fort Vancouver, 107, 108
Fort Victoria, 135
Fort William, 49, 107
Forth and Clyde Canal, 170
Fox River, 175
France, 28, 35, 86
Franklin, 204
Franklin, Benjamin, 67, 68, 70, 83, 85
Franklin Institute, 56
Fraser, Simon, 105
Fraser, William, 208
Fraser Highlanders, 49, 58
Fraser and Chalmers, 160
Freehold, 60
Frémont, John Charles, 133
French and Indian War, 8, 48, 51, 66, 76
Friends of the People, 86
Friendsborough, 37
From Soda Fountain to Moonshine
    Mountain, 212
Fugitive Slave Act, 120, 141
Fulton, Robert, 122
fur trade, 104–09
Furnas, JC, 175

Gaelic, 43, 61, 108, 149, 166, 202, 207,
    208–10
Gàidheal, An, 209
Galt, John, 2, 16, 18, 101, 195
Geddes, James, 123
Geddes, General James, 142
General Assembly of the Church of
    Scotland, 61
Gentle Shepherd, The, 195
George III, 17, 47, 71, 73, 76, 82, 85
Georgia, 7, 28, 32-4, 36, 43, 61, 64, 65, 81,
    93, 94, 129, 131, 140, 141, 204

Geronimo, 151-52
Gertrude of Wyoming, 26
Gettysburg, 144
Ghost Dance, 152
Gibson, Walter, 6
Gigha, 42
Gilchrist, John, 126
Gilchrist, Mary, 194
Glasgow, 2, 5, 6, 7, 8, 10, 15, 21, 22, 31, 41,
    45, 51, 53, 55, 58, 62, 64, 73, 86, 88, 89,
    95, 98, 103, 113, 114, 115, 117, 118, 120,
    121, 122, 128, 135, 136, 142, 153, 175,
    179, 180, 184, 199, 212, 214, 215
Glasgow Botanic Garden, 128
Glasgow Linen Company, 124
Glasgow Mercury, 1
Glasgow and New York Steamship
    Company, 95
Glasgow University, 60, 61, 69, 70, 73, 86,
    88, 114, 179, 180
Glassford, John, 55
Glassford Street, Glasgow, 55
Glen Urquhart, 49
Glencoe, 107
Glenelg, 15
Glenfinnan, 205
Glengarry, 49, 50
Glengarry County, 47, 50
Globe, 130
gold, 135, 147, 155
Golden Gate Park, 183
Goold, William, 184
Gorbals, 175
Gordon, Lord Adam, 35
Gordon, Charles, 4, 5
Gordon, James, 36-7
Gordon, Roderick, 47
Gourock, 32
Gow, Niel, 203
Grafton, 124
Graham, Isabella, 125, 128
Graham, John, 56
Graham, RB Cunninghame, 21, 150–51, 153
Graham, Stephen 187
Grahame, William, 98-9
Grandfather Mountain, 147, 204, 205, 215
Grangemouth, 181
Granite Cutters' Journal, 185
Grant, Anne, 51-3, 197
Grant, Sir Archibald, of Monymusk, 35
Grant, George, 154
Grant, Dr James, 132
Grant, James, of Ballindalloch, 35

Grant, General Ulysses S, 142, 144
Gravesend, 4, 135
Great Falls, 166
Great Northern Railroad, 166
Great Plains, 148, 158
Great Wagon Road, 43
Greece, 35
Greeley, Horace, 148
Greenock, 1, 2, 3, 17, 22, 26, 42, 50, 54, 89, 99, 103, 106, 122, 185
Greig, John, 126
Grierson, John, 212
Grieve, Miller, 129
Griffith, DW, 146
Guthrie, Woody, 187, 202

Halifax, 79, 95
Hallidie, Andrew, 183
Hamilton, 90
Hamilton, Alexander, 83, 84
Hamilton, Andrew, 30, 31
Hamilton, Thomas, 87-8, 90, 97-9, 100, 118-19, 196
Hamilton, William, 88
Hancock, Forest, 104
Hancock, John Lee, 132
Hardie, George, 184
Harmonie. See New Harmony
Harper's Ferry, 141
Harrower, John, 13
Hawick, 165
Hayes, President Rutherford, 145
Hays City, 161
Helena, 201
Henderson, 45
Henderson, George, 164
Henderson, James, 12
Henry, Alexander, 182
Henry, Joseph, 126-27
Henry, Patrick, 75
Hermosillo, 134
Hibernia Savings and Loan Society, 136
Highland Boys of North Carolina, 142
Highland Clearances, 15, 16, 19, 42, 108, 121
Highland Games, 204-06
Highland Guard, 142
Highland Land League, 19
Highland Rangers, 142
Highland Societies, 204, 207
Highlanders, 42nd, 9
Highlanders, 79th, 142
Hill, James J, 166, 181
Hillsboro, 43, 44

Historical Register, 86
Hogan, Kitty and Thomas, 170, 171
Hogg, James (land speculator), 43-4, 45
Hogg, James (poet and novelist), 195
Hogg, Robert, 43, 45
Hogg's Instructor, 26
Holland. See Netherlands
Home, Henry, Lord Kames, 68
Home, John, 195
Homestead Act, 154
Homestead Steel Works, 173-75, 178
Hook, Andrew, 198
Hooker, Professor William, 128
Houston, 134
Houston, Samuel, 132, 133
Hubbard, Tom, 212
Huckleberry Finn, 199
Hudson Canal Company, 122
Hudson River, 17, 47, 49, 101, 170
Hudson's Bay Company, 107, 108-09, 135, 152
Hull, 80
Humboldt Mountains, 158
Hume, David, 65, 68, 84, 86
Huntly, 185
Huron people, 8
Hutcheson, Francis, 69, 70

Iberville River, 36
Idaho, 151, 165
Illinois, 91, 95, 99, 113, 117, 120, 129, 134, 147, 155, 159, 180, 183, 184, 185, 199, 208
Illinois Central Railroad, 181
Illinois Company, 180
Illinois Investment Company, 180
Illinois Scotch Regiment, 142
Inchinnan, 11
Independence, 117
Independent, The, 202
India, 9
Indian Territory, 148, 154, 161
Indiana, 99, 114, 122, 155, 160, 177, 182
Information to Emigrants, 11
Inglis, John, 45
Ingram Street, Glasgow, 55
Innes, James, 38
Intruder in the Dust, 200-01
Inverness, 31, 34, 93, 94, 165
Inverness, Illinois, 130
Inverness-shire, 33, 49, 122, 208
Iowa, 109, 130, 142, 147, 155, 159
Iowa Volunteers, 8th, 142
Ireland, 60, 66, 86

Iroquois people, 8, 49
Irving, Washington, 106, 196
Islay, 7, 38, 41, 42, 48
Italy, 35
Ivanhoe, 194

Jackson, President Andrew, 93, 94, 95, 131, 132
Jackson, Thomas 'Stonewall', 143
Jacobites, 7, 8, 9, 48, 76, 77, 194, 205
Jamaica, 37, 62, 91
Jamaica Street, Glasgow, 55
James VII, 3, 28, 31, 52
James brothers, 177
James, Duke of York. See James VII
James, Henry, 24
James, Jesse, 201
James River, 54
Jamieson, Neil, 56
Jefferson, John, 128
Jefferson, President Thomas, 44, 67, 68, 70, 92, 103, 104, 119
Jeffrey, Francis, 198
Jersey City, 23, 155
John Glassford & Co, 56
Johnson, President Andrew, 144, 145
Johnson Country War, 164
Johnson, John, 50
Johnson, Sir William, 17, 35, 48-9
Johnston, General Joseph E, 143
Johnston, John, 181
Johnston, Gabriel, 37, 38
Johnstone, John, 30
Jones, John Paul, 79-80
Journal of a Tour to the Hebrides, 203
Jura, 15, 38, 42

Kames, Lord. See Home, Henry, Lord Kames
Kane County, 175
Kansas, 129, 143, 147, 152, 154, 161
Kansas City, 160, 161
Kansas-Nebraska Act, 141
Kansas Pacific Railroad, 161
Keith, 129
Keith, George, 118
Kelman, James, 214
Kelso, 139, 167
Kelvingrove Museum, 153
Kennedy, John, 181
Kentucky, 44, 45, 91, 93, 98, 104, 132, 133, 141, 145
Kentucky River, 44
Kidnapped, 13
Kilmarnock, 193

King, Rev Mitchell, 191
King's Mountain, 81, 82
King's Royal Regiment, 79
Kingsburgh, 76
Kingussie Record, 210
Kinross, 180
Kintyre, 38, 130
Kiowa people, 148
Kirkbean, 79
Kirkcaldy, 84
Kirkintilloch, 85
Kirkwall, 36, 37
Kirkwood, James, 123
Knapdale, 82
Knox College, 199
Knox, Henry, 92
Knoxville Journal, 113
Ku Klux Klan, 145-46

Lady's Life in the Rocky Mountains, A, 158
Laggan, 197
Laing, David, 182
Lainshaw, 55
Lake Champlain, 9, 49, 122
Lake George, 48
Lake Superior, 207
Lanark, 14
Lanarkshire, 15, 45, 56, 90, 120, 125, 181
Laramie County, 164
Largo, 14
Lauder, 122
Laurel Hill, 89
Laurie, James, 123
Lavender, David, 105
Lawrie Todd, 16, 101-03
Lay of the Last Minstrel, The, 195
Lazarus, Emma, 25
Lee, General Robert E, 144
Leggat, Robert, 21
Leiper, Thomas, 45, 56
Leith, 16, 76, 80, 95, 101, 182
Leith, Alexander, 45
Lewis, 10, 207, 208
Lewis, Meriwether, 104
Lexington, Kentucky, 44
Lexington, Massachusetts, 75
Limekilns, 170
Lincoln, President Abraham, 141, 144, 176, 177
Lincoln County, 162
Lindsay, John, 47
Liston, Sir Robert and Lady, 43
Little, Andrew, 165-66

Little Bighorn River, 152
Little River, 37
Liverpool, 7, 54, 95, 98, 196
Livingston, Philip, 73
Livingston, Robert, 52, 73
Loch Arkaig, 107
Loch Inver, 1
Loch Linnhe, 49
Loch Norman, 205-06
Loch Norman Games, 205-06
Lochwinnoch, 59
Locke, John, 70
Loco Engineers Union, 184
Logan, 117
Logansport, 182
London, 6, 26, 35, 114, 181
London Financial Observer, 173
Lone Ranger,The, 200
Lone Star Swing, 214
Long Island, 29, 122
Longbaugh, Harry, 177
Loon Mountain, 206
Los Angeles, 134
Los Angeles Star, 135
Louisiana, 141, 142
Louisiana Purchase, 92, 103, 140
Lowell, 124
Lower Canada. See Quebec
Lowrie, William, 129
Loyalists, 45, 47, 50, 51, 57, 76, 77, 78, 79,
    81, 88, 94, 129
Lundie, John, 181
Lynchburg, 144

MacAlester, Alexander, 27, 42
Macalester, Charles, 182
Macalester College, 182
MacArthur, Arthur, 142
MacArthur, General Douglas, 142
McArthur, John (architect), 121
McArthur, John (soldier), 141
McBeath, John, 10
McBryde, Archibald, 129
McCall, Catherine, 45
McCall, George, 45
McCall, Samuel, 45
McCallum, Donald,123
McClellan, General George, 143, 144, 176
McClellan, Robert, 106
McClure, Samuel, 199
McClure's Magazine, 199
McComb, John, 121
McCosh, James, 126

McCowan, James, 111
MacCrimmon's Lament, 154
McCutcheon family, 134
McDonald, Alexander, 183
McDonald, Allan, 40
MacDonald, Captain Allan of Kingsburgh,
    76-8
MacDonald, Angus (soldier), 142
MacDonald, Angus (fur trader), 108, 149
MacDonald, Archibald, 107
MacDonald, Catherine, 108
MacDonald, Donald, 116
MacDonald, General Donald, 76, 77, 78
MacDonald, Duncan, 149
MacDonald, Farquhar, 153
MacDonald, Finan, 107
MacDonald, Flora, 77
MacDonald, George Sandfield, 189
Macdonald, James, 161
Macdonald, Lord, 19
McDonalds restaurants, 212
MacDonnell, Alexander, 49
MacDonnell, Allan, 49
MacDonnell, John, 49, 50
McDougald, Archibald, 82
MacDougall, Duncan, 106
McGillivray, Alexander, 93-4
McGillivray, Lachlan, 93-4
McGillycuddy, Dr Valentine, 152
MacGregor, Rev James, 118
Macgregor, John, 132
McGregor, Robert, 99
McGregor, Thomas, 149
McIlwaine, William, 45
McIntosh, 165
McIntosh, Archibald, 152
McIntosh County, 33
McIntosh, Donald, 165
MacIntosh, Ebenezer, 66
McIntosh, John (from Manitoba), 155
McIntosh, John (poet), 186
McIntosh, John (sheep rancher), 165
McIntosh, William (Creek leader), 94
McIntosh, William (sheep rancher), 165
McIntosh, Captain William, 94
MacIver, Charles, 95
MacIver, David, 95
Mackay, Aeneas, 10
McKay, Alex, 165
McKay, Alexander, 106
Mackay, Donald, 122
McKay, Donald, 152
Mackay, Lieutenant Hugh, 33

Mackay, George, of Mudal, 41
McKay, WA, 165
McKean, Thomas, 73
MacKenzie, Alexander, 105, 106, 107
Mackenzie, Compton, 204, 215
MacKenzie, Donald, 106
Mackenzie, Eneas, 91, 96–7, 98, 100, 118, 121
Mackenzie, Gordon, 185
Mackenzie, Kenneth, 107
Mackenzie, John, 162
Mackenzie, Marianne, 130
Mackenzie, Murdo, 162–63
Mackenzie, Colonel Ranald, 148
McKinley, Jim, 135
Mackintosh, Hemphill & Co, 179
Mackintosh, John, of Borlum, 33
McLaglen, Andrew, 162
Maclaren, Ian, 199–200
McLaren, John, 183
McLean, 214, 215
MacLean, Dr Angus, 126
McLean, Duncan, 213, 215
MacLean, Murdo, 166
Maclean, Norman, 201
MacLeod, Rev Alexander, 118
MacLeod, Daniel, 49
McLeod, James, 10–11
McLeod, Norman, 9, 10
MacLeod, Rev John, 61
McLoughlin, Dr John, 107, 108
Maclure, William, 127–28
Macmillan, Duncan, 208
MacMillan, James, 107
McMillan, John, 91
McNeill, Hector, 82
MacNeill, Neil, 38, 41
Macpherson, Angus, 122
Macpherson, James, 195, 203
MacRae, David, 143
McRitchie, Finley, 209
Mactalla, 209
MacVicar, Captain Duncan, 51–2
Madison, President James, 68, 84, 198
Madison River, 105
Maine, 28
Makemie, Rev Francis, 60
Malcolm III, 205
Manchester, 5
Manhattan, 23, 28, 29, 186
Manitoba, 155
Mansfield, Earl of, 128
Manson, William, 37
Maple Leaf, The, 207

Marchand, Sehoy, 93
Marieta, 99
Marischal College, 69
Martin, Josiah, 27, 42
Maryland, 3, 11, 13, 28, 53, 54, 56, 59, 62, 65, 79, 89, 110, 119, 127, 133, 140, 144, 211
Massachusetts, 4, 59, 75, 86, 124, 142, 185
Matador Land and Cattle Company, 162-63
medicine, 61–2, 71
Mediterranean Sea, 56, 189
Melrose, Richard, 183
Melville, Herman, 200
Memoirs of an American Lady, 52, 197
Memphis, 116
Menomonee, 184
Menzies, William J, 159
Mercer, Hugh, 76
Metropolitan Museum, 185
Mexican War, 133, 135, 144
Mexico, 34, 132, 133, 134
Michigan, 96, 152, 166, 184, 189
Middleton, Peter, 51
Midlothian, 45, 59
Millar, John, 86
Millar, John Craig, 86
Millar, Robina, 115
Miller, Alfred Jacob, 109
Milnathort, 180
Milwaukee, 181
Milwaukee and St Paul Railroad, 181
Minneapolis, 180, 182
Minnesota, 147, 159, 160, 165, 207
Minorca, 35
mining, 120–21, 160, 177-78, 183–84
Mississippi, 141, 142, 147
Mississippi River, 34, 35, 91, 92, 97, 98, 104, 131, 140, 144, 155, 163, 184
Missouri, 96, 106, 107, 110, 117, 134, 141, 143, 147, 159, 160, 177
Missouri Compromise, 140, 141
Missouri River, 104, 148, 150, 156
Mitchell, Alexander, 181
Mobile, 90
Moffat, 126, 165
Moffat, Dr Joseph, 110
Mohawk River, 47, 49, 102
Mohawk Valley, 9, 17, 47, 48–51, 79
Molly Maguires, 178
Monmouth, James, Duke of, 31
Monarch of the Glen, The, 204, 215
Monongahela River, 97, 173
Monro, William, 10

Monroe, Bill, 202
Monroe, James, 198
Montana, 108, 143, 149, 151, 163, 166, 201
Montcalm, General Louis Joseph, 51
Montgomerie, James, 7
Monterey, 135, 200
Montreal, 105, 175, 180, 189
Montrose, 160
Monymusk, 35
Moore, Annie, 24
Moore County Scotch Riflemen, 142
Moore, Colonel James, 77
Moore's Creek, 77, 78, 79, 80
Morayshire, 155
Mormons, 117, 185, 200
Morrison, Alexander, 78, 79
Morrison, David, 142
Morrison, Margaret, 95, 170, 171
Morrison, Tam, 170, 175
Morton, William, 204
Moultrie, John, 62
Mudal, 41
Muir, Daniel, 166
Muir, John, 155, 166–67
Muir, Thomas, 86
Muir, Samuel, 130, 149
Mull, 42, 118
Mumford, Lewis, 22
Murdo, 163
Murray, Charles Augustus, 150, 171, 194, 211
Murray, James, 36
Murray, John, Lord Dunmore, 50, 75
Murray, Robert, 135
Murray, William, 135
Murthly Castle, 109
Museum of Science and Art, 126
Museum of Scotland, 8, 122
music, 201–03, 206, 209, 213
My Life on the Range, 164
Mylne, William, 63, 65, 66, 80

Nairne, Thomas, 39
Napoleonic Wars, 14, 101, 109
Nashoba, 116–17, 128
Nashville, 213
Nassau Water Works, 123
National Conservation Commission, 162
National Tartan Day, 191–92
Navigation Acts, 3, 31
Nebraska, 139, 156
Nelson, Thomas, 159
Neshaminy, 61
Netherlands, 3, 6, 28

New Amsterdam, 3, 28, 29
New Brunswick, 78, 88
New England, 4, 5, 28, 59, 88, 124, 184
New Hampshire, 11, 206
New Hampshire Gathering of the Scottish
 Clans Inc, 206
New Harmony, 114, 116, 128
New Inverness, 33
New Jersey, 4, 29–31, 36, 60, 76, 79, 102,
 118, 120, 124, 127, 135
New Lanark, 114, 124
New Mexico, 133, 160, 161, 162, 165
New Orleans, 88, 91, 97, 98, 123, 150, 202
New Providence, 7
New Smyrna, 35
New York Chronicle, 129
New York City, 3, 7, 11, 20, 21, 28, 29, 31,
 47, 49, 50, 51, 52, 53, 57, 60, 62, 67, 75,
 76, 78, 81, 87, 90, 91, 94, 95, 96, 101,
 102, 103, 113, 114, 115, 121, 122, 123,
 125, 130, 142, 148, 155, 167, 170, 177,
 181, 185, 186, 188, 189, 194, 196, 208,
 210, 211
New York Enquirer, 129
New-York Gazetteer, 13
New York Herald, 129
New York Highlanders Shinty Club, 210
New-York Journal, 50
New York Literary Gazette, 195
New York Magdalen Society, 125
New York Observer, 196
New York State, 9, 12, 16, 47, 48, 49, 50,
 71, 79, 81, 90, 101, 118, 120, 122, 123,
 126, 141, 143, 185, 186
New York Times, 208
Newark, 124
Newcastle, 37
Newcastle, Pennsylvania, 60, 179
Newcastleton, 122
Newfoundland, 186
Nez Perce people, 108, 149
Nicholson, David, 180
Nicol, John, 60
Norfolk, 53, 56, 75, 76
North Carolina, 7, 9, 10, 11, 13, 16, 20, 27,
 28, 37–44, 45, 47, 56, 65, 76, 77, 78, 79,
 81, 82, 89, 90, 93, 126, 129, 130, 140,
 141, 142, 143, 145, 146, 147, 162, 191,
 202, 205, 208, 209
North Dakota, 152, 155, 159, 189
North Platte, 139
North West Company, 105, 106–07
Northern Indian Department, 48

Northern Ireland. See Ulster
Northern Pacific Railroad, 165
Northwest Ordinance, 140
Norwich and Worcester Railroad, 123
Nova Scotia, 71, 78, 88, 118, 129, 189, 202

Oakland, 207
Ochiltree, 32
Ogden, 117
Oglethorpe, James, 32
Ohio, 91, 99, 110, 116, 120, 143, 144, 151,
   155, 170, 183
Ohio and Erie Canal, 170
Ohio River, 35, 44, 49, 88, 91, 97, 103, 121,
   140, 171
Oklahoma, 131, 161, 214
Old Deer, 181
Old Scots Charitable Society, 192
Old Statistical Account, 15
Oliver, James, 122
Omnibus Railroad Company, 136
Onderdonk, Robert J, 133
Ontario, 9, 47, 189
Oracle, 165
Ord, George, 127
Oregon, 104, 107, 108, 109, 110, 128, 154,
   159, 208
Oregon and Washington Investment Trust, 160
Orkney, 16, 36, 37, 196, 215
Orr, Hugh, 59
Ossian, 195, 203
Oswald, Richard, 118
Oswald Street, Glasgow, 55
Owen, Robert, 114, 116, 117, 128
Owen, Robert Dale, 117
Owen, William, 116, 117

Pacific Ocean, 104, 105, 127, 133, 137,
   154, 163, 185
Paisley, 14, 18, 63, 71, 102, 113, 124, 129,
   149, 175, 184
Panama, 31
Paris, 80, 82
Parker, James, 57, 76
Passenger Acts, 14
Paterson, 135
Patriots, 50, 73, 75, 76, 77, 78, 80, 81, 85
Patterson, George, 185
Patuxent River, 54
Pawnee people, 150
Pawtucket, 124
Peninsular War, 88
Penn, William, 4, 28, 29

Pennant, Thomas, 5, 6
Pennsylvania, 4, 11, 26, 36, 43, 61, 63, 79,
   95, 122, 127, 129, 165, 170, 173, 177,
   182, 187, 209
Pennsylvania Gazette, 36, 80
Pennsylvania Railroad, 171
Pentland Firth, 16
Perth, 99, 128, 165
Perth Amboy, 30, 31
Perth, Earl of. See Drummond, James, Earl of
   Perth
Perthshire, 107, 109, 111, 118, 123, 174, 180
Peru, 136
Philadelphia, 1, 28, 31, 35, 36, 43, 44, 45,
   46, 53, 56, 60, 62, 67, 71, 73, 74, 76, 78,
   80, 88, 96, 98, 120, 121, 124, 127, 177,
   182, 192, 203, 209, 210
Philip, Scotty, 155
Philippines, 142
Phillips, William, 129
Pictou, 118
Pine Ridge, 152
Pinkerton Agency, 173, 175, 176–78
Pinkerton, Allan, 95, 120, 175–78
Pinkerton, Billy Ray, 213
Pinkerton, Joan. See Joan Carfrae
Pinkerton, Robert, 177
Pinkerton, William, 177
Pitsligo, 76
Pittencrief, 171, 174
Pittsburgh, 62, 91, 95, 96, 97, 113, 130,
   155, 171, 172, 173, 174, 179, 186, 210
Port Glasgow, 2, 3, 6, 54, 57, 89
Port Royal, 32
Port Tobacco, 55
Porter, Jane, 195
Portland, 154, 180
Potomac River, 54, 56, 57, 141
Prairie-Bird, The, 150
Prairie Cattle Company, 161, 162
Presbyterian Church, 59-61, 64, 73, 81, 85,
   118, 129, 182, 191
Preston, Sir Robert, 128
Prince Edward Island, 209
Princeton University, 61, 71, 84, 121, 126
Promontory Point, 155
Providence, 180
Puget Sound Agricultural Company, 108
Pulaski, 145
Pulteney, Sir William, 90
Quakers, 4–5, 29
Quebec, 9, 107
Queen Street, Glasgow, 55

Quincy, 185

railroads, 123, 155, 177, 181-82
Ramsay, Allan, 195
Randolph, Edward, 53
Rankin, Brayton & Company, 160
Rappahannock River, 20, 54, 143
Raritan River, 30
Ray, Duncan, 82
Red River, 108
Reed family, 134
Regan, John, 113
Regiment, 77th, 51
Reid, Hugo, 134–35
Reid, James, 172
Reid, John, 211
Reid, Robert Gillespie, 185
Reid, Thomas, 69
Reid, Victoria, 134
Reminiscences of a Ranchman, 152
Renfrew, 14
Renfrewshire, 11, 123
Reno gang, 177
Revolutionary War, 3, 17, 37, 38, 51, 56, 57, 58, 75–83, 84, 94, 129, 196
Rhode Island, 124, 140, 180
Richardson, James, 117
Richmond, 55, 82, 111, 141
Rio Grande, 132, 135
River Clyde, 1, 2, 3, 6, 16, 22, 26, 53, 54, 55, 58, 88, 89, 90, 95, 97, 103, 170, 175, 181
River Humber, 80
River Runs Through It, A, 201
Robb, Lydia, 213
Robertson, Alexander, 129
Robertson, James, 129
Robertson, William (engineer), 162
Robertson, William (historian), 68
Rob Roy, 5
Rochester, 123, 186
Rocking Chair Ranch, 162
Rocky Mountains, 95, 104, 106, 107, 109, 158
Roosevelt, Theodore, 162
Ross, Betsy, 73
Ross, George, 73
Ross, John (Cherokee chief), 131, 132, 149
Ross, John (merchant), 45
Ross, Peter, 121, 125, 184, 185
Ross-shire, 106, 107
Roxburghshire, 122
Royal American Gazette, 129
Royal Botannic Garden, 183
Royal Highland Emigrants, 79

Royal Horticultural Society, 128
Royal Pennsylvania Gazette, 129
Rucker, Edward, 175
Ruff, Professor Willie, 202
Rush, Benjamin, 71, 73
Russia, 80, 187
Rutherford, General, 82
Rutherford, Fanny, 20
Ryegate, 12, 51

Sabhal Mór Ostaig, 208
Sac-Fox people, 149, 191
Sacramento River, 135
St Andrews, 73
St Andrews Golf Club (NY), 211
St Andrews Societies, 74, 76, 125, 191–92, 207
St Andrews University, 37, 51, 73
St Louis, 98, 104, 107, 121, 180, 210
St Louis Missouri Fur Company, 105
St Paul, 180
Salem, 86
Salina, 129
Salt Lake City, 117, 185
Salt Lake Valley, 117
Samoa, 129
San Antonio, 132
San Carlos, 152
San Francisco, 135, 136, 154, 160, 167, 182, 183, 200, 210
San Francisco and San Jose Railway, 136
San Gabriel Valley, 134
Sandwich Islands, 128, 134
Santa Anna, General Antonio Lopez de, 132–33
Saratoga, 81
Savannah, 33, 36, 37, 81, 129
Schaw, Janet, 20, 40, 42, 63, 65
Schaw, Robert, 65
Schenectady, 102
Scone, 128
Scotch Greys Artillery, 142
Scotch Grove, 109, 130
Scotch Rifles Pennsylvania Reserves, 142
Scotch Tigers, 142
Scots American Company of Farmers, 11, 17, 51
Scots Magazine, 72, 78, 84
Scots Thistle Society, 192
Scotsman, The, 18, 161
Scotsman, The (USA), 195
Scott, Sir Walter, 101, 146, 194–95, 199, 200
Scott, William, 180
Scottish-American Investment Company, 159

Scottish American Investment Trust, 160, 179
Scottish-American Journal, 130, 195
Scottish-American Mortgage Company, 161
Scottish Chiefs, The, 195
Scottish Enlightenment, 68, 73, 74, 193
Scottish Illinois Land Investment Company, 181
Scottish Land League of America, 208
Scottish Pacific Coast Mining Company, 160
Scottish Tartans Museum and Heritage
    Centre, 204
'Scotus Americanus', 41, 59
Scranton, 122
Seattle, 154, 186, 210
Second Continental Congress, 44
Sehoy, 94
Selkirk, 29
Selkirk, Earl of. See Douglas, Thomas, Earl
    of Selkirk.
Seminole people, 93, 131, 148
Shapinsay, 196
Shap's Landing, 91
Sharp, John, 185
Shaw, Margaret Fay, 209
Shaw House, 206
Shawnee people, 62, 93
sheep farming, 165–66
Shenandoah Valley, 91
Sherman, General William T, 142, 148
Sherriffs, James, 184
Shetland, 13, 16
shipbuilding, 6, 122
ships
    Amity, 115
    Atlas, 21
    Bachelor, 16
    Betty and Matty, 1
    Carolina Merchant, 32
    Charming Sally, 49
    City of Glasgow, 95
    Clermont, 122
    Clyde, 21
    Columbia, 135
    Commerce, 13
    Devonia, 22
    Esmeralda, 134
    Fame, 42, 89
    Fortune, 21
    George, 50
    Georgia Packet, 37
    Glasgow Packet, 79
    Ironsides, 122
    Jamaica Packet, 20
    Janet, 1

    John and Sara, 4
    Marlborough, 37
    Marloch, 207
    Metagama, 207
    Mohawk, 98
    Monongahela, 98
    Nancy, 20, 50
    Pearl, 49
    Pelican, 7
    Prince of Wales, 33
    Robert Fulton, 122
    Thistle, 38
    Tuscania, 188
    Walter Scott, 199
    Wiscasset, 170
    Unity, 4
Sierra Nevada, 134, 148, 167
Silliman, Benjamin, 195–96
Silverado, 200
Simpson, Sir George, 107
Sinclair, John, 155
Sinclair, Rev John, 208
Sioux people, 143, 147, 151 152, 153, 154
Sitting Bull, 153
Skibo Castle, 174
Skye, 9, 19, 21, 42, 77, 78, 89, 153, 208
slavery, 34, 36, 41, 98, 115, 118–20,
    140–41, 145, 175, 176
Sleat, 19
Small, William, 69, 70, 73
Smith, Adam, 68
Smith, George, 181
Smith, Robert, 121
Smith, William, 69, 73, 74
Smith, Huie & Alexander, 89
Smithsonian Institution, 126-27
Snake River, 106
Society for the Propagation of Christian
    Knowledge, 60
Solway Firth, 1, 4, 16, 79, 121
Sonoma County, 136
South Bend, 122
South Carolina, 13, 28, 32, 43, 56, 62, 65,
    81, 89, 90, 93, 140, 141, 204, 208
South Dakota, 152, 155, 159, 162, 189
South Uist, 209
Southern Pacific Railroad, 186
Southern Recorder, 129
Spain, 28, 33, 34, 132
Spanish American War, 142
Speirs, Alexander, 55
sport, 210-11
Spy of the Rebellion, 176

Stamp Act, 66
Statist, The, 160
Steel, William, 120
Stephen's Creek, 64
Stephenson, George, 184
Stevenson, Sir Daniel Macaulay, 180
Stevenson, John, 179
Stevenson, Robert Louis, 22-4, 73, 155-58,
   187-88, 199, 200
Stevenson House, 200
Stewart, Charles Edward, 76, 205
Stewart, John, 164
Stewart, John, Earl of Bute 71
Stewart, Sir William Drummond, 109
Stiles, Ezra, 72
Stirling, 68, 180, 183
Stirlingshire, 12, 122
stone masons, 185
Stornoway, 105
Stornoway Gazette, 207
Stowe, Harriet Beecher, 120, 141
Strachan, Patrick, 180
Strange Case of Dr Jekyll and Mr Hyde, 199
Strathaven, 45
Strathglass, 49, 93, 162
Strathspey, 50
Stromness, 16
Stuart, David, 106
Stuart, James, 208
Stuart, Jeb, 143
Stuart, John, 34
Stuart, Robert, 106
Stuart's Town, 32
Susquehanna River, 36, 49
Sutherland, 10, 33, 50, 109, 174
Sutherland, Alexander, 16
Sutherland, Duchess of, 120
Sutter's Mill, 135
Swan Land and Cattle Company, 162, 164
Sweetwater River, 164
System of Moral Philsophy, 69
Szasz, Ferencz, 165

Tacoma, 210
Tain, 122, 162
Tait, James, 163
Tama County, 130
tartan, 203, 204
Tartan Day. See National Tartan Day
Tartt, Donna, 200
Taylor, Robert, 165
Tecumseh, 93
Tennent, William, 61

Tennessee, 81, 91, 93, 116, 141, 142, 145, 213
Texas, 132, 133, 134, 141, 150, 154, 160,
   162, 163, 214, 215
Texas Land and Cattle Company, 162
textile production, 123-24
Thirteen Colonies, 9, 17, 28, 44, 50, 64, 66
This House of Sky, 201
Thompson, David, 106, 107
Thomson, Alexander, 63
Thorburn, Grant, 86, 101
Thurso, 16
tobacco trade, 28, 53-8, 67, 72
Tod and McGregor, 95
Tongue, 10
Toronto, 99, 130
Torridon, 108
Tour in Scotland 1817, 196
Tour of Scotland in 1769, 5
Tour Thro' the Whole Island of Great
   Britain, 5
Trail of Tears, 131
Transylvania, 44
Transylvania Company, 44
Travels in North America, 150
Travis, William, 133
Treaty of Fort Stanwyx, 49
Treaty of Guadalupe, 133
Trendle, George W, 200
Trent, James, 31
Trent, Maurice, 31
Trent, William, 31
Trenton, 31
Troy, 122
Truckee City, 158
Turnbull, Dr Andrew, 35
Twain, Mark, 199
Tweedmouth, Baron, 163
Tyrone, 36
Tytler, James, 86

Ulster, 4, 8, 64, 73, 107, 201, 202
Ulster Scots, 4, 8, 17, 29, 31, 36, 48, 59, 60,
   66, 69, 73, 81, 93, 103, 104, 132, 133,
   134, 141, 145, 199, 206
Uncle Tom's Cabin, 120, 144
Union. See Act of Union
Union Iron Works, 135
Union Pacific Railroad, 155, 156, 165
United Company of Farmers of Perth and
   Stirling, 12
University of the Highlands and Islands, 108
University of North Carolina, 44
University of Pennsylvania, 73

University of Toronto, 126
University of Wisconsin, 167
Upper Canada. See Ontario
Urie, 29
US Congress, 83, 113, 129, 133, 181
US Steel, 179
US Supreme Court, 73
Utah, 117, 134, 155, 158, 160, 185

Vailima, 200
Vancouver Island, 108, 135
Vermont, 12, 45, 49, 185
Vicksburg, 142, 144
Victoria, 108
Victoria, Queen, 203
Views of Society and Manners in America, 115
Virginia, 3, 4, 5, 6, 10, 11, 26, 28, 29, 53,
    54, 56, 57, 58, 59, 61, 62, 65, 72, 75, 79,
    80, 81, 82, 89, 104, 110, 111, 118, 120,
    132, 140, 141, 142, 211
Virginia Convention, 28
Virginia Gazette, 57
Virginia Street, Glasgow, 55
Voyageurs, 106, 212
Wales, 114
Wall Street Journal, 208
Wallace, William, 195, 214
Walls, 16
War of 1812, 88, 93, 107
Ward, Nahum, 99
Wardrop Street, Glasgow, 55
Warren, Sir Peter, 17
Wasatch Mountains, 134
Washington, 108, 127, 159
Washington, DC, 43, 88, 126, 141, 143, 144
Washington, President George, 76, 80, 83,
    85, 94
Washington Street, Glasgow, 55
Washita River, 152
Watson, Rev John. See Ian Maclaren
Watson, Peter, 29
Wayne, John, 29, 162
Weatherford, William, 94
West Indies, 5, 7, 56, 72, 81, 83, 89, 118,
    136, 140
West Point, 204
Westchester County, 211
Wester Ross, 166
Western American Cattle Company, 163
Western Farmer and Gardener, 129
Westland, John, 185
Wheeling, 97
Wheelman, The, 199

Whitby, 36
Whitelaw, James, 11, 12, 17
Whitman, Walt, 117, 188, 200, 212
Wichita, 161
Wigtown, 121
Wigtownshire, 129
Wilderness Road, 44
Wilkes, Captain Charles, 127
William Allason & Co, 57
Willamette River, 110
Williamsburg, 59
Williamson, Charles, 90–1
Williamson, Peter, 45
Williamstown, 50
Wilmington, 37, 38, 39, 41, 42, 43, 53, 65,
    77, 89
Wilson, Alexander, 18, 127
Wilson, Daniel, 126
Wilson, George, 126
Wilson, James, 71, 73, 74, 83, 84
Wilson, President Woodrow, 191
Windsor Locks, 123
Winnipeg, 109
Winton, Alexander, 181–82
Winton Motor Carriage Company, 182
Wisconsin, 99, 142, 147, 160, 166, 180, 184
Wisconsin Marine and Fire Insurance
    Company, 181
Wisconsin Regiment, 11th, 142
Witherspoon, Rev John, 71–2, 84
Wolf River, 116
Woodbridge, 4
Wooden Leg, 151
World War II, 213
Wounded Knee Creek, 153
Wright, Camilla, 114–16
Wright, Frances, 114–17, 128
Württemberg, 116
Wyoming, 107, 143, 151, 154, 158, 162,
    163, 164, 194
Wyoming Cattle Ranche Company, 163
Wyoming Stock Growers Association, 164, 165

Yale University, 72, 195, 202
Yorkshire, 36
Yorktown, 76, 82
Yosemite National Park, 167
*You Have to Be Careful in the Land of the
    Free*, 214
Young, Brigham, 117
Younger brothers, 177

Some other books published by **Luath Press**

Scots in Canada
Jenni Calder
ISBN I 84282 038 9 PB £7.99

The story of the Scots who went to Canada, from the seventeenth century onwards.

In Canada there are nearly as many descendants of Scots as there are people living in Scotland; almost five million Canadians ticked the 'Scottish origin' box in the most recent Canadian Census. Many Scottish families have friends or relatives in Canada.

Thousands of Scots were forced from their homeland, while others chose to leave, seeking a better life. As individuals, families and communities, they braved the wild Atlantic ocean, many crossing in cramped under-rationed ships, unprepared for the fierce Canadian winter. And yet Scots went on to lay railroads, found banks and exploit the fur trade, and helped form the political infrastructure of modern day Canada.

Meticulously researched and fluently written... it neatly charts the rise of a country without succumbing to sentimental myths
SCOTLAND ON SUNDAY

Calder celebrates the ties that still bind Canada and Scotland in camaraderie after nearly 400 years of relations.
THE CHRONICLE HERALD, NOVA SCOTIA

Not Nebuchadnezzar: In search of identities
Jenni Calder
ISBN 1 84282 060 5 PB £9.99

'I'm not Nebuchadnezzar and I'm not Macbeth.' If you know who you are not, do you then know who you are?

In these unusual and searching essays, acclaimed author Jenni Calder examines the theme of identity through non-identity, determining who she is by exploring who she is not. Surmounting the feelings of displacement that characterised her childhood in the USA and Scotland, her days striving to be the perfect English schoolgirl, and the desire to resolve her identity as a non-practising Jew with her family's rabbinical background, Calder thematically approaches the contributions made to her identity through experiences in four continents.

This is a life study more than an autobiography, the search for every woman – and indeed every man – to define themselves as an individual within the structure of family, gender, occupation, and nation or nations. The traditional concept of roots is rapidly fading; this outlook on how to find one's self in the midst of the fray could not be more timely.

...excellent series of autobiographical essays... Calder's lash at the various presumptions placed on women in the 20th century is sincerely felt and timely.
SCOTLAND ON SUNDAY

...a touching and highly resonant account of what it means to have several identities... This is an intelligent, personal, yet universal tale.
THE SCOTTISH STANDARD

Scottish Roots: The step-by-step guide to tracing your Scottish ancestors
Alwyn James
ISBN 1 84282 090 7 PB £6.99

For anyone interested in researching family history, *Scottish Roots* is a fundamental tool in tracing your Scottish ancestry.

In this excellent step-by-step guide, Alwyn James illustrates just how easy it is to commence the research process and gradually compile a meaningful family tree. James navigates the reader through the first steps of sourcing family details, making contact with distant relatives and collating new information.

This easy-to-use guide explains how to begin searching for family records in New Register House, the Scottish Record Office, and local libraries and folk museums. In detailed but user-friendly terms, James provides information on the costs associated with record searching, along with useful advice on maintaining realistic expectations during your research. This new and updated edition includes information on how to utilize electronic resources and the internet to access family data – a must if conducting research from an overseas base – is essential for anyone interested in discovering their Scottish roots.

Indispensable.
CALEDONIA MAGAZINE

Mr James writes entertainingly and clearly, guiding the enquirer step by step through the Scottish archives.
FAMILY TREE MAGAZINE

Braveheart: From Hollywood to Holyrood
Lin Anderson
ISBN 1 84282 066 4 PB £7.99

Braveheart was the best movie of 1995, winning five Oscars and re-establishing the historical epic as a film genre, paving the way for the successes of *Gladiator* and *Lord of the Rings* that followed.

Braveheart reached a global audience with its powerful re-telling of the almost forgotten story of William Wallace and his struggle to defend Scotland's freedom. Described as 'the most politically influential movie of the 20th century', it also had a part to play in the political change that swept Scotland, mobilising public opinion to aid the return of a Scottish Parliament after a gap of 300 years.

Braveheart: From Hollywood to Holyrood is the first book about this movie phenomenon, discussing the life and legacy of William Wallace through the modern image of the hero as presented in the film. Written with the co-operation of Randall Wallace, author of the screenplay and novelisation of *Braveheart*, and including never before published photographs, this is the long-awaited handbook for *Braveheart* fans around the world.

I am proud to be a Scot and proud to have been part of Braveheart.
The late IAN BANNEN writing to the 1997 Braveheart Convention.

Those in whose veins the love of freedom and/or Mel Gibson runs will thrill to the vox pop plaudits here from cinemagoers worldwide, recorded on the author's own Braveheart *website.*
THE SCOTSMAN

Reportage Scotland: Scottish history in the voices of those who were there
Louise Yeoman
Foreword by Professor David Stevenson
ISBN 1 84282 051 6 PB £7.99

Events – both major and minor – as seen
and recorded by Scots throughout history.

Which king was murdered in a sewer?
What was Dr Fian's love magic?
Who was the half-roasted abbot?
Which cardinal was salted and put in a barrel?
Why did Lord Kitchener's niece try to blow up Burns's cottage?

The answers can all be found in the eclectic mix covering nearly 2000
years of Scottish history. Historian Louise Yeoman's rummage through
the manuscript, book and newspapers archives of the National Library
of Scotland has yielded an astonishing range of material from a letter to
the king of the Picts to Mary Queen of Scots' own account of the murder
of David Riccio; from the execution of William Wallace to accounts of
anti-poll tax actions and the opening of the new Scottish Parliament. The
book takes pieces from the original French, Latin, Gaelic and Scots and
makes them accessible to the general reader, often for the first time.

The result is compelling reading for anyone interested in the history that
has made Scotland what it is today.

Marvellously illuminating and wonderfully readable.
Angus Calder, SCOTLAND ON SUNDAY

A monumental achievement in drawing together such a rich historical harvest.
Chris Holme, THE HERALD

Global Scots: Voices from Afar
Kenny MacAskill and Henry McLeish
ISBN 1 905222 37 8 PB £9.99

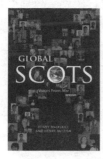

Why leave Scotland?
What has Scotland provided?
What has Scotland failed to provide?
What does it mean to be Scottish
elsewhere in the world?

Global Scots is a series of over thirty interviews with highly successful expatriate Scots around the world. The interviewees, all of whom grew up in Scotland – including iconic photographer Harry Benson; Chairman of Walt Disney Consumer Products, Andy Mooney; and comedian/ presenter Craig Ferguson – reflect on issues such as identity, sectarianism and dour Scottish Sundays.

Although the interviewees vary in age, background and profession, certain values and feelings are universal. They all remain committed to the land in which they were brought up, remaining distinctively Scottish no matter where they are in the world, be it Toronto or Tallinn.

These voices from afar provide valuable insights into Scotland's role in the modern world. Reflective and often hard-hitting, the perspectives they offer on their native country are enlightening, entertaining and potentially beneficial to a new devolved Scotland.

Scotland has, and it's no secret, an identity problem... Now we have a Parliament and I think it's a question of establishing where Scotland wants to be in a globalised world.
David Speedie, Special Advisor to the President of the Carnegie Corporation of New York

SOCIAL HISTORY

This City Now: Glasgow and its working class past
Ian R Mitchell
ISBN 1 84282 082 6 PB £12.99

HISTORY

Desire Lines: A Scottish Odyssey
David R Ross
ISBN 1 84282 033 8 PB £9.99

Plaids and Bandanas
Rob Gibson
ISBN 0 946487 88 X PB £7.99

A Passion for Scotland
David R Ross
ISBN 1 84282 019 2 PB £5.99

Blind Harry's Wallace
William Hamilton of Gilbertfield, with an introduction by Elspeth King
ISBN 0 946487 33 2 PB £8.99

FOLKLORE

Luath Storyteller: Highland Myths & Legends (new edition)
George W Macpherson
ISBN 1 84282 064 8 PB £5.99

Luath Storyteller: Tales of the Picts
Stuart McHardy
ISBN 1 84282 097 4 PB £5.99

Tales of the North Coast
Alan Temperley
ISBN 0 946487 18 9 PB £8.99

LANGUAGE

Luath Scots Language Learner [Book]
L Colin Wilson
ISBN 0 946487 91 X PB £9.99

Luath Scots Language Learner [Double Audio CD Set]
L Colin Wilson
ISBN 1 84282 026 5 CD £16.99

BIOGRAPHY

Willie Park Junior: The man who took golf to the world
Walter Stephen
ISBN 1 905222 21 1 HB £25.00

Think Global, Act Local: The life and legacy of Patrick Geddes
Edited by Walter Stephen
ISBN 1 84282 079 6 PB £12.99

THE QUEST FOR

The Quest for Arthur
Stuart McHardy
ISBN 1 84282 012 5 HB £16.99

The Quest for the Nine Maidens
Stuart McHardy
ISBN 0 946487 66 9 HB £16.99

The Quest for the Celtic Key
Karen Ralls-MacLeod and Ian Robertson
ISBN 1 84282 084 2 PB £7.99

The Quest for Charles Rennie Mackintosh
John Cairney
ISBN 1 84282 058 3 HB £16.99

The Quest for Robert Louis Stevenson
John Cairney
ISBN 0 946487 87 1 HB £16.99

The Quest for the Original Horse Whisperers
Russell Lyon
ISBN 1 84282 020 6 HB £16.99

ON THE TRAIL OF

On the Trail of the Pilgrim Fathers
J. Keith Cheetham
ISBN 0 946487 83 9 PB £7.99

On the Trail of Mary Queen of Scots
J. Keith Cheetham
ISBN 0 946487 50 2 PB £7.99

On the Trail of John Wesley
J. Keith Cheetham
ISBN 1 84282 023 0 PB £7.99

On the Trail of William Wallace
David R. Ross
ISBN 0 946487 47 2 PB £7.99

On the Trail of Robert the Bruce
David R. Ross
ISBN 0 946487 52 9 PB £7.99

On the Trail of Robert Service
GW Lockhart
ISBN 0 946487 24 3 PB £7.99

On the Trail of John Muir
Cherry Good
ISBN 0 946487 62 6 PB £7.99

On the Trail of Robert Burns
John Cairney
ISBN 0 946487 51 0 PB £7.99

On the Trail of Bonnie Prince Charlie
David R Ross
ISBN 0 946487 68 5 PB £7.99

On the Trail of Queen Victoria in the Highlands
Ian R Mitchell
ISBN 0 946487 79 0 PB £7.99

On the Trail of Scotland's Myths and Legends
Stuart McHardy
ISBN 1 84282 049 4 PB £7.99

ISLANDS

Lewis and Harris: History and Pre-History
Francis Thompson
ISBN 0 946487 77 4 PB £5.99

The Islands that Roofed the World: Easdale, Belnahua, Luing & Seil:
Mary Withall
ISBN 0 946487 76 6 PB £4.99

Rum: Nature's Island
Magnus Magnusson
ISBN 0 946487 32 4 PB £7.95
282 088 5 PB £5.99

FICTION

Deadly Code
Lin Anderson
ISBN 1 905222 03 3 PB £9.99

The Burying Beetle
Ann Kelley
ISBN 1 905222 08 4 PB £6.99
ISBN 1 84282 099 0 PB £9.99

The Berlusconi Bonus
Allan Cameron
ISBN 1905222 07 6 PB £9.99

The Golden Menagerie
Allan Cameron
ISBN 1 84282 057 5 PB £9.99

Selected Stories
Dilys Rose
ISBN 1 84282 077 X PB £7.99

Lord of Illusions
Dilys Rose
ISBN 1 84282 076 1 PB £7.99

Torch
Lin Anderson
ISBN 1 84282 042 7 PB £9.99

Heartland
John MacKay
ISBN 1 905222 11 4 PB £6.99

The Blue Moon Book
Anne MacLeod
ISBN 1 84282 061 3 PB £9.99

Driftnet
Lin Anderson
ISBN 1 84282 034 6 PB £9.99

Milk Treading
Nick Smith
ISBN 1 84282 037 0 PB £6.99

The Kitty Killer Cult
Nick Smith
ISBN 1 84282 039 7 PB £9.99

The Road Dance
John MacKay
ISBN 1 84282 024 9 PB £6.99

But n Ben A-Go-Go
Matthew Fitt
ISBN 1 905222 04 1 PBK £7.99

The Glasgow Dragon
Des Dillon
ISBN 1 84282 056 7 PB £9.99

Six Black Candles
Des Dillon
ISBN 1 84282 053 2 PB £6.99

Me and Ma Gal
Des Dillon
ISBN 1 84282 054 0 PB £5.99

The Underground City
Jules Verne
ISBN 1 84282 080 X PB £7.99

POETRY

Parallel Worlds: Poems in Shetlandic and English [book]
Christine De Luca
ISBN 1 905222 13 0 PB £8.99

The Souls of the Dead are Taking the Best Seats: 50 Poets on War
compiled by Angus Calder and Beth Junor
ISBN 1 84282 032 X PB £7.99

Jane
Anita Govan
ISBN 1 905222 14 9 PB £6.99

The Wallace Muse: Poems and artworks inspired by the life and legend of William Wallace
compiled and edited by Lesley Duncan and Elspeth King
ISBN 1 905222 29 7 PB £7.99

Tweed Rivers: New writing and art inspired by the rivers of the Tweed catchment
edited by Ken Cockburn and James Carter
ISBN 1 905222 25 4 PB £9.99

Tartan & Turban
Bashabi Fraser
ISBN 1 84282 044 3 PB £8.99

The Ruba'iyat of Omar Khayyam, in Scots [book]
Rab Wilson
ISBN 1 84282 046 X PB £8.99

The Ruba'iyat of Omar Khayyam, in Scots [audio CD]
ISBN 1 84282 070 2 CD £9.99

Kate o Shanter's Tale and other poems [book]
Matthew Fitt
ISBN 1 84282 028 1 PB £6.99

Kate o Shanter's Tale and other poems [audio CD]
Matthew Fitt
ISBN 1 84282 043 5 CD £9.99

Bad Ass Raindrop
Kokumo Rocks
ISBN 1 84282 018 4 PB £6.99

Scots Poems to be Read Aloud
introduced by Stuart McHardy
ISBN 0 946487 81 2 PB £5.00

The Luath Burns Companion
John Cairney
ISBN 1 84282 000 1 PB £10.00

The Whisky Muse: Scotch whisky in poem & song
Robin Laing
ISBN 1 84282 041 9 PB £7.99

Parallel Worlds: Poems in Shetlandic and English [audio cd]
Christine De Luca
ISBN 1 905222 38 6 CD £9.99

Details of these and other Luath Press books are to be found at www.luath.co.uk